IN THE
LION'S DEN

IN THE LION'S DEN

AN EYEWITNESS ACCOUNT OF WASHINGTON'S BATTLE WITH SYRIA

ANDREW TABLER

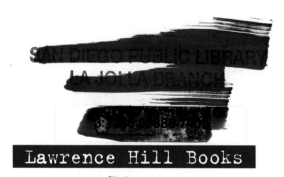

Lawrence Hill Books

Chicago

Library of Congress Cataloging-in-Publication Data

Tabler, Andrew.

In the lion's den : an eyewitness account of Washington's battle with Syria /
Andrew Tabler. — 1st ed.

p. cm.

Includes bibliographical references and index.

ISBN 978-1-56976-843-3 (pbk.)

1. United States—Foreign relations—Syria. 2. Syria—Foreign relations—
United States. 3. Bush, George W. (George Walker), 1946- 4. Assad, Bashar,
1965- 5. Tabler, Andrew. I. Title.

E183.8.S95T33 2011

327.7305691—dc23

2011024015

Cover and interior design: Jonathan Hahn
Cover photo: Phil Smith
Map design: Chris Erichsen

First edition
Published by Lawrence Hill Books
An imprint of Chicago Review Press, Incorporated
814 North Franklin Street
Chicago, Illinois 60610
ISBN 978-1-56976-843-3
Printed in the United States of America
5 4 3 2 1

For my parents, Clarence and Lucille; my brother, Bill; and my grandmother Helen, whose unconditional love made my long journeys possible.

You have retired to your island, with, as you think, all the data about us and our lives. No doubt you are bringing us to judgment on paper in the manner of writers. I wish I could see the result. It must fall far short of *truth*: I mean such truths as I could tell you about us all—even perhaps about yourself.

—**Lawrence Durrell,** ***Balthazar***

CONTENTS

ACKNOWLEDGMENTS

I would not have been able to tell this story without the help of friends and institutions that encouraged me to write about my experiences in Syria and Lebanon. A good portion of this book was essentially written while I was a fellow with the Institute of Current World Affairs (ICWA). My fellowship, which began only days before the former Lebanese prime minister Rafik Hariri was assassinated, allowed me to travel and write for over two years as I "followed my nose"—in the ICWA tradition—around Syria and Lebanon. Special thanks go to Joseph Battat, a former ICWA fellow in China who noticed me while on a mission for the World Bank in Syria and encouraged me to apply to the institute. ICWA executive director Steven Butler, as well as his predecessor, Peter Martin, helped me learn to put myself back into my writing after years of writing and editing dry news. Completing that process was Victoria Rowan, the New York–based writing coach and editor. Through my work with Victoria, I learned a lot about story-telling and how to manage myself through the writing process. I also learned how dilemmas not only define characters but American and Syrian presidents as well.

I could not have endured my sojourn in Syria and Lebanon without the friendship of Michael Karam and Nicholas Blanford, two outstanding Beirut-based writers whose kindness helped me deal with the stress of living in Syria. During our weekly gatherings in Beirut, Mike and Nick, together with friends Norbert Schiller, Anissa Rifai, and Mona Alama, helped me put my experiences in perspective. As did Lee Smith, a good friend and great writer who then called Beirut home. Last but not least, I would like to thank Andrew Lee Butters, my flatmate in Beirut, who helped keep me mentally and physically fit, and Katherine Zoepf, my flatmate in Damascus, who treated me with good food and even better stories.

A number of Syrians made a lasting impact on my stay in Damascus. Special thanks go out to Kinda Kanbar, businessman Abdul Ghani Attar, Abdul Kader Husrieh of Ernst & Young Syria, Ibrahim Hamidi of *Al Hayat* newspaper, and Ayman Abdel Nour of all4Syria, as well as to Francesca De Chatel, a wonderful writer and editor who ultimately succeeded me as editor in chief of *Syria Today*. Because of the Syrian regime's current crackdown, I would like to collectively thank all those at *Syria Today* for all you taught me and allowed me to teach you. I would also like to recognize the diplomats of the US embassy in Damascus who spent considerable time helping me understand Syria and US-Syria policy, including Daniel Rubinstein, Mary Brett Rogers-Springs, Chris Stevens, Steven O'Dowd, Brian O'Rourke, Todd Holmstrom, Andrew Abell, Maria Olson, Katherine Van De Vate, Pamela Mills, and Tim and Tracy Pounds.

After I left Syria, the Washington Institute for Near East Policy provided me with a platform in Washington to write about the country. Special thanks go to Robert Satloff, Patrick Clawson, David Makovsky, David Schenker, Simon Henderson, Matt Levitt, Dina Guirguis, Michael Jacobson, Michael Singh, Mike Eisenstadt, Steve Borko, and Larisa Baste, whose input on my work has helped me expand from journalism into policy research. Thanks also go to Kathy Gockel and the Stanley Foundation, who first helped get my ideas into Washington policy circles, and *Foreign Policy*'s David Kenner.

My biggest appreciation goes to those who took the time to read and comment on the book's draft. They include Andrew Abell, Syria desk officer, US Department of State; Itamar Rabinovich, former Israeli Ambassador to the United States and former representative in peace talks with Syria; and Levant experts Amr al-Azm, Jon Alterman, Nicholas Blanford, Steven Heydemann, and David Schenker. I would also like to thank my friends in government who have shared their thoughts with me about the Levant, including the State Department's Ruth Citrin and Matt Irwin and the National Security Council's director for Lebanon and Syria, Hagar Hajjar. Thanks also go to Susan Betz and Kelly Wilson of Lawrence Hill Books, who edited the manuscript, and Mary Kravenas and Meaghan Miller, who aided me in the book's promotion. Last but not least, I thank my fantastic research assistant, Andrew Engel, and my intern, Maya Gebeily. Together their comments and hard work made this a much better book.

Ankara

TURKEY

CYPRUS

Latakia

Mediterranean
Sea

Beirut

LEBANON

Damascus

Golan
Heights

West Bank

ISRAEL

Jerusalem

Gaza Strip

Suez
Canal

Cairo

EGYPT

Aleppo

SYRIA

Euphrates R.

Baghdad

IRAQ

Amman

Dead Sea

JORDAN

SAUDIA
ARABIA

Nile R.

Red Sea

0		125		250 miles

0	125	250 kilometers

INTRODUCTION

I only planned to work in Damascus for a few months and engage an Arab country I didn't know. Instead, I stayed seven years and got an unexpected front-row seat to a fight.

This book is a firsthand account of the confrontation between the administration of US president George W. Bush and the regime of Syrian president Bashar al Assad. The Bush administration called its Syria policy "isolation," while the Assad regime portrayed it as an American plot to overthrow Syria's leadership and remake the Middle East in America's image.

No attempt will be made in this book to argue either way, as details of decision makers' plans and intentions have yet to emerge. (Britain's former prime minister Tony Blair writes in his book, *A Journey: My Political Life*, that Bush and former vice president Dick Cheney had machinations to remake the Middle East, using "hard power" to take down the regimes in Iraq, Iran, and Syria. While certain members of the Bush administration may have advocated using military force against Syria, I have been unable to find any formal US government plans to bring down the Assad regime.) Nevertheless, much of this story is part of the United States' invasion and occupation of Iraq—America's largest-ever military adventure in the Middle East.

I saw the conflict between Washington and Damascus—which I generally refer to as a "cold war"—from an unusual and privileged vantage point. I lived and worked in Damascus between 2001 and 2008, served as a media adviser for nongovernmental organizations (NGOs) under the patronage of President Assad's wife, Asma, and had the honor to cofound Syria's first—and still best—English-language magazine, *Syria Today.* By virtue of my work, I had a rare journalist multiple-entry visa that allowed me to travel back and forth to Lebanon—often on a weekly basis—to cover the dramatic events leading up to and following the February 2005 murder of the late Lebanese prime minister Rafik Hariri by car bomb in Beirut. I was able to travel freely in and out of Syria and speak my mind without the threat of being banned from the country—at least until the very end of my stay.

This book is also a personal account of an American's engagement with the regime of the "Lion of Damascus"—"Assad" being Arabic for "lion." While I wouldn't compare my experience to that of the Bible's Daniel, my sojourn in Syria was a series of crises and dilemmas that sculpted my view of engagement and confrontation with what are commonly referred to in America as "rogue regimes." My personal and professional experiences in Syria were so intertwined I didn't know how else to write a book that wasn't a hybrid of memoir and foreign policy analysis. Following my departure from Syria in the autumn of 2008, the regime began its harshest crackdown on dissidents and journalists during Bashar al Assad's reign. With an eye toward protecting my friends and associates in Syria, in this book I have changed nearly all their names and some details of their identities.

I went to Syria in 2001 with an open mind about a country and a regime that the United States and the West had struggled to change the behavior of for decades. (This long process even gave birth to "Syriana"—the term for the idea that a big power can remake nation-states in its own image. The term was made internationally famous when it was adopted as the title for the 2005 box-office thriller of the same name.) The regime's long alliance with the Soviet Union; its support for Hezbollah, Hamas, and other groups on the US list of terrorist organizations; its pursuit of weapons of mass destruction (WMD); and its horrible human rights record had led some US administrations and their allies over the years to attempt to change the Assad regime's behavior via confrontation or sanctions. Other administrations had attempted to engage Syria diplomatically, most notably centered on Arab-Israeli and Syrian-Israeli peace talks, based on the idea that America could gain more with rewards than punishments. Neither approach solved the problems. Underlying each policy was the idea that the Assad regime only cared about politics. As Damascus's oil revenues declined and Assad opened his country to the outside world, I watched firsthand as economics became a bigger and bigger part of the Assad regime's calculations for survival.

Multilateral pressure shepherded by the Bush administration brought about some of the greatest changes in Syrian policies in decades. Damascus withdrew its troops from Lebanon, implemented long-delayed economic reforms, and eased—at least for a time—restrictions on the Syrian opposition. A major impetus for these changes is the fact that Syria, like all globalizing rogue regimes, increasingly needs the international community more than the international community needs Syria.

Other changes in Syrian policy were not to Washington's liking, however. Damascus deepened its alliance with Iran, turned a blind eye to jihadi fighters entering Iraq, and stepped up a nuclear program now under investigation by the International Atomic Energy Agency (IAEA). While Washington and its allies' responses to the latter two policies ultimately curbed their impact, the Bush administration proved far less skillful in countering Assad's moves in Syria and Lebanon—historically a key battleground between Iran and the United States.

Engaging regimes like Assad's might seem an easy solution to America's problems in the Middle East, including dealing with Iran's nuclear program or fostering Arab-Israeli peace. But engaging the

Assad regime is historically far harder done than said. It's not just that Syrian and US policies are now more opposed to each other than ever. Based on my experiences in Syria, the prospects of America's underwriting a Syrian-Israeli peace treaty are not promising unless Damascus acts decisively to support human rights, institute rule of law, and curb corruption in the country. This is particularly the case following the outbreak of protests throughout Syria in March 2011. Meanwhile, Washington policy makers and analysts are also finding difficulty moving beyond the unsuccessful but still deeply entrenched "peace process or pressure" arguments of the last four decades. Until the US government learns to "think like a lion" and develops a dilemmas-driven policy that (a) promotes human rights, (b) effectively addresses Syria's increasingly problematic policies, and (c) maximizes economic as well as political leverage in conjunction with allies—all while keeping the door open someday for a Syria-Israel peace agreement—Assad is unlikely to change his detrimental policies anytime soon.

In the Lion's Den: *An Eyewitness Account of Washington's Battle with Syria* is organized into two parts. In part 1, I use my personal story in Syria to talk about the country itself, its relations with the United States and the West, and its economic and social problems. I take a step back in part 2 and tell the story of the confrontation between the United States and Syria as it appeared from my desk at *Syria Today*. In this section, I describe in detail Assad's defiant response to the allegations of his regime's involvement in Hariri's murder; his outreach to the Islamic Republic of Iran, Hezbollah, and Sunni Muslims and their institutions in Syria; and his crackdown on the country's domestic opposition. I also describe the Assad regime's skillful political use of sectarian chaos in US-occupied Iraq, the civilian deaths of the 2006 Lebanon War, and the mysterious February 2008 assassination in Damascus of Hezbollah operative Imad Mughniyeh—perhaps the world's most-wanted terrorist prior to the attacks of September 11, 2001.

In the epilogue, I enter into the Washington policy debate over Syria. I describe the "expectations gap" between the kind of engagement Syria sought and ultimately received from the United States following the passing of the presidential baton from Bush to Obama, the advent of the Arab Spring, and the approach that I believe would be most effective in the future.

PART I

1

THE ARAB WORLD'S
TWILIGHT ZONE

I had no idea where to start. That morning in July 2001, Oxford Business Group (OBG), at that time a publishing company start-up, had sent me from my base in Cairo to Damascus to carry out "the most comprehensive study of Syria ever compiled." Getting projects of that magnitude off the ground in an Arab country was always hard, but after eight years of study and journalism in the Middle East, I understood this better than most. Many Arab countries had local independent English-language publications of reasonable quality that were softly critical of the state and society. So it was normally just a matter of taking the editor out to lunch or buying a few drinks and asking for a few names of people with whom to speak. The ball would then soon start rolling, and six to eight months later, we would somehow manage to publish our report.

This wasn't going to work in Syria, however. The state's virtual monopoly on media ownership, as well as its tight control of access by foreign journalists, meant that no such publication existed. A colleague from OBG gave me the number of Leila Hourani—a young Syrian woman with whom he had once worked, and who, he said, knew her way around. I had given her a call that morning, and, to my surprise, she agreed to meet me for lunch at Gemini, an upmarket restaurant in Damascus's Abou Roumaneh district.

Leila turned the head of every man as she entered the restaurant's front door. Her doll-like face, curly brown hair in the bouffant style, form-fitting clothes, and five-inch heels made it easy to understand why many Arabs regarded Syrian women as the region's most beautiful. What I learned that lazy afternoon in Damascus, however, was that Leila's best quality was her candor, a rare attribute to be found under a dictatorship where most people are afraid to speak their mind.

Leila got right down to business and gave me a summary of the biggest unfolding story of the year: President Bashar al-Assad's promise to reform Syria. The thirty-four-year-old ophthalmologist had taken the reigns of control in Syria exactly one year ago that day upon the death of his father, the infamous "iron man" dictator Hafez al-Assad. In his inauguration speech—delivered only days after the Syrian parliament had had to change the constitution to lower the minimum age for a Syrian head of state from forty to thirty-four years to allow Bashar to assume his post—the young Assad urged Syrians to "accept the opinion of the other." Like many Syrians during what became known as the "Damascus Spring," Leila was excited with the idea of change and loved her new president. Nevertheless, every time she mentioned his last name, Leila lowered her voice and looked over her shoulder.

Bashar's coming to power was a story that I had followed from afar. After Assad's acceptance speech, scores of "discussion groups" formed throughout the country to address a whole host of Syria's political and social problems. At first, the state tolerated the forums—after all, many forum organizers believed that they were carrying out the discussions in Bashar's name. But as the discussions got increasingly critical of the regime, it struck back. A group of officials who had been close to Bashar's father—known as the "old guard" and led by vice president Abdel Halim Khaddam—were said to have advised the president to close the groups. Forum participants who were critical of regime corruption were imprisoned. While some discussion groups continued to function, Leila said that most, if not all, Syrians had no idea what was going on.

As we finished our appetizers, Leila turned the subject of the conversation to her family. By her style of dress, I thought Leila was Christian, as followers in the Arab world were not subject to Islam's conservative dress codes. In fact, Leila was Sunni—the daughter of Hassan Hourani, an agricultural engineer from the Houran region, which is south of Damascus. After joining the Baath Party in the late 1950s, Hassan was sent on a United Nations (UN) scholarship to France to study desertification—the loss of arable land to the desert, which was damaging Syria's agricultural production. After returning to the Houran in the mid-1960s, Hassan married Samia, an English teacher from a nearby village. The couple moved to Damascus in 1970, where Leila was born six years later.

The Baath Party was something I had only really read about. Based on the Arabic word for "renaissance," Baathism was a secular ideology that called for the unification of the Arab world into one country as the quickest way to solve its problems—most notably liberation from Israel, created from the former British Mandate of Palestine, whose flag the party even adopted as its own. Baathism functioned in another way on Syria's domestic scene: as a vehicle for minority rule over Syria's majority Sunni Muslim population. In the 1950s, Alawites—members of an obscure offshoot of Shiite Islam—filled the ranks of Syria's Baath Party and the army's officer corps. When the Baath seized power in a military coup in March 1963, Syria's Christian, Circassian, Druze, Ismaili and Shiite minorities, amongst others, saw the Baath as a path to freedom and a means to power. Under four hundred years of Ottoman rule, Syria's majority Sunni population had set the rules of the game, keeping minorities under the yoke. The Baath's secularism provided an ideological bulwark against traditional Islam.

The "Renaissance Party" was vulnerable to Syria's most virulent political disease, however: its penchant for military coups. Between independence in 1946 and 1970, various juntas and factions had overthrown or changed the government no less than seventeen times—making it one of the world's most unstable political entities.

One man figured out how to stop it. In November 1970, defense minister Hafez al-Assad seized power in a bloodless coup—much like his predecessors. But instead of relying on the Baath's minority base, Leila said, Assad reached out to two key constituencies of Syria's Sunni population that didn't like each other. The first was Damascus's historically powerful trading families. As merchants on the Western terminus of the Silk Road, these Damascene families were extremely rich, were educated abroad, and often spoke foreign languages at home. Many lost their businesses to the state's program of nationalizations in the late 1950s and 1960s. By selectively reversing some of these nationalizations through what he called the "Correctionist Movement," Assad won over a good portion of Damascus's merchant class.

The second were rural Sunni farmers like Leila's extended family. For centuries, these families eked out an existence in the Euphrates Valley to the east and the Houran area south of Damascus. Like Syria's minorities, these peasants didn't fare well under Ottoman rule and were generally regarded as uncivilized by Damascus's trading elite. Assad offered peasants who joined the Baath Party and its professional associations an education, jobs in the public sector, state financing for houses, and, for the most talented, a chance to live and work in the capital.

Assad's policies earned him respect among a majority of Syrians, and the regime quickly stabilized. He buttressed his domestic moves with aggressive moves on the regional level as well—he joined Egypt in a surprise attack on Israel in the October War of 1973. Syrian forces were ultimately defeated, but international intervention to stop the war transformed Syria's conflict with Israel into a cold war battlefield. The Soviet Union provided Syria with millions of dollars in military equipment and financial aid. Persian Gulf states, led by Saudi Arabia, provided Syria with billions of petrodollars in aid—money that had resulted from the war's boom in the price of oil. The United States engaged Syria as well, extending $534 million in foreign assistance between 1975 and 1979 to coax Syria to the peace table with Israel and out of the eastern camp.

From what I could remember of recent regional history, the courting didn't last long. When Egypt signed a peace treaty with Israel and moved into an American orbit, Syria formed the "rejectionist front" of groups opposing what became known as Camp David. The same year, Syria formed an alliance with the leaders of Iran's Islamic Revolution against their common rival, Iraqi president Saddam Hussein. As Iran continued to rail against America as "the Great Satan," the United States's Gulf allies, led by Saudi Arabia, cut off aid and investments to Syria. The country's economy contracted, and discontent set in.

It was then that Assad's new order was challenged by the Muslim Brotherhood, an organization with a strong following in the conservative northern Syrian cities of Hama, Idlib, and Aleppo. Branding the Alawite-dominated Assad regime as "apostates," the militant wing of the Brotherhood waged a terrorist war against regime figures and government institutions. Leila said she remembered her father taking her out of her first-grade classroom after the Brotherhood car bombed the Ministry of Information across the street from her family's apartment.

In February 1982, Assad ordered Syrian special forces to surround the Brotherhood's headquarters in Hama. What happened next was something that featured prominently in almost every Syria domestic news story I had ever read. Using artillery, the regime leveled the Brotherhood's warren in the backstreets of Hama's Old City. Tens of thousands of people were killed. The regime also launched a sweeping campaign of arrests—not only of suspected Brotherhood members but virtually all regime opponents, including communists and Arab nationalists who hated the Brotherhood as much as the regime. Acute fear gripped the country as the economy fell deeper into recession.

Nearly a decade later, Syria emerged back on the international scene, due largely to tectonic shifts in the international balance of power and shifts in its regional alliances. With its Soviet patron in political and economic chaos, Assad joined the American-led alliance to oust the forces of his Baathist rival, Saddam Hussein, from Kuwait. In return, the United States gave its tacit consent for Syria to use its forces in neighboring Lebanon to implement the Lebanese National Reconciliation Accord, otherwise known as the Ta'if Accord, named after the city in Saudi Arabia where the agreement was negotiated to end Lebanon's civil war.

After the war, Leila and her family expected that, given the regime's strong position and good terms with the West, Assad would release political prisoners and launch sweeping reforms to overhaul the country's moribund public sector. In the end, economic reform was limited to a single law for foreign investment. The prisoners who emerged from jail were mostly communists and Arab nationalists, which left thousands of others associated with the Muslim Brotherhood "disappeared." And while I didn't fully realize it then, it was the specter of those who never emerged from Syria's prisons that kept Leila's—and every other Syrian's—voice to a whisper when they spoke about the Assad family.

After lunch, Leila took me for a tour of Abou Roumaneh. The architecture of the district's buildings looked like certain quarters of Cairo—a city I had grown tired of. When I had arrived in Egypt to study political science at the American University in Cairo in 1994, I thought that if I just learned Arabic, life in Cairo would be easy. Boy, was I wrong. With better Arabic came better comprehension of the growing number of personal questions from Cairenes I didn't know. Often they asked why I hadn't converted to Islam. It would also be nothing for a taxi driver taking me and a female colleague somewhere to ask if we were married. An increasing number of Egyptians just simply seemed to jeer at Westerners as we walked down the street. While it was hard to point to any one reason for Egyptians' slow shift toward this kind of conservative, in-your-face interpretation of Islam, it coincided with the return home of thousands of Egyptians who had traveled to Saudi Arabia as guest workers in the 1980s. Egyptians told me that many of their countrymen brought Saudi Arabia's less-tolerant interpretation of Islam, Wahhabism, back home and were now disseminating it around the country.

Walking down a street in Abou Roumaneh was a completely different experience. No one asked about my relationship with Leila, who, despite her risqué dress, garnered only glances from passers-by. Shopkeepers were friendly and asked no questions about our religion. People just minded their own business. Car traffic was far less than Cairo, where the air constantly smelled of exhaust fumes. In American terms, it was more like walking down a street in Pittsburgh than New York.

We decided to take a breather in a nearby café. As we sipped on strong cups of Arabic coffee scented with cardamom, Leila asked me about OBG's project in Syria. When I finished explaining all that was involved, she asked me if we had all the proper government permissions. I told her that we had all the paperwork in hand, as well as the backing of the Ministry of Economy and Trade.

"What about the American government?" she asked.

I laughed and told her we didn't need clearance from Washington to work in Syria—journalism was exempt from US sanctions on the country.

"Oh yeah?" Leila said, putting her hand on my shoulder and giving me a big smile. "Remember, Andrew, everything about Syria is political. Go and see your embassy and tell them what you are up to."

I called the economic and commercial section of the US embassy in Damascus the next morning. The secretary immediately patched me through to Mary Brett Rogers, an American diplomat whom I had met the previous week. To my surprise, she set an appointment to see me that afternoon. US embassies officially represent American interests abroad, but they are still an arm of the federal government's bureaucracy. A recent request to see an officer at the US embassy in Cairo had taken about two weeks to set up, due to the need to obtain security clearances and fit the appointment around diplomats' extensive vacation time.

The US embassy in Damascus sits atop Rouda Circle, the center of the Syrian capital's top residential district. The Tora River—one of seven small tributaries that trickle through Damascus—feeds the square's large water fountain. The embassies of other countries, including Turkey, China, and Iraq, are also in the square. President Assad's residence—a common apartment—sits a few hundred meters northwest.

As I passed through "Post One"—the embassy's business gate—I was immediately filled with a sense of irony. Here I was, entering the US embassy in Syria—one of the original nations on the United States's "State Sponsors of Terrorism" list. The list, created by Congress in 1979, "designated" countries that supported groups carrying out car bombings, hijackings, and other terrorist operations—an official mantra tattooed on the inside of my skull after writing it hundreds of times in news stories on Syria.

However, of the scores of US embassies that I have visited in the Arab world, this was the only one that didn't resemble Fort Knox. The August 1998 bombings of the US embassies in Dar Es-Salam and Nairobi spurred the State Department to build a slew of new, more secure embassies in the Arab world. Each had thick concrete walls and crash barriers camouflaged as large concrete planters; some had watchtowers. The design—called "setback"—was based on the recommendations of a 1985 report into another tragic attack: the April 1983 bombing of the US embassy in Beirut (Lebanon was then partially occupied by Syrian forces). Seven months later, another truck bomb destroyed the US marine barracks at Beirut's airport. The 241 marines who perished in the rubble marked the largest one-day death toll for the US Marine Corps since the battle of Iwo Jima.

To protect the American diplomats and staff from car bombs, the new embassy buildings were constructed several hundred feet inside the compound's outer walls. The interior of the US embassy in Amman, Jordan, about three hours by car from Damascus, looked and felt like a futuristic high school somewhere in southern California.

The embassy building—with tiled roofs and sidewalks—even featured its own restaurant. Security on the perimeter was as tight as a drum.

Stepping through the gate of the US embassy in Damascus, in contrast, was like traveling back in time—to a world before car bombs. For starters, the embassy building directly touched the embassy compound's outer wall. The chancery—the part of the embassy that houses the US ambassador and staff—was a 1920s-era villa. An American flag foisted at the villa's highest point, above the gate, was surrounded by a bird's nest of barbed wire. The texture of the embassy's stucco exterior was uneven, like a cheap New York apartment whose walls have been plastered over too many times. Two small windows served as the embassy's only portholes to the outside world. Gigantic cypress trees ringed the inside of the compound's outer wall, enclosing a small garden centered on a marble oriental fountain, whose basin held a pool of stagnant green water.

The embassy's security procedures were remarkably relaxed. When I accidentally set off the gate's metal detector—presumably with the cassette recorder in my briefcase—two Syrian guards just waved me through without searching the bag. The marine guardsman, finding my appointment in his logbook, smiled and traded me a clip-on ID for my passport. They all waved me through a heavy blast door into a waiting room, which appeared as though it had once served as the villa's front porch.

I soon found myself staring at a row of old yellowed photographs on the waiting room wall. A 1947 photo, labeled "The American Legation in Damascus," showed the villa at its prime, ringed on three sides with covered terraces resembling an old shopping arcade. The compound's front gate led to the villa's front porch, which, as far as I could tell, was exactly where the waiting room now stood. A number of massive 1940s-era cars were parked along the curb. The villa was virtually unchanged in another photo from 1982, apart from the natural growth of the garden's trees and the comparatively streamlined 1970s American cars. Neither structure resembled the building I had just entered.

"Like another world, huh?" said a man standing at my right. Extending his hand, he introduced himself as Daniel Rubinstein, the embassy's economic and commercial officer. Standing to his left was Mary Brett, whose slight giggling hinted to me that she knew I had been lost in the bygone world of the photos on the wall.

Thus began what, to this day, remains the most succinct—and sober—depiction of US-Syrian relations I have ever heard. Daniel explained that since Syria's independence in 1946, US policy toward Syria oscillated between isolation and engagement. Damascus broke diplomatic relations with the United States when it sided with Israel against Syria during the Six-Day War of June 1967. Syria lost its highest peak in the conflict: the Golan Heights, a strategic plateau overlooking the plains of Israel's Galilee.

I knew from my study of modern Middle Eastern history that the first watershed event in US-Syrian relations was following the next regional war in October 1973. Egypt and Syria counterattacked, inflicting heavy Israeli casualties. While the United States agreed to resupply Israel, US secretary of state Henry Kissinger used active American mediation to broker a ceasefire. Kissinger helped conclude a disengagement agreement the following May between Israeli and Syrian forces on the Golan that remains in effect to this day. A much lesser-known part of the story was that the United States had offered Syria economic and military aid to conclude peace treaties with Israel. The strategy, dubbed "constructive engagement," was based on the assumption that the ability of the United States to reward "good behavior" far exceeded its capacity to punish "bad behavior."[1] A similar approach worked with Egypt, paving the way for the conclusion of both the 1978 Camp David Accords and the 1979 Egypt-Israel Peace Treaty.

Syria, however, was a different story. At first things seemed to be going well. In 1976, the United States brokered the Red Lines Agreement—a tacit understanding between Syria, Israel, and the United States that facilitated Syria's military intervention in Lebanon as part of the Arab Deterrent Force to end that country's civil war.

Damascus opposed Camp David, however, by forming the "rejectionist front" of countries opposed to peace talks with Israel. As part of that policy, Syria continued to host a number of radical Palestinian groups opposed to Israel that had carried out a series of hijackings and other terrorist acts against US targets. In response, Washington added Syria to its first list of state sponsors of international terrorism in 1979. Because US law bans economic assistance to nations on the list, Washington terminated constructive engagement with Damascus. Washington also leveled trade sanctions against Syria, including restrictions on US exports of "dual-use" materials.

Relations between Damascus and Washington quickly turned frosty. In June 1982, shortly after the last photo on the waiting room's wall was taken, US ally Israel invaded Lebanon to uproot fighters of the Palestinian Liberation Organization (PLO). During the three-month onslaught, Syrian forces fought pitched battles against the Israeli Army. Tensions increased between the two countries after Damascus and the Palestinian groups that it hosted opposed a UN-brokered evacuation of the PLO from Beirut.

The massive truck bombings of the US embassy and marine barracks in Beirut the following year was a further watershed event in US-Syrian relations. While Damascus was never directly accused of involvement in the attacks, the Assad regime openly opposed US policy in Lebanon at the time and helped Washington's nemesis, Iran, form Hezbollah—a Shiite Muslim group originally set up to fight Israeli occupation of Lebanon. The attacks were widely believed to have been organized by Imad Mughniyeh, a senior Hezbollah operative. As relations continued to sour, the walls outside the US embassy were heightened and fortified.[2]

Despite often tense US-Syrian relations, the United States kept an ambassador in Damascus. The only exception occurred in 1986 when Washington withdrew its ambassador following "evidence of direct Syrian government involvement" in an attempt by a Jordanian of Palestinian origin, Nezar Hindawi, to blow up an Israeli airliner. A

US ambassador returned to Damascus the following year after Syria expelled the most radical of the Palestinian factions that it hosted—the Abu Nidal Organization—and helped free an American hostage held in Beirut.[3]

We left the waiting room and ascended the stairs toward Daniel's office in the embassy's chancery, the formal offices of the ambassador. A long row of eight-by-ten-inch photos of past US ambassadors to Syria lined the stairwell's left-hand wall. Along the way, Daniel casually pointed his finger at the photo of ambassador Edward Djerejian. In 1988 President Reagan prepared the groundwork for engaging Syria to help solve the deteriorating situation in Lebanon, where fighting raged out of control and US hostages languished in captivity. To carry out this difficult task, he assigned Djerejian, an American of Armenian descent, as ambassador to Damascus with strict orders to gain Hafez al-Assad's trust.[4]

When we arrived in Daniel's office, we stood in front of a yellowed wall-size topographical map of "Greater Syria" that stood to the right of the door. It had been rescued from the US consulate building in Aleppo after a mob torched the building following the 1967 War, abruptly shutting down America's oldest consulate in the Middle East. Pointing at Syria's long eastern border with Iraq, Daniel explained that Djerejian's talks with Assad bore fruit in the autumn of 1990 when Saddam Hussein invaded Kuwait. Syria sealed its border with Iraq and participated in the US-led alliance to oust Iraqi forces from Kuwait the following January. While Daniel didn't make the link, I remembered that, around the same time, Washington gave its tacit approval for Syrian troops to end Lebanon's civil war, based on the Ta'if Accord. Washington had subsequently referred to Syrian troops in Lebanon not as an occupation, but as a "presence."

As Syrian troops took control of Lebanon and US forces withdrew from Kuwait, Washington called for Middle East peace talks to take place in Madrid, Spain. Getting Assad to attend the talks was not easy, however. Secretary of state James Baker traveled to Damascus sixteen times for talks with Assad, finally earning the president's trust and approval. Direct negotiations between Syria and Israel under American auspices began in 1994 in Washington, DC.

I knew this part of Daniel's story pretty well, as my first job at the *Middle East Times*'s Cairo bureau focused on the peace process. The talks made substantial progress, most notably with agreements over security guarantees, water rights, and "normalization" of relations. The major area of division was over the extent of Israel's withdrawal from the Golan. When Israel captured the plateau in June 1967, Syrian territory began at the northeast shore of the Sea of Galilee. Extensive irrigation projects in Israel and surrounding countries had caused the lake's water level to recede substantially, however. Israel offered to return the Golan up to the lake's 1967 waterline, which was now several hundred meters east of the water's edge. Syria demanded that the border be set at the current waterline. Reports circulated widely that Assad wanted to put his feet in the Sea of Galilee like he did when he was a boy.

The talks ended without agreement after the assassination of the Labour Israeli prime minister, Yitzhak Rabin, in 1995 and the coming to power of the Likud Party's Benjamin Netanyahu the following year. After further years with little progress in talks between Israel and the Palestinians, Labour returned to power in May 1999, pledging progress on the peace process. Labour leader Ehud Barak sought progress on talks with Syria to offset limited gains in the negotiations with the Palestinians. Direct negotiations between Israel and Syria began in December 1999, leading to a summit in Geneva between Assad and president Bill Clinton in March 2000. In the end, Assad rejected Israel's final offer: a full withdrawal apart from a one-hundred-meter strip of land along Galilee's northeastern shore.

While the negotiations were ongoing, the US embassy in Damascus officially returned to the "constructive engagement" policy of the

1970s. However, there were limits this time: a mere day before delegates convened in Madrid, the US State Department issued regulations banning "defence services" to Syria, effectively cutting off the possibility of any bilateral military cooperation.[5] US law also continued to ban American economic assistance to and restrict trade with Syria due to its designation as a state sponsor of terrorism. Nevertheless, Syria remained the only country on the US terrorism list with which the United States maintained full diplomatic relations.[6] Private-sector cooperation developed to unprecedented levels, as the embassy worked with Syria's business community to arrange export licenses for American products. The Syrian government awarded a $430 million gas-development project to Conoco, an American energy company, to be carried out in conjunction with French energy giant Total.

Relations were generally businesslike, but there were still flare-ups. Syrian youths stormed the US ambassador's residence in December 1998 and ripped down the flag in response to the United States and United Kingdom's bombing of Iraq that month in Operation Desert Fox—an attempt to cajole Iraq to comply with weapons inspectors. Washington virulently protested the Syrian incident and requested that the government sell it land to build a new, secure embassy in a suburb of Damascus.[7]

When Assad died three months later, Washington adopted a "wait and see" approach with his son and successor, Bashar. For a while, the situation was uncertain. In October 2000, Syrian protestors tried to storm the US embassy after the Israeli prime minister, Ariel Sharon, controversially led a Likud Party delegation around the al-Aqsa Mosque, effectively bringing a decade of peacemaking to an end.

It was then that diplomats in Damascus began to notice some changes. Syria's oil exports increased dramatically, leading Washington and London to accuse Syria of violating UN sanctions on Iraq by accepting up to one hundred fifty thousand barrels per day of Iraqi crude through a derelict section of the Kirkuk-Banias oil pipeline (which was built in the 1940s to carry crude from Iraq to Syria's Mediterranean coast) in return for exports of poor-quality Syrian products.[8] The Syrians, for their part, attributed the increase to having converted its power stations from oil to natural gas, which was now more plentiful in Syria due to the government's project with Conoco. In his first visit to Damascus in February 2001, US secretary of state Colin Powell had raised the pipeline issue with the Syrian leadership, but the oil and other goods kept flowing.

As it was the end of the working day, Daniel and Mary Brett invited me for a drink at the Marine Bar, located across the street from the embassy. We each grabbed a draft beer from the smiling Syrian bartender and took a table in the bar's paved garden. Syrian women, all wearing tight-fitting Western-style clothes like Leila, mixed freely with American diplomats and staff, playing pool and darts.

As the beer flowed, I began to ask more and increasingly direct questions. How could OBG produce an objective report on Syria? I explained how hard it had been to carry out research in Egypt—a US ally and a country relatively open to the world. And who would be a good local partner?

Daniel and Mary Brett just looked at each other and laughed. "I don't know," Daniel said. "Go and see the Syrian-European Business Center [SEBC]. While we don't help them, we quietly support their goal to help Syria's private sector. They also seem to be the only international project really doing anything."

I called the SEBC the following morning to set up an appointment. After a few minutes on hold, I was patched directly through to the project's director, Alf Monaghan. I briefly introduced myself and explained why I was calling.

"Come on over," he said. "I have nothing on my plate this afternoon."

When I showed up around 2 PM, the SEBC receptionist greeted me with a smile and asked me to take a seat. Unlike the décor of the US embassy, the SEBC's waiting room was all about the future. Full-sized posters advertising books on such things as starting a business and quality-control measures dotted the room's stuccoed walls. Business books and literature filled a corner cabinet behind the front door. In the right-hand corner was the center's logo, complete with European Union (EU) and Syrian flags side by side in seeming harmony.

Five minutes later, the reception area came alive as the building's staff, leather briefcases in hand, headed home for the day. Male staff sported dark, well-fitted suits; bright, wide cravats; and meticulously polished shoes. The women wore skirts, white blouses, and high heels. All spoke Arabic with a Levantine accent, which was far different from the Egyptian I had learned in Cairo. Their physical features looked hardly Arab at all, however. Most, if not all, had pearly white skin, mousy or blond hair, and piercing blue or dark-green eyes. I guessed that they were Alawites or other minorities.

Alf greeted me with a warm handshake in the lobby ten minutes later and escorted me up to his office. The top of his desk contained a penholder, nameplate, and a simple notebook. As I took a seat, I noticed the walls were covered with posters similar to the ones in the reception.

With his dark-blue silk suit and black lace-up shoes, Alf seemed the quintessential well-paid European bureaucrat. After only a few minutes into the conversation, however, I realized he took his job very seriously. He had spent a lot of time trying to come to grips with Syria's festering economic problems and the critical decisions now facing the regime. Alf explained that the regime's battle with the Muslim Brotherhood in the 1980s had had a deep impact on the country's demographics and economy. In the three decades following independence in 1946, the Syrian government encouraged couples to have large families, based on the idea that Syria had the resources to provide for a much larger population. By 1975, population growth rates reached 5 percent—one of the highest in the world at that time. The regime's crackdown on the Muslim Brotherhood in 1982 was so fearsome that many Syrians were forced to stay at home, causing a decade-long increase in birthrates. During the 1980s and early 1990s, Syria was among the top twenty fastest-growing populations in the world.

After the regime crushed the Brotherhood insurrection, Assad fell ill from exhaustion and was hospitalized. It was then that his brother, Rifaat, commander of the "special companies" brigades that had ruthlessly battled the Muslim Brotherhood in Hama, attempted to stage a coup d'état. Eventually Rifaat lost and was forced into exile, but it was costly; around the same time, nearly all of Syria's foreign currency reserves disappeared from the Central Bank, plunging the country into a crisis.[9]

As the smoke cleared and the regime consolidated its hold on power, the regime realized the scale of the population "time bomb" and quickly introduced measures to bring fertility rates down. To get more hard currency back into the country, Syria instituted a draconian foreign-exchange policy and banned nearly all imports, including even tissues and toilet paper. The regime also concentrated on boosting oil production, the revenues of which directly filled the state's coffers. It invited energy giants Shell and Total to develop Syria's light-oil production along the Euphrates River. By 1996, oil production topped six hundred thousand barrels per day, providing the state with more than enough money to fund the budget and accumulate billions of dollars in hard currency revenues. The state felt so confident of its economic position that between 1997 and 2000, parliament did not even bother to pass a state budget. As President Assad fell ill, however, and key decisions were deferred, the Syrian economy contracted 7 percent by 2000.

There were other problems as well. Syrian oil production declined as the country's oil fields slowly ran dry. Assad had also realized that the state's tired socialist public sector would be unable to create enough jobs for the waves of Syrian youngsters that were soon to enter the job market. So, in 1996, Damascus called on the European Union's help to "rehabilitate" Syria's ancient trading and capitalist systems. Brussels, trying to engage Syria to help support the peace process, was only too happy to help. The SEBC was born.

I explained to Alf all about OBG and presented him with some of our publications on Lebanon, Turkey, and Egypt. After flipping through each one, Alf confirmed that this was just what Syria needed: a quality publication on the country that dealt more with the economy than the country's difficult political issues. When I proposed a partnership with SEBC, similar to our work with chambers of commerce and business associations in other countries, he immediately agreed that it was a great idea.

To my surprise, however, Alf said the decision to set up a partnership was not his. It was up to Rola Bayda—one of several administrators. Alf set up a meeting and escorted me to Rola's office.

Rola shook my hand, smiled, and asked me to sit down. Like the SEBC staff I had seen earlier, Rola had ivory skin, brown hair, and light eyes, which, while initially kind, also appeared cold and calculating. I briefly introduced OBG and showed her some of our other reports on authoritarian countries in the Arab world. I explained that we normally partner with organizations like SEBC and that the center had come highly recommended. After flipping through our report on Egypt, Rola closed the cover and stared intently at me for what seemed like an eternity.

"Great," she said, finally breaking the silence. "When do we start?"

Two months later I was back in Cairo, finishing up a long day of organizing and writing at OBG's offices at the American Chamber of Commerce in Egypt (AmCham). Getting stuff done at AmCham, which was funded by the US Agency for International Development (USAID), was a hell of a lot easier than it was in Syria. The Internet was fast, nearly everyone seemed to have a cell phone, and take-out food deliveries arrived in less than thirty minutes. Maybe I was being too hard on old Egypt, I thought as I walked home.

My cell phone rang when I reached the front of my apartment building in Agouza. "Where are you?" my mother said as quickly as

I picked up. "CNN is reporting two planes have hit the World Trade Center in New York."

Two planes didn't sound like an accident. I had canceled my satellite TV connection when I started working in Syria to save a few dollars, so I jumped in a cab and headed back to AmCham. Along the way I dialed as many American friends in Cairo as I could. The fact that no one answered unnerved me.

I immediately headed to the executive director's office—the only one I knew who had a television. As I entered the room, I saw half a dozen senior AmCham staff gathered around a blaring television, which was showing footage of a jet ploughing into the World Trade Center's south tower. My heart seemed to move into my throat as I panicked. I immediately dialed everyone I knew in New York, but all the lines were busy. As I put the phone down, I noticed I was the only one in the room saying anything. Some paced back and forth, while others just stared at the screen in disbelief. But the same thing was on all our minds: nothing would ever be the same again.

I loved Egypt and had made many great Egyptian friends. Nevertheless, there were issues coursing through Egypt and the Arab world that were not only anti-American but against Western civilization as a whole. When I left AmCham a few hours later, everything seemed normal. Shopkeepers and passers-by gathered around radios and TVs, listening to news coverage of the attacks. I headed over to the home of an Egyptian-American friend who subscribed to CNN.

On TV, pundits were already speculating about who was responsible for the attacks. At first it seemed related to the Arab-Israeli struggle. An anonymous source had tipped off an Abu Dhabi newspaper that the attacks were carried out by the Democratic Front for the Liberation of Palestine—a leftist offshoot of the PLO. But a stark condemnation of the attacks by the organization's leader, Nayef Hawatmeh, quickly refuted the claim. The longer the night wore on, though, the more fingers pointed toward Osama bin Laden, the son of a Saudi construction magnate and leader of the Sunni radical militant group al-Qaeda. Instead of liberating Palestine, bin Laden set his sights on "liberating" the Arabian Peninsula from American forces.

As we listened, an American journalist friend sitting beside me leaned over and whispered into my ear that our host's Egyptian family didn't really have a problem with the attacks. "They said this is what we get for so blindly supporting Israel," he said. A few minutes later, another American friend arrived, saying a taxi driver had told him that the attacks were "payback" for America's foreign policy in the Middle East. The news ticker at the bottom of the TV screen stated that Palestinians were celebrating in their camps in Gaza and Lebanon, even going so far as to pass out congratulatory sweets.

This reaction didn't surprise me. Palestinians had suffered extensively from what was then fifty years of Arab-Israeli conflict; many lived in squalid conditions. But Egyptians? In the two decades following president Anwar el-Sadat's signature of the Camp David Accords, Egypt had received upwards of $2.2 billion per year from the American taxpayers. Hundreds of American businesses invested in Egypt as well, and American advisers played a key role in helping the government reform its bloated public sector. Now not only did I feel sorry that I had spent seven years in the Middle East, but I felt exploited as well.

Needing a good stiff drink and some secular solace among Westerners, I visited an upmarket bar-restaurant in Zamalek, normally an island of Western tranquility. Halfway through a whiskey, I saw two Egyptian girls in Westernized dress jump up and start dancing and singing. As the patrons also sang along, I finally realized that they were singing about how "Sylvester Stallone couldn't save the World Trade Center." I couldn't tell for sure, but the girls looked like they could have been students at the American University in Cairo. Angry, I paid the bill and went home.

The next morning at the office, I sat staring blankly at my laptop screen, my eyes tired from sifting through stories of who might be responsible for the attacks. Speculation had evolved into outright accusations that the attacks were the handiwork of Osama bin Laden, whose organization had ties to similar organizations in Egypt and the Taliban in Afghanistan. Throughout the day, I received phone call after phone call from American friends in the region asking if my friends and family were OK.

I hadn't slept well the previous night, so I headed home early to take a nap. As I stepped into the elevator, I realized that not a single Egyptian member of staff at AmCham had expressed any sorrow about the attacks. The only person who asked me if my family was safe was the building's security guard, whom I spoke with each day on the way into the office.

I then asked myself the question, Why am I living here? Egyptians always told me they differentiated between their opposition to the American government and the American people themselves. But their reactions indicated otherwise. I knew that the United States supported Israel and that its sponsorship of the peace process had yet to solve the problem. But did anything justify ploughing jets full of innocent passengers into skyscrapers? No, I thought. Standing on my terrace, overlooking the office buildings and slums that make up the Cairo skyline, I suddenly realized that I couldn't stand living there anymore. I called my travel agent and asked her to get me on the next flight to Damascus.

Stepping off the bus ferrying passengers from the Cairo International Airport terminal to the Syrian Arab Airlines jet the following afternoon, I immediately sensed that this was going to be a strange ride. Instead of participating in the normal mad dash for the stairway leading up to the aircraft's door, we stopped as an airline employee screamed at us to wait. Before us, all the passenger luggage sat in a long row on the tarmac beside the plane. One by one, we had to identify our bags and confirm the luggage tags against our boarding passes and passports before getting on the plane.

The dirty Boeing 727 looked like something out of an early 1970s airport-disaster film—it provided a window into the era before US sanctions restricted sales of American aircraft to Syria. The décor inside the plane was timeworn, and the stuffing in the seat cushions was so compacted in the center that it felt like sitting on a toilet seat. As the plane took off and the weight of my body was thrust backwards, the back of my seat gave way and slammed into the knees of the passenger behind me. All over the plane it was the same story: the seats' decades-old gearing was stripped bare from overuse.

Ideas started to race through my head. If the suspected attackers were part of a Sunni radical group led by a Saudi, and if they had links to similar terrorist groups who had been attacking Western tourists in Egypt, I began to wonder if the United States was betting on the wrong people in the Arab world. After all, didn't the Syrian regime battle with the same groups in the 1980s?

Upon arrival in Damascus, almost everyone I spoke with asked me about my family. The driver from the airport asked about my "loved ones." Checking in at the Cham Palace Hotel, a five-star hotel in Syria where I had basically lived for five months, the receptionist said she hoped "everyone was fine" as she handed me back my passport. When I called Leila, she invited me to come over to her apartment and have dinner with her parents. They were worried: Leila's brother, Tarek, had just graduated from Tufts dental school and was now practicing in Boston. While they knew by now that he was safe, they didn't know how it would affect the status of his green card in the United States. "Do you think they will kick him out?" Leila's mom asked me. I didn't know what to say.

The following morning, I met up with a few OBG analysts already in the country carrying out research. I told them about the response of Egyptians to the attacks and how much more sympathetic Syrians had seemed. Most agreed with me. The only sympathy for the attackers they had heard had been the previous morning in the SEBC's kitchen. As the Syrian staff ate a midmorning breakfast and discussed the attacks, one OBG analyst said that he had heard an SEBC employee—who was rumored to be the former girlfriend of Bashar al-Assad before he married his wife, Asma—say the attacks "made her proud to be an Arab." According to the analyst, the other SEBC employees hurriedly averted their eyes before changing the subject.

Of everyone I met, Rola seemed the most sympathetic. She sat me down in her office and asked me if my family and friends were safe.

"It's just unbelievable," she said, and she launched into a diatribe against "Sunni fundamentalists" and in favor of "our war" against the Muslim Brotherhood in the 1980s. "We have a common cause now," she said. "Maybe we always did, but some other factors got in the way."

This message was almost exactly the one that the Syrian government gave to Washington. The Syrian ambassador to the United States, Imad Moustapha, contacted US security agencies immediately and offered Syria's help, saying, "We have been fighting against al-Qaeda and other extremist fundamentalist groups for the past thirty years, and we have a wealth of information."[10] Washington accepted the offer. In the year following the September 11 attacks, Damascus provided to American security forces information on Mohammed Haydar Zammar, later identified as a planner in the September 11 attacks, who had been taken into Syrian custody after he was extradited from Morocco. Damascus also gave information to US authorities on a planned al-Qaeda attack on a US Navy unit in Bahrain that was so useful that a senior administration official told a congressional panel that "the cooperation the Syrians provided in their own interest saved American lives."[11] What Washington gave Damascus in return was not clear, but when Syria was nominated the following month for a rotating seat on the UN Security Council, the Bush administration said nothing.[12]

I do not know whether it was Syria's new-found cooperation with Washington or my growing appreciation for Damascus's secular lifestyle, but my research on Syria progressed extremely well from then onward.

The Ministry of Information told me that the only "red lines"—issues that we were not allowed to write about, or we risked being banned from the country—in my coverage concerned the president and his family and the pipeline from Iraq to Syria, which the Syrian government insisted it was only "testing."

Rola made arrangements with "new guard" reformers loyal to the president to write a number of opinion pieces for the report. These reformers included Ayman Abdel Nour, an Assyrian Christian engineer who served as an adviser to the president on finance, and Samir Seifan, a Christian economist trained in East Germany, who served as the Damascene representative of the oil company Petrofac. Both produced well-argued pieces on time.

By rubbing shoulders, I was able to attract some really talented people to the project. Abdul Kader I. Husrieh, a lawyer with the Arthur Andersen accounting office in Damascus, wrote the entire legal and accounting sections of the report himself. Husrieh loved Syria, but he also loved the power of the American education he had received at the American University in Beirut. Of all the Syrians writing for OBG's first Syrian report, it was Husrieh who believed that only legal and tax reforms would eventually change the way the Assad regime ruled, essentially taming it by necessity.

When it came to finding a politics writer, I asked Ammar Abdulhamid, an SEBC translator and compiler of the organization's newsletter, to participate. I first met Ammar when he served as my interpreter for an interview with his mother, the renowned Syrian actress Muna Wassef. Sporting a long blond bushy ponytail and baggy clothes, Ammar did not conform to the SEBC's fashion code. In this instance, however, Ammar failed to write the section and instead subcontracted a friend to do it.

In the month before we went to press, I circulated drafts of each section to various local economists and diplomats as part of the fact-checking process. Daniel Rubinstein at the US embassy liked the draft and appreciated that we were critical of the country while outlining its strengths. He reminded me that Syria's $534 million debt to the United States should be added into our section on Syria's external accounts.

When the report was finally launched in February 2002, the Ministry of Information was pleased and passed the report through the country's strict censorship bureau in one day. This was surprising, given that the report basically told the international community that while good things were going on in Syria, it was hardly a place to invest until much deeper reforms had taken root. Syrian TV covered the book's launch at the Meridien Hotel as if it were the Academy Awards.

Sitting in the hotel bar with OBG senior staff after the launch, I realized that I had reached a tipping point. At first I thought it was just my desire for the Levant's more secular lifestyle. But it was more than that. I had stumbled into what seemed to be a great story—the transformation of a brutal dictatorship into a developing country with great potential. I knew I already had access to Syria, but I couldn't live there due to the country's visa restrictions for foreign journalists. So I flew to Cairo the next day, said good-bye to my friends, and closed my apartment.[13] I moved everything I owned to Syrian-controlled Beirut, where the liberal Western lifestyle was a welcome relief after seven years in an increasingly conservative and radicalized Arab regime. In Lebanon there were beautiful mountains, forests, wine châteaus, Roman ruins, and rain—the first I had seen in years. And while it wasn't Pennsylvania, it felt like home.

2

THE GREAT UNRAVELING

Almost a year to the day after the launch of OBG's Syria report, I was back in Damascus working on another one. As I entered my rented apartment in East Mezze, a few blocks from the SEBC, the air was so cold that I could see my breath. I threw the switch to the apartment's boiler, which let out a roar as it ignited ten seconds later. The apartment filled with the smell of diesel—the cheap subsidized fuel Syrians use for everything, from heating their homes to keeping irrigation pumps running.

I turned on the television and cranked the volume up to drown out the boiler's drone. Secretary of state Colin Powell was beginning a presentation to the UN Security Council concerning allegations that Iraq was attempting to conceal its weapons of mass destruction (WMD) program from UN inspectors. His slide presentation, entitled "Failure to Disarm," was peppered with English translations of Iraqi radio transmissions that helped make Washington's case. In one transcript, an Iraqi officer said, "Nerve agents. Stop talking about it. They are listening to us. Don't give any evidence that we have these horrible agents." Another showed computer animations of "mobile labs"—railcar and truck-sized trailer facilities that US intelligence claimed could produce as much biological agent in one month as the whole of Iraq had produced in "all the years prior to the Gulf War." I knew that Iraq had no missiles or planes that could deliver such agents to Europe or the United States. But they could make their way into the hands of terrorist groups set on America's destruction. For the first time in my life, I thought about the possibility of an anthrax attack on my hometown near Pittsburgh.

While Powell didn't prove any of his claims, he did demonstrate that Iraq was attempting to conceal something regarding a biological, chemical, or nuclear weapons program.[1] This was in violation of Security Council Resolution 1441, a measure passed the previous November that declared Baghdad in "material breach" of its disarmament obligations following the 1990–1991 Gulf War and gave Baghdad "a final opportunity to comply with its disarmament obligations."[2] Powell's presentation was the Bush administration's opening diplomatic salvo to try to pass another UN resolution giving international legal justification for the use of military force against Saddam Hussein's regime.

From afar, Damascus's reactions to Washington's plans might have seemed mixed. Syria voted in favor of 1441, allowing the resolution to be adopted unanimously and giving it a wider range of support than had been achieved leading up to the US-led liberation of Kuwait in the 1990–1991 Gulf War.[3] Powell's presentation seemed to change Syria's tune, however. In prepared remarks, Syria's representative to the UN, Mikhail Wehbe, read a statement by the Syrian foreign minister, Farouk al-Shara, implying a new resolution was not needed.[4]

In the weeks that followed, there were signs that perhaps Washington and Damascus were still working together behind the scenes. Syria ordered the withdrawal of around four thousand troops from Lebanon. Damascus threw all its troop- and tank-transport trucks onto the Damascus-Beirut highway at the same time, jamming the road and raising the redeployment's profile.

From my office in Damascus, however, it was clear that relations between Syria and the West were worsening. The euphoria surrounding Assad's promised reforms had vanished, as scores of new legislative initiatives remained unimplemented. Many held Syria's "new guard" reformers responsible, as well as the EU and UN projects designed to assist them. The pressure was so strong on many reformers that they wouldn't even meet with me.

The Ministry of Information was less friendly as well. It limited the duration of my visa from six months to three, giving the government the option of not renewing it, in case OBG operations got out of line. We were told that, shortly following the release of OBG's first report, a local economic research firm published a report that severely criticized our work, as well as the Ministry of Information for allowing it. While the matter seemed to have been resolved by the time that I first arrived in Damascus in the autumn of 2002, my first meeting with the director of the ministry's public relations office, Mounir Ali, told me exactly what worried the government most. "I don't want to read anything about the pipeline from Iraq," he said.

Reports continued to make it into the Western press that Syria received up to two hundred thousand barrels per day of Iraqi crude at discounted prices. For proof, most diplomats pointed to figures showing Syrian oil exports rising—quite an anomaly for a country whose oil fields were well known to be in slow decline. The extra top-up from Iraq helped the regime not only to export more crude but to continue subsidizing diesel, food stuffs, and other basic goods far below market prices. Businessmen close to the regime, whose factories produced poor-quality goods, were rumored to have dealings with Iraq as well.

Suddenly, anything to do with Iraq became a red line. On December 23—while most Westerners in Syria were home spending the holidays with their families—security forces arrested Ibrahim Hamidi, Damascus bureau chief of *Al Hayat* and author of the main political commentary in our OBG report the previous year. No one knew where he was for about a week—Syria's emergency law allowed the state to detain any Syrian citizen indefinitely without charge. A few days before his arrest, Ibrahim had written a story about Syria's preparations to receive up to one million Iraqi refugees should American forces invade Iraq and oust Saddam Hussein. His arrest was finally confirmed by the official Syrian Arab News Agency (SANA), which stated that he was being held on charges of "publishing false news," a crime that carried a possible term of three years in prison and a fine of one million Syrian pounds (twenty thousand US dollars).[5]

I knew Ibrahim well, and his arrest upset me greatly. When I returned to my desk at the SEBC in January, I reread Ibrahim's article, "Modernizing Syria's Image," in OBG's last report. The article was one of the most concise summaries of the clampdown on the "Damascus Spring" during Bashar's first two years in power. He concluded the article with a certain degree of optimism about the release of political prisoners and the closing of Syria's most notorious gulags. I hated to think of the one in which he now found himself.

With reforms frozen, people avoiding my phone calls, and the story of Syria's opening up to the outside world fading, I could see from my edition-planning sheet that this year's report would be remarkably thin. So I called a meeting with Rola to ask for her advice on what to do. She agreed with me that there had been setbacks in Syrian reform, due largely to the "regional situation." However, unlike most Syrians and foreigners involved in reform that year, Rola was optimistic that reform would continue. She said a number of new NGOs under the patronage of the president's wife, Asma al-Assad, showed the president's dedication to reform. "Would you like to see their operations in action?" she asked.

Two days later, I found myself sitting in the backseat of a black SUV speeding down a windy dirt road that cut through the lush green countryside outside Aleppo. I was there to tour the development projects of the Fund for Integrated Rural Development of Syria (FIRDOS), an NGO dedicated to tackling rural poverty that was supported by Mrs. Assad. As I read through the NGO's introductory pamphlet, I remembered that "firdos" was Arabic for "paradise."

The SUV slowed down as we entered a village southwest of Aleppo. Before the driver could put it into park, villagers gathered around the car to greet us. I stepped down from the car, and my polished shoes immediately sloshed into four inches of deep red mud that carpeted the village's town square. A village representative from FIRDOS greeted me with a handshake and a smile and asked me to follow him to the village's project site.

They called it a dental clinic, but it looked more like the window-less concrete shell of a would-be gas station that you might find in the mountains of Pennsylvania. The representative described the building as a former "municipal complex." He said that FIRDOS had provided enough funds to cover the current renovations and the purchase of state-of-the-art dental equipment. Syria's Ministry of Health would be responsible for providing the dentists.

In the next village, it was a different version of the same story. FIRDOS had purchased scores of computers and created a computer lab in a village municipal building. The eyes of smiling students sitting at every computer terminal greeted me as I entered the room. When I tried to make small talk and ask them what they were working on, I noticed that most had Microsoft Word documents open on-screen and were practicing their typing; a few were playing with blank Excel spreadsheets. The representative told me the center was one of twelve FIRDOS-sponsored labs throughout the country. The organization had a "mobile information center" (MIC)—a bus that had been turned into a sort of mobile computer lab.

In the next village, I interviewed a recipient of a FIRDOS scholarship, a bright girl named Amira who had scored particularly well on her high school exams. "I could never go to college without FIRDOS," she told me nervously. "I want to study English literature and return to my village and teach."

Late in the afternoon, while taking lunch with FIRDOS representatives, I started to have mixed feeling about what I had seen that day. On the one hand, I strongly identified with the stories of the Syrians we had visited. I grew up in rural western Pennsylvania, where my mother and father had bettered themselves through a combination of hard work and higher education. They often told me about the "chances" they had been given with the help of scholarships or benefactors. I had received similar help as well: more than one scholarship fund in my hometown had helped me pay college tuition, and a number of foundations had paid my way through MA study at the American University in Cairo, launching me on a career in journalism in the Middle East.

On the other hand, FIRDOS programs seemed tightly controlled and its beneficiaries' stories too good to be true. At first I chalked it up to a language barrier: five years of English-language journalism and office work at OBG had eroded my Arabic language skills. Nevertheless, my journalistic experience in Cairo had taught me that development projects in the Arab world seldom went according to plan. For example, FIRDOS's pilot microfinance program to support small business ventures had a payback rate of 100 percent—an unlikely percentage given the risks of starting thousands of microenterprises. After all, what were the chances that every business would succeed? The obstacles that beneficiaries had overcome sounded genuine and compelling, but the ending of each story was apparently always the same: FIRDOS was their ticket to paradise.

When I returned to Damascus, I stopped by to thank Rola for arranging what I felt was a very interesting trip. "Yes, I know," she said knowingly. "The first lady would like to meet you for a 'chat' about what you saw."

Asma al-Assad's secretary called me a few days later to schedule an appointment. She told me to wait at 6 PM on the corner outside my apartment building, where a car and escort from the palace would meet me. When I tried to offer my address, the secretary politely cut me off midsentence. "We know where you live, Mr. Tabler," she said.

At 6 PM sharp, a man with dark hair, bright-blue eyes, and ivory skin, dressed in a black wool trench coat, met me at the side of the curb and motioned me into the backseat of a black Honda Accord. I knew who I was going to meet, but I had no idea where I was going. As the car snaked up the road from Mezze to Mount Qassioun, the heights overlooking Damascus, I tried to make small talk with the drivers in Arabic about the cold and rainy weather that winter. Both acknowledged with a glance that I was talking to them, but they said nothing, their faces stern. Halfway up the hill, along a right-hand bend in a thicket of willow trees, the car veered off the highway onto an old country road whose passage was obscured by dangling branches. Men with machine guns appeared among the trees at both sides of the car as we approached an iron gate. A guard with features nearly identical to my escort's looked at the driver's face, then glanced at mine. Without saying a word, he motioned with one hand, and the gate in front of us swung open. Fifty meters ahead was a small dacha with a classical facade. The car pulled up to the building's front door. Another guard, looking identical to the first, opened the car door. "Up the stairs to your left, sir," he said.

This wasn't my first meeting with a head of state or his wife in the Arab world, so I had a good idea what to expect. This usually involved waiting, sometimes for hours, in an antechamber while staff served strong cups of Arabic coffee or tea. Sometimes the VIP's aides would try and spin stories as well. Once, while waiting to meet the Palestinian president Yasir Arafat in Gaza, for example, one of his staff tried to convince me that the Monica Lewinsky scandal was a Jewish plot to undermine the peace process.

As I entered the room, I saw Asma al-Assad sitting behind her desk, quietly writing. I was shocked—no one had asked me for my ID or searched my bag. She glanced up, put down her pen, and greeted me with a tender handshake and smile. It was clear why she had caught the president's eye: standing about five foot eight with bobbed blond hair and friendly eyes and in good shape, Mrs. Assad was a vision of refined Levantine beauty.

I also soon understood why he had married her. In a place where few things were as they seemed, she was surprisingly open and genuine, telling me all about her life within the first hour of our discussion. Asma was born in London in 1975 to Fawaz Akhras, a well-regarded cardiologist who hailed from a prominent Sunni family from the Syrian city of Homs, and his wife, Sahar, a former first secretary in the Syrian embassy in London. After a public-school education in Britain, Asma entered King's College, University of London, earning high marks and graduating with a first-class-honors bachelor of science degree in computer science and a diploma in French literature. The following year, she started work at Deutsche Bank as an analyst in a hedge fund. In 1998, she joined J.P. Morgan's London office, where she became an investment banker specializing in mergers and acquisitions for biotechnology and pharmaceutical companies.[6]

The reasons for her next step she didn't explain. After three seemingly successful years in the world of finance, Asma returned to Syria and married Bashar al-Assad. The marriage raised eyebrows in Syria for one particular reason: Asma was Sunni, and Bashar was Alawite.

No photographs of the wedding appeared in local newspapers, which some Syrians told me was a sign of the Assad family's displeasure with the president's choice. Asma told me that the secrecy surrounding her wedding allowed her to get to know her homeland better. So while the British press speculated that the president's wife was now living the life of luxury, Asma instead made an incognito journey around Syria. She said she wanted to talk to and meet Syrians openly, not as the wife of the president. She said she needed to talk to people in a normal environment to listen to and understand their problems. She said she visited around one hundred villages in all but one of Syria's fourteen governorates. Since Israel occupied the Golan, that probably meant all Syrian territory under the regime's control.

Asma said, "Villagers are very pure, very willing. Young people don't want to leave their villages, but economic opportunities don't exist there." While this seemed hard to believe, I understood her point: Syrian cities were already crowded and full of shantytowns. During the 1980s and early 1990s, Syria had one of the world's highest population growth rates in the world. If they all came to Damascus and Aleppo for work, life would be miserable for everyone.

Some of the "discussion forums" of Bashar's early days in office were rumored to have tried to register under the associations law, the statute governing civil-society organizations that dated back forty years—long before NGOs existed. But the reason why NGOs couldn't register was political; some of the "discussion forums" of Bashar's early days in office had tried to register under the associations law, which alarmed many in the regime. They had probably followed the Egyptian government's legal battles with Western-funded NGOs in the 1990s that tried to promote democratic change. Some in the Syrian regime were rumored to believe that the NGOs were "Trojan horses" designed to bring down the regime.

To protect FIRDOS, Mrs. Assad explained that she registered the NGO as a charity, which legally restricted its work but allowed it to operate. She also placed the organization under her "patronage," a term that I knew, from my years of working in the Arab world, meant that she called most, if not all, the shots.

I suddenly felt confused. If we had had this conversation during my first project in Syria, when reform euphoria still gripped the country, it would have been consistent. However, times had changed. The legislation to open private banks in Syria, passed in April 2001, had yet to be implemented—in fact, not a single bank had even been named. Those who had originally written about the potential of private banks wouldn't write for me anymore, and my buddy Ibrahim was in jail.

So I asked her about these recent setbacks and the reasons behind them. She smiled and said reform in Syria would continue, but it was taking longer than expected. "When you are in our situation, you come to depend on people you would not have to elsewhere," she said impenetrably. Did she mean that the Syrian regime was next on Washington's hit list? Or was it because it was a minority regime? "If we opened the market to private banks now, and the staff at the Central Bank was not prepared to handle it, there could be chaos. Would that be good for the country?"

I had experienced the incompetence of Syrian public officialdom firsthand. Only a few weeks previously, the Syrian Central Bank governor—the Syrian equivalent of the Federal Reserve chairman—had grilled one of our analysts on last year's OBG report. During a three-hour meeting, he read aloud every line of the financial services section in Stalinist fashion, screaming "This is a lie!" at the end of every sentence. While I didn't doubt that OBG was capable of making mistakes, the notion that everything we wrote was untrue was simply nonsensical.

I didn't agree with everything she said, but Asma al-Assad seemed genuine and was very likable. After working in Syria on and off for two years, it was just refreshing to meet a talented person in such an interesting—and powerful—position. While many of her projects seemed naïve, her motivation to improve her fellow man in such a tough environment was seductive. I felt so comfortable with her that when I shook her hand to say good-bye, I nearly called her by her first name.

Excited by my visit with Syria's first lady, I began writing my article on FIRDOS the next morning. I was familiar with NGO activities in Egypt as well as the problems associated with Cairo's sprawling shantytowns, so it was an easy task. When I visited Mounir Ali at the Ministry of Information that week and told him about my interview with the "first lady," he looked surprised. "Just a point of clarification," he said pedantically. "Officially, the first lady of Syria is Anissa al-Assad, the late president's wife and President Bashar's mother. Asma should be referred to as 'the wife of the president.'"

After the article had been edited, I sent a copy to Rola to forward on to Mrs. Assad. After a few days, Rola reported back that the "first lady" loved the article and handed me a memory pen containing an electronic copy of an amended version. The only addition was a quote from FIRDOS's external relations coordinator Nouar al-Shara, the daughter of foreign minister Farouk al-Shara, reading, "FIRDOS is different because we work with people, not for them."

Shortly after my meeting with Asma, US policy toward Syria began to change. On March 3, 2003, Secretary of State Powell declared in a speech before Congress that it was the objective of the United States to "let Lebanon be ruled by the Lebanese people without the presence of the Syrian occupation army."[7] Since Washington's tacit "deal" with Assad over Lebanon in the autumn of 1990, Powell's words marked the first time that a US official referred to Syria's "presence" in Lebanon as an occupation.

On March 17, Powell withdrew a draft resolution from the UN Security Council, which had called for the use of military force to compel Saddam Hussein to disarm. Washington announced that existing resolutions were enough to justify the use of military force in Iraq. War was coming fast, so I hurriedly cleaned out my Damascus apartment and prepared to fly the following morning to OBG's other project, which was located in Tunis. Most Syrians I knew warned me that during the Gulf War, international telephone lines and other communications with Syria were disconnected for over a week—which was time I could not afford to be cut off from OBG while it was going through frantic regional expansion.

I stopped by to see Rola. I wanted to tell her about my early departure and thank her for all her help. After a few minutes of small talk, she suddenly surprised me by saying that she had been talking with Bouthaina Shaaban about ways to improve Syria's image. She was referring to the spokeswoman for the Ministry of Foreign Affairs—a former translator for Hafez al-Assad. "We'd like to hear your ideas on how to do that. Once the war is over, come to Damascus and we will talk about it."

Before leaving Damascus, I stopped by the US embassy to say good-bye to a few friends. The thoroughfare in front of the embassy, normally filled with cars, was jammed with people, queuing in front of the Iraqi embassy. Buses were parked nearby, with scores of Syrian youths sitting inside. When I finally made it into the chancery, a friend pointed out of the window toward the Iraqi embassy. "They say they are volunteering to go fight us in Iraq," he said, eyebrows raised.

In Tunis, I returned to the chaos of OBG's global expansion. From my hotel room, I followed the story of US troops invading Iraq via CNN.

Reports from journalists and camera crews embedded within US troop units dominated the news coverage, which eclipsed Syria's response to the invasion. The Tunisian government's restrictions on the Internet made checking the news difficult. I was also suffering from a sort of "burnout" regarding Syria that OBG staff often experienced immediately after a report. However, from what I could see, US-Syrian relations seemed to be taking a turn for the worst.

Syria's response to the invasion was defiance. Volunteers to wage "jihad" against occupation forces continued to gather in front of the US embassy in Damascus. When Washington protested diplomatically, the gathering point was moved to the old Damascus International Fairgrounds.

On March 27, Assad officially confirmed Syria's support for resistance against US forces in Iraq. In an interview with Lebanon's *As-Safir* newspaper, Assad said that "if the American-British designs succeed—and we hope they do not succeed . . . there will be Arab popular resistance."[8]

Later the same day, Syria's grand mufti, the elderly Sheikh Ahmad Kuftaro, called on "Muslims everywhere to use all means possible to thwart the aggression, including martyr operations against American, British and Zionist invaders. . . . Resistance to the belligerent invaders is an obligation for all Muslims."[9] A few days later, Syrian foreign minister Farouk al-Shara announced before the Syrian parliament that Syria had a "national interest in the expulsion of the invaders from Iraq," and praised Iraqis' "courageous resistance" to the US-led invasion.[10]

Syria's change in policy elicited a corresponding change in Washington's approach to Syria. Under Washington's constructive engagement policy, the State Department had eschewed criticizing Syrian policy in public in favor of private but frank discussions. But when battlefield reports came in of Syrian-supplied Russian Kornet anti-tank missiles and night-vision goggles being used to attack US forces, the Department of Defense adopted a new, harder line with Damascus. On March 28, defense secretary Donald Rumsfeld told reporters that the United States had information regarding the shipment of military supplies from Syria to Iraq that pose "a direct threat to the lives of coalition forces." When asked if the regime itself was responsible for the shipments, Rumsfeld simply replied, "They control their border."[11]

Two days later, Powell hardened the State Department's line on Damascus as well. Since Bashar had taken the reigns of power in 2000, the State Department's assumptions were that the young president was not fully in charge of the regime he had inherited from his father and that certain rogue elements were able to carry out security-related activities without the knowledge of the presidential palace. With evidence piling up of Syrian support for resistance to the US invasion, however, Powell laid blame directly at Assad's doorstep. "Syria faces a critical choice," Powell told an audience at the American Israel Public Affairs Committee. "Syria can continue direct support for terrorist groups and the dying regime of Saddam Hussein, or it can embark on a different and more hopeful course. Either way, Syria bears the responsibility for its choices, and for the consequences."[12]

On April 2, Bouthaina Shaaban, the Ministry of Foreign Affairs spokesperson, gave the world an indication of how Syria's support for resistance would work, at least rhetorically, for years to come. On the one hand, the regime would continue to exercise the Arab world's most liberal visa policies for Arab nationals. On the other, the regime did not accept responsibility for patrolling its border with a US-occupied Iraq. "If anybody is going, it is beyond our control as the government," she said. "We have long borders with Iraq and we can't put a policeman on every single meter."[13]

As American forces continued their assault on Baghdad, the war of words escalated between Washington and Damascus. On April 11, President Bush warned Syria not to offer safe haven to Iraqi officials. The warning was based on US intelligence that convoys of vehicles had crossed from Iraq to Syria in the first week of the war, possibly carrying members of Saddam Hussein's family and key members of the regime. US forces later fired on a Russian diplomatic convoy from Baghdad to Syria that reportedly had been carrying Iraqi officials as well. On April 14, Powell said that the United States "will examine possible measures of a diplomatic, economic or other nature as we move forward."[14] In the days that followed, US special forces shut down the last Iraqi pumping station on the Kirkuk-Banias pipeline, cutting off the flow of sanctions-busting oil flowing from Iraq to Syria.[15] They also bombed the Syrian Trade Center in Baghdad. This kicked off speculation that the Department of Defense was drawing up contingency plans for a US attack on Syria.[16]

The Syrian leadership's comments resonated not only with Syrians opposed to the invasion but also with a lot of people across the Arab world. At a rally in Egypt's al-Azhar Mosque, a center for Islamic jurisprudence, protestors shouted, "Bashar, Bashar, set the world on fire!"[17] For anyone familiar with Syrian history, Assad's turn away from the United States and toward jihadists and Salafists—who hated the Syrian regime—was surprising to say the least. Many Islamists in the Arab world regarded the minority Assad regime as apostates, especially after the regime's bloody suppression of the Muslim Brotherhood's uprising in 1982.

As Iraqi resistance to the US invasion fell apart, there were signs that Assad appeared to be complying with Washington's demands and that a diplomatic resolution to the crisis was in the cards. On April 16, the US Central Command (CENTCOM) in Qatar announced that the numbers of people moving between Syria and Iraq had fallen sharply, due in part to the deployment of US forces along the frontier. Later the same day, Powell announced that he would soon visit Damascus for a "very vigorous diplomatic exchange" with President Assad. Two Iraqi regime members who had taken refuge in Syria—including Saddam Hussein's bodyguard and a son-in-law—showed up back in Iraq a few days later. By April 20—a mere month after US forces invaded Iraq—President Bush announced that there were "positive signs" coming out of Damascus regarding American demands.[18]

For most of the summer, tensions seemed to ease between Washington and Damascus. On May 3, Powell made his third and arguably most high-profile visit to Damascus. During the discussions, Powell addressed the issues of (1) Iraqi border security; (2) Damascus's harboring of high level Baathists from Saddam Hussein's regime; (3) Hamas, Islamic Jihad, and other Palestinian militant group offices in Damascus; and (4) Syria's WMD program. A number of Bush administration officials, led by undersecretary of state for arms control John Bolton, expressed concern about Syria's stockpiles of chemical weapons, most notably sarin nerve gas, which could be loaded onto Syria's large stockpile of Scud missiles. Bolton also expressed concern about Syria's development of biological weapons as well as its pursuit of nuclear cooperation with Russia, which "provides opportunities for Syria to expand its indigenous capabilities, should it decide to pursue nuclear weapons." In an interview on April 15, Bolton said, "I'm not saying they're doing anything specific. . . . I'm just saying it's a worrisome pattern that we've seen."[19]

Powell's visit had mixed results. Powell cited "some closures" of the offices of Islamic Jihad, the Popular Front for the Liberation of Palestine–General Command (PFLP-GC), and Hamas following his visit, but calls to these facilities indicated they were still open.[20] The number of foreign fighters continued to be lower than during the first weeks of the war, but the issue of Iraqi Baathists fleeing to Syria remained a sore point. On June 18, US forces in "hot pursuit" of a convoy of SUVs suspected of carrying Iraqi officials penetrated some twenty-five miles into Syrian territory. Iraqi officials were not found in the convoy.

Nevertheless, with increased reports of foreign fighters crossing the Syrian frontier into Iraq as well as accusations that Syria was harboring remnants of Saddam Hussein's regime and arsenal, those voices within the administration advocating a hard line with Damascus won out. In September, the Bush administration allowed Bolton to testify before a congressional subcommittee hearing on Syria's efforts to develop weapons of mass destruction (having prevented him doing so two months earlier). While much of the information was not new, the hearing marked the first time that the Bush administration, in the words of the *New York Times*, "presented a detailed, public assessment of such activities." Bolton said that Syria had developed "a stockpile of the nerve agent sarin that can be delivered by aircraft or ballistic missiles, and has engaged in the research and development of more toxic and persistent nerve agents such as VX" and "is continuing to develop an offensive biological weapons capability." Bolton also reported on Syrian efforts to acquire nuclear technology, adding that Russia and Syria "have approved a draft program on cooperation on civil nuclear power"—all expertise that could be applied to a nuclear weapons program.[21]

As OBG expanded into more countries, the pace of expansion was getting to be too much for me. Traveling every week to a new country might sound glamorous, but it takes its toll. I spent most of my time at OBG's production facility in Istanbul, Turkey, far away from the Arab world that I had come to the region to learn about. Around the time that Powell visited Damascus, I knew that I was ready to leave OBG.

Looking for a way out, I took a week's vacation in July and traveled from Amman, Jordan, to Damascus to talk with Rola. Sitting in her office at the SEBC, I explained my novel idea for improving Syria's image: create an English-language, privately owned magazine and give its writers freedom to write critically on issues in Syria. Much of OBG's success in the Arab world was simply based on the fact that well-edited English-language articles, based on in-country research, were virtually nonexistent. Creating high-quality articles wasn't simply a matter of editing, however. The uncertain red lines governing media in Syria would have to be thrown out of the window as well. The only restriction that we would observe would be avoiding harsh criticism of the president and his wife.

When I finished my presentation, Rola looked into my eyes, took a deep breath, and exhaled. "Interesting," she said. "Can you draw up plans to create such a magazine?"

As I worked on the plans at a friend's house in Damascus, I watched the news carefully to see which way the wind was blowing between Washington and Damascus. Everything seemed quiet, and there was no news of any fallout from Bolton's WMD testimony. It seemed that Powell's more stern diplomatic approach with Syria had worked and that Washington's interests in preserving intelligence cooperation in the war on terror trumped other issues.

A week later, I handed Rola a business plan to create *Syria Today*—a quarterly magazine on Syrian affairs—before returning to my work with OBG in Jordan. Soon after I arrived at my hotel in Amman, Rola called me from Damascus. "The first lady loved your proposal," she said. "Can you make it here next week to go over the details with her?"

As soon as Rola and I walked through her office door, I sensed something was different about Asma al-Assad. She seemed tired and preoccupied. The first characteristic I could chalk up to the fact that she was pregnant; the second I couldn't tell, but I guessed it was a result of the political situation.

After a bit of casual chat, she got right down to business. She told me she had read the business plan and liked the idea. During the week that I was in Amman, Asma and Rola had agreed that *Syria Today* would be set up as a start-up company in the business incubator of a new NGO being established under Asma's patronage: Modernizing and Activating Women's Role in Economic Development (MAWRED). Leila, with whom I had developed the business plan, would be the lead entrepreneur, legally hosted in the incubator.

I would be hired as the media adviser for FIRDOS, the NGO I had written about six months before. While I would have duties editing materials for FIRDOS, I would be seconded to MAWRED to advise Leila on founding *Syria Today*. After reading through the business plan together, she only had one question: "Are you sure you will have enough time to advise FIRDOS and work on *Syria Today* at the same time?" I assured her that I would.

After a half an hour of discussing the details, Rola and I said good-bye to the first lady and piled into the palace car for the ride back down the hill. As we rolled out of the front gate, I turned to Rola and blurted out, "Strange, she didn't talk about the costs I outlined. I was going to say something, but I was afraid to ask." Rola suddenly looked serious and shushed me by putting a finger to her lips, then pointed to the palace drivers in the front seat.

After a few seconds, her smile returned. "She likes you," she said. "You are going to do well here."

3

PARADISE LOST

It was October 5, 2003—two weeks to the day after I began work at FIRDOS. I sat in the NGO's kitchen reading the Syrian broadsheets on my morning coffee break. On most days, I was able to read the main pages of Syria's state-owned broadsheets in a mere fifteen minutes. This wasn't because my Arabic was that good or that the articles were that well written—it was that all Syrian newspapers ran the same stories, word for word, that SANA, the state's official mouthpiece, produced.

Looking up from a story on a council of ministers meeting, I saw Nouar al-Shara—daughter of foreign minister Farouk al-Shara and the NGO's external relations coordinator—staring at me while nibbling on a carrot. Of all my colleagues at FIRDOS, Nouar was always the most polite, so I greeted her with a smile and asked her how she had spent her evening the day before.

"Didn't you hear? They bombed us last night," she said in between bites. Then she raised her eyebrows, grabbed her coffee mug, and walked out of the kitchen.

As the first lady's premier NGO, FIRDOS's office had one of Syria's fastest Internet connections, so I jumped online and checked the English-language media. After a bit of frantic searching, I finally found the story on the English-language site of the Israeli paper *Haaretz*.

Israeli planes had bombed a Palestinian camp at Ain Saheb, fifteen miles outside Damascus. The raid was in response to a suicide bombing in a Haifa restaurant that had killed nineteen people two days before; responsibility for the bombing had been claimed by the Palestinian terrorist group Islamic Jihad. Israel held Syria responsible for the attack because Islamic Jihad's offices in Damascus remained open, despite Assad's pledge to Powell a few months earlier. Syria claimed that it had in fact closed the offices but that only "media representatives" remained in each office's information bureaus.

My heart started to race. The last time Israel had bombed Syria was during the October 1973 War, which happened to have begun nearly the same day thirty years before. The surprise attack by Syria and Egypt against Israel had been thwarted a few days later by a massive Israeli counterattack. After countless rounds of "shuttle diplomacy" by Kissinger, both sides had signed a disengagement agreement in May 1974, and since then, Syria's border with Israel was the country's quietest one.

I ran a few hundred yards down the street to the SEBC offices to see Rola. Through her open office door, I could see her frantically wading through the stacks of papers on her desk. Without looking up from her desk, she simply said, "I heard," and motioned for me to sit down. For the next ten minutes, she said nothing; instead she nervously searched through the drawers of her desk, then slammed them shut. She then wheeled her desk chair over to me, looked me in the eyes, and said, "We might need to go to Jordan to support the president and the first lady from there."

I swallowed hard and thought, Jordan? Why would that be necessary? Is the regime about to fall?

"I know it's hard to understand," Rola said. "But everyone knows that the Assad regime is based on a sort of understanding between Israel and the Assad family. That understanding was broken last night."

Panic filled my head. My Syrian friends had told me countless times about the "rules of the game" between Israel and Syria: the Assad family rules Syria, it doesn't directly attack Israel, and it keeps Syria stable and the Muslim Brotherhood in check. In return, Israel agrees not to attack Syrian soil. Up until this point, however, I had just chalked this up to the conspiratorial nature of politics in the Levant, which often attributed events to the playing out of a sinister plot. Throughout Bashar's early years in power, there were constant rumors of conflict between the president and the "old guard"—political and security officials appointed by Bashar's father who continued to serve the new president. While no one was able to specifically name members of this "old guard," most believed that the group was headed by the Syrian vice president, Abdel Halim Khaddam, the man many held as responsible for the crackdown that ended the Damascus Spring shortly after Bashar came to power. Driving the panic home, Rola said, "I'm going to pay you before the Syrian pound crashes."

I bid Rola good-bye and ran downstairs, one floor below, to the offices of MAWRED, which the SEBC officially "hosted." Inside a small room in the MAWRED business incubator, Leila sat at her desk, working on *Syria's Today*'s marketing strategy. I told her in a hushed voice what Rola had just told me. She wrinkled her eyebrows, looked at me, and yelled, "What!" Then she became uncharacteristically quiet and just stared out of the window for a few minutes. Without saying a word, she then packed her bag and headed home.

Syria is seven hours ahead of Washington, so when I arrived home I switched on the TV expecting to hear Washington's response—none was forthcoming. Before heading to bed, I listened to the BBC World Service's *Newshour* on my short-wave radio. The program's host interviewed Tom Lantos, then chairman of the House Committee on Foreign Affairs and a Holocaust survivor who had helped draft the Syria Accountability and Lebanese Sovereignty Restoration Act of 2003 (SAA)—a bill designed to tighten trade sanctions on Syria because of its support for terrorism, foreign fighters entering Iraq, and its WMD program.

Because of Syria's intelligence sharing after the attacks of September 11, the Bush administration opposed the SAA on the grounds that it tied the president's hands in waging the war on terror. As Lantos ranted against the Syrian regime and its sponsorship of terrorism, the announcer reminded Lantos that Bush opposed the SAA and had asked the committee to block its passage. "Oh no they don't," Lantos retorted. "I just got off the phone with the national security adviser. They are going ahead with it." The radio suddenly fell silent, and I drifted off into sleep.

I had a dream. I was running through the streets of Koreitem, the Beirut neighborhood that was home to the Lebanese prime minister, Rafik Hariri. Bombs were falling from the sky around us as we ran by a nearby lighthouse. Scores of Lebanese around me were ducking for cover. As I approached the Hariri compound's rear entrance, I stopped and looked up at the sky to see who was bombing us. It was an American plane. Somewhere deep down, I realized that I now worked in the newest member of the "axis of evil." I also understood that the battle between the United States and Syria would take place in Lebanon.

The following morning it was official: President Bush described the Israeli attack as "justified" and announced that he was lifting his administration's opposition to the SAA. News coverage speculated that the new sanctions would have little impact, given Syria's small trade volume with the United States. Politically, however, the sanctions were billed as a turning point in US-Syrian relations. When I visited a contact at the US embassy that morning for background information on the new sanctions regime, he concluded our conversation by saying, "We need to talk about whether your work helps or hurts the new situation." As I exited the embassy and walked across Rouda Square, I contemplated ways that I might leave the country.

I had never realized my work in Syria was so precarious. It wasn't just that I was an American working with the leader of a regime whose fortunes were fading with Washington. It was also that the NGOs that I worked for had no clear legal foundation. When Syria passed its associations law in the late 1950s during its political union with Egypt, economic assistance to developing countries like Syria was through bilateral aid agreements—that is, transfers from states to states. Begin-

ning in the 1980s, most Western countries began funding NGO programs in developing countries instead of the states themselves because
their programs were not meeting their goals. There were also concerns
of corruption surrounding bilateral programs as well as manipulation
of development statistics. For example, a developing country's literacy
rate might appear high on paper, but a visit to the country in question—especially to rural areas—made it apparent that many, if not
most, people could not even read a newspaper.[1]

Syria and other authoritarian Arab countries such as Egypt took
issue with development assistance falling outside state control. In the
1990s, the Egyptian state shut down many Western-funded NGOs in
Egypt, which were dedicated to promoting rule of law or democracy,
for "improper registration." In reality, however, the Egyptian state saw
these organizations as Trojan horses for inducing regime change. Foreign funding of NGO operations became particularly sensitive. To
deal with the problem, the Egyptian state passed a new associations
law that required foreign NGOs to gain government permission for all
foreign-funded activities.

After Bashar al-Assad came to power in 2000, and the state openly
recognized its development problems (which it hadn't under Hafez al-
Assad), NGOs remained politically sensitive. During the Damascus
Spring, a number of "discussion forums" tried to register under the
associations law as "advocacy NGOs" and were rejected. Operational
NGOs, which are associations dedicated to addressing societal problems, were kept in limbo by the state's unwillingness to reform the
associations law—modern NGOs simply didn't exist when the law was
passed in the 1950s, so their applications could not even be accepted.
Some operated illegally but were tolerated by the government because
they were run by known regime figures.

It was in this legal limbo that Asma al-Assad began building a
network of NGOs under official patronage. Because they were under
regime control, they were permitted to register as charities under the
associations law, even though their activities transcended the bound-

aries of what traditional charities do. Perhaps the best example was FIRDOS's rural microfinance project. In villages in which FIRDOS operated, Syrians applied for loans to buy anything to start a business. Some bought cows to produce milk and cheese; others bought computers to open Internet cafés. However, there was a catch: because establishing a microbusiness is risky, and many are therefore bound to fail, microfinance institutions in other countries were forced to charge a small rate of interest to ensure their program's sustainability. Since FIRDOS was registered as a charity, however, it could not charge interest on the loans.

When I inquired about this to the FIRDOS administration, I was told that it wasn't an issue, because not a single Syrian borrower had defaulted on a loan. In times of crisis—if the cow died or a power surge knocked out a computer—other program beneficiaries would take up a collection to repay the loan. The FIRDOS administrators chalked this up to the integrity of rural Syrians. Others said that 100-percent repayment rates were only ever seen in the realm of loan-sharking.

After returning to Damascus, I edited FIRDOS's quarterly newsletter. The first to work on the newsletter was Ammar Abdulhamid—the same writer I had contracted to write the politics section of OBG's Syria reports. With his wife, Ammar also set up another business, Dar Emar, in the MAWRED incubator. To meet the incubator's requirements, Dar Emar was established in his wife's name. Ammar's project— Tharwa, the Arabic word for "wealth"—sought to talk about diversity in the Arab world. After a bit of editing, I sent the final version of the newsletter, using the FIRDOS mailbag, to the palace for final approval, along with a letter outlining my work and a few ideas I had about how to improve the way FIRDOS communicated with the outside world.

With things moving ahead at FIRDOS, the Israeli strike and looming US sanctions were increasingly an afterthought. The first lady seemed committed to reform in Syria, and her NGOs, which were just getting off the ground, were everything the West wanted to see in Syria. Nevertheless, a lingering sense of stasis, which I couldn't explain, permeated FIRDOS's operations. Everyone seemed to be waiting on approval from the palace for whatever project they were working on—but the word was not coming. So, as things slowed down, I turned my attention to *Syria Today*.

As I worked for the first lady, and MAWRED and its business incubator would soon be officially opened, we had all the political cover we needed to produce our sample edition. Other, more fundamental obstacles stood in our way, however. Decades of authoritarianism and isolation meant that English speakers and writers were few, and those who could write effectively were even fewer. The only Syrian writers that I could remember from my work at OBG were Ammar and Amr al-Azm, an archaeologist and son of renowned Syrian intellectual Sadiq Jalal al-Azm. Given that the Israeli strike had just occurred and Syrians were keeping quiet about political reform, Leila and I decided that we should therefore write about something people could talk about openly. Because we were in one of Syria's new NGOs under the first lady's patronage, we thought we would use our experience to talk about NGOs in Syria and what they could do, if they had some legal reform. I assigned Ammar the NGO article and gave assignments on the country's poverty problems and its wealth of mosaics to Amr. I would write on the slow pace of banking reform in Syria as well as writing the news notes and editing the magazine.

With *Syria Today*'s plan in place, Leila and I were optimistic that the first lady's efforts would push reform forward in Syria. For Leila, the first lady was a role model for what a woman could aspire to in Bashar al-Assad's Syria. As for me, while US sanctions seemed to be on the way, US-Syrian trade was so small that some of the sanctions' proposed measures, including a trade or investment ban, seemed to have little threat. Consultancy and journalism—my professional fields—would be unaffected by the sanctions. So I decided to stay the year in Damascus with Leila and take my chances. The only way was up.

On December 11, 2003, President Bush signed the Syria Accountability and Lebanese Sovereignty Restoration Act (SAA) into law. The bill demanded that Damascus "halt Syrian support for terrorism, end its occupation of Lebanon, stop its development of weapons of mass destruction, [and] cease its illegal importation of Iraqi oil and illegal shipments of weapons and other military items to Iraq." The text added that Syria "will be held responsible for attacks committed by Hezbollah and other terrorist groups with offices or other facilities in Syria." Under the SAA, the president was required to choose at least two of six outlined penalties within six months of the bill's signature. The options included a reduction of diplomatic relations with Syria, a ban on US exports to Syria, a US investment ban, a restriction on Syrian diplomats within twenty-five miles of Washington and the United Nations, a ban on Syrian flights to the United States, and a freeze on Syrian assets under American jurisdiction.[2]

In a public statement, Bush said the bill was "intended to strengthen the ability of the United States to conduct an effective foreign policy," but there were tensions surrounding the decision as well. Under the American constitution, foreign policy is the domain of the executive branch. Bush's statement added that "a law cannot burden or infringe the president's exercise of a core constitutional power by attaching conditions precedent to the use of that power." Just like his predecessors, Bush didn't want his hands tied when dealing with Damascus. In response, Syria's state news agency blamed the law's passage on "the partisans of Israel in the American Congress . . . who want more than anything for Syria to end its support for the resistance of the Palestinian people."[3]

At MAWRED, no one even noticed—the staff was busily preparing for Mrs. Assad's official opening of MAWRED's business incubator on December 13. Until then, the incubator, which consisted of three offices in a corner of the SEBC's ground floor, operated "unofficially" as a "pilot project." In the days leading up to the opening, Rola rallied the NGO's staff to finish the organization's website and tape up some posters on the walls. The key person on this was Dunya Istanbuli, a Syrian-American SEBC analyst whom I had met in 2001. She was now the daughter-in-law of a senior Syrian military officer. Dunya and I worked marathon sessions editing and rewriting the website's English text, which had been poorly translated from Arabic.

As Asma al-Assad walked into the NGO that Saturday, the SEBC's staff, dressed in their best attire, greeted her at the door. Standing behind the staff were representatives of the European Commission, which sponsored the SEBC, as well as the ambassadors and their wives from Greece, the Netherlands, and a few other countries. In the days leading up to the opening, Rola had given the European representatives guided tours of the incubator, after which their countries were thanked on the NGO's website for their "support" of MAWRED.

After a brief collective hello, Rola then guided the first lady around the incubator and introduced her to its projects, which, like *Syria Today*, she had already approved. As Mrs. Assad walked into Ammar's office in her turquoise silk dress, only the sound of rustling clothing could be heard as staff members scrambled to open doors for her or get out of the way. This was the first time I had seen Mrs. Assad since my interview and the first time she had been seen in public since the birth of her second child, Zein.

Mrs. Assad shook hands and rubbed shoulders with the European diplomats and representatives for about half an hour before waving a friendly good-bye and heading gracefully out of the front door. There was an air of excitement in the room, which frequently happens in the Arab world where the people seldom see their leaders. It wasn't just that she was the wife of the leader of Syria—she was the only remaining hope for her husband's reform promises. For me and the European diplomats, Asma al-Assad was also a comprehensible and reasonable individual in an opaque regime.

I went upstairs to find Rola, who was sitting on a chair in her office surrounded by a handful of SEBC senior staff. She was writing down figures frantically on pieces of paper and handing them over to one of her colleagues, who was sitting at her computer terminal. The staff quietly watched in awe as Rola provided estimates for the NGO on everything from electricity to seed capital for small businesses. She put down her pen and looked me in the eye. "Next year is going to be a good year, Andrew," Rola said, a sly smile on her face.

I stopped by Rola's office a few days later to say hello. The confident person of MAWRED's opening now sat slumped over her desk, leafing through the pages of her passport. Her fingers were cocked back like the hammer on a revolver.

"I need to go to Switzerland for treatment," she said. "I suffer from a rare disease that will eventually kill me."

I was shocked. I had noticed that she had certain minor physical limitations, but I had not thought that they were due to an underlying disease.

"I'll be back in a few weeks," she said. "Keep working on the magazine."

When I arrived back in Syria after the Christmas break, I talked with all the writers about their progress on the articles and the approaching midmonth deadline. Amr told me that he was still working on his assignments but didn't discuss his progress in detail. Ammar simply said he had done nothing on his article at all. "Every time I sit down to write, I just start attacking the regime," he said. I reminded him that if he did a bit of research and conducted some interviews, he should have lots of raw material for an article. "I can't write it, but I know someone who can," he said. "He's written on this before."

The lack of activity by the Syrian writers filled me with a sense of dread. It wasn't fear of the authorities—I was confident of our political cover—or worry about the magazine's design and concept, which had already been finalized through a Dutch friend and former colleague in Istanbul. It was the sense that the Syrians were making no progress—even energetic Leila, my business partner and guide to Syria, seemed to be doing little on marketing and other research. I was confident that I could put together a magazine and edit it, but how could I do anything if I had no raw material to work with? And how could it turn into a viable venture if we had no idea of the market?

The mid-January deadline came and went without a single writer's achieving it. After a few more days of haranguing Ammar, he presented me with an Arabic text by a Syrian writer on civil society and NGOs in Syria. It had no discernable argument, covered none of the NGOs under the first lady, and gave no references or quotes to support its points. The only article that I had in hand was my own on Syrian banking and a few news notes.

So I began work on the NGO article myself from scratch, interviewing people from FIRDOS and some of the other NGOs under the first lady's patronage. Getting information was like pulling teeth, but what I found was interesting and helped me understand the layout of the "limbo land" in which I was working.

Since marrying Bashar, the first lady had quietly built a network of what are internationally referred to as operational NGOs: bodies dedicated to the design and implementation of development projects. These NGOs mirrored the Baath Party's "popular unions," organizations formed in the 1960s when Syria's civil-society associations and other clubs were consolidated under the Baathists' control. Legally, Asma's charities were the same as the hundreds of charities that had sprung up since Hafez al-Assad passed a law in 1974 that gave these organizations tax-exempt status. They were dedicated to specific causes: FIRDOS addressed rural poverty; MAWRED, women; the Syrian Young Entrepreneurs Association (SYEA), entrepreneurialism; Qawz Qaza ("rainbow" in Arabic), abused children; and AMAL, the disabled. As charities, they officially steered clear of advocacy activities such as the defense or promotion of a specific cause in order to influence public policy, which is the very activity many of the discussion forums sought to do when they tried to register under the associations law during the Damascus Spring. However, because these NGOs were "from the first lady," all those that I interviewed actively lobbied the Syrian government on their field of expertise. As a result, Syrians and the international community now had two ways to lobby the Syrian government to reform: through the state or through Asma's NGOs.

After a month of writing, working with external copyeditors in Beirut, and traveling to Turkey for design-layout discussions, we printed our sample edition (legally in Syria called "zero edition") in Beirut in the first week of March 2004. I illegally smuggled a hundred or so copies in my suitcases over the Lebanese frontier to our office in Syria, where I passed them out to everyone at MAWRED and FIRDOS. I sent thirty copies to the palace through the FIRDOS mail system; I included a letter from Leila and me to Mrs. Assad, which thanked her for her quiet support for our project. I also asked her if the NGO would like to import the magazine from Lebanon.

A few days passed, and I didn't hear back from the palace. So I called the first lady's secretary, Lina Kinaye, to see if she had received the copies I had sent. She confirmed that they had arrived and said that I should send thirty more, which I immediately did. When three days passed and I didn't hear from the palace, I called Rola. I had been in touch with her about once a week during her absence to give her updates on the magazine's progress. Each time she was encouraging and asked lots of questions on the publication date and marketing plan. During this call, however, I asked most of the questions. She broke it to me a few minutes into the conversation: the first lady didn't want to help to import the publication into the country. In an instant, I reviewed the magazine's contents in my mind. I had read and reread the text countless times with an eye to avoid the only red lines I knew: criticism of the president and his family or anything that promoted sectarianism. Nothing came to mind, but we had been very critical of the Syrian government's population policy as well as the government's unwillingness to reform. I then asked Rola if there was something specific we could remove and gain the first lady's support. "No, it's not that," Rola said sadly, then said she had to go.

Leila arrived at my house half an hour later. As I told her that the first lady didn't want to help us import the magazine, Leila's tears poured down her face. I put a finger to my lips and pointed at the ceiling, not knowing where a listening device might have been planted in my apartment. We ran out of my apartment and onto the street to talk privately.

Leila kept looking over her shoulder into the darkness and ahead of us into the areas illuminated by streetlights. "Do you see someone there?" she asked me. When I said no, she still insisted someone was watching us. "It's *mukhabarat* [intelligence agents], don't you see them," she said in complete panic, tears streaking her face. Not knowing what to do, I held her hand and told her not to worry. "I will talk with the first lady personally," I said. "Don't worry, we haven't done anything wrong."

The next morning I sent a letter in the company mailbag up to the palace requesting a meeting with the first lady. As I knew she wasn't helping us with the magazine's import procedures, Leila called the Ministry of Information and made an appointment with deputy minister Taleb Kadi Amin. A rotund man with a thick grayish-brown mustache and sporting a 1970s-style comb-over haircut, Taleb was known to be among the ministry's "reformers"—officials who, supposedly, were not closely aligned with the country's intelligence services.

Taleb greeted us with a firm handshake and asked us to sit down. After a few minutes of introductions, Taleb looked at Leila and me and said, "Where is Ms. Rola Bayda?"

Surprised he knew Rola and that we worked with her, we told him she was out of the country recovering from an illness.

"What about the money from the UNFPA [United Nations Population Fund]?" he asked.

Leila just stared at me, not knowing what to say. We were there to talk about importing the magazine, and he was asking us about money from a UN agency.

After we made it clear that we didn't know what he was talking about, Leila presented him with our sample edition for submission to the ministry's censorship bureau. Syrian law stated that no printed material could enter the country without approval from the Ministry of Information, so we needed permission in order to clear the magazine's shipment from Lebanon through Syrian customs. He shook our hands as we left and asked us to call him the next day for the verdict.

In the ministry's rickety elevator, whose stainless-steel sides scraped the sides of the elevator shaft as we descended, I remembered that the UNFPA was listed among the bodies supporting MAWRED. I also remembered that the agency's Syrian director, Dalia Hajjar, was a good friend of Rola's. Dalia was smart and well educated; she was also from the ruling Alawite elite. It was widely rumored that the first lady would soon promote Dalia to be the head of Syria's "Family Council"—an umbrella institution that the first lady was creating to deal with the myriad problems facing Syrian families.

Thoroughly confused and not knowing what to do, I initiated a process of damage control. After Leila received the censor's approval the following day, I also requested that she obtain all permissions to distribute the magazine as well. Next, we imported the sample edition's five thousand copies into the country and stored them at my apartment, well out of the way of anyone snooping around *Syria Today's* offices at the MAWRED incubator. I then drafted a letter with Leila introducing the magazine. Finally, we sent introductory copies to all the embassies, the EU and UN agencies, and all the ministries.

Letters of support started to fill our e-mail in-boxes. One impassioned e-mail from the chief of the UN Development Program's office in Damascus urged us to push forward "no matter what obstacles we faced." It made us feel good to hear that people enjoyed the publication's writing, editing, and layout—but underlying every message was something else: what we were doing was unprecedented and needed to continue at all costs.

Two weeks later, Rola suddenly returned to Syria. When I stopped by her office to welcome her back, I found Rola sorting through stacks of papers a foot or higher on her desk. While she was superficially chipper, she looked as if she had aged considerably since I last saw her three months ago. I asked her about what had happened with the sample edition of *Syria Today*. She said that all she knew was that the first lady didn't want to help with importing the magazine. That was it.

Down in the incubator, however, rumors ran wild regarding some kind of problem between Rola and the first lady. At first, Leila heard someone saying that the first lady was angry with Rola for running the NGO badly, while someone else said that the first lady was just keeping everyone at arm's length because US sanctions were being put in place. Some of the rumors were coming from Dunya; others were coming from known Rola supporters.

With the fate of the *Syria Today* project uncertain, I turned my attention to writing for Beirut's English-language broadsheet, the *Daily Star*. I tackled Syria's recent announcement to cut taxes, the implications of US sanctions on Syrian business and its oil industry, and, while I visited home in Pennsylvania, the impact that spiraling US casualties in Iraq was having on local politics.

In April, Leila and I assisted a team from the World Bank to evaluate Syria's investment climate. The group was led by Joseph Battat, a Lebanese American and well-known China expert. A few days after their arrival, Joe asked me to a dinner at Arabesque, at that time the best restaurant in Damascus's Old City. Between entrées, our conversation quickly moved on from Syria to me.

"I've been watching you," Joe said, looking intently at me. My spine immediately stiffened, thinking for sure that this was a pitch to work for a foreign-intelligence agency.

Seemingly reading my mind, he said, "No, no, it's not CIA stuff. I know what it's like to be you—a rare person in a strange place. I was one of the only foreigners allowed to be in China after Mao died, during the Gang of Four time. I worked with the State Council, the country's highest decision-making body, to reform China."

As he continued, I relaxed. "During that time, I was a fellow with the Institute of Current World Affairs, an old American fellowship that supports writers willing to go deeply into a subject. If you had two years of your life to investigate a topic thoroughly, what would it be?"

Without hesitating, I said, "I would look at how these pressures and threats from the United States and the West impact Syrian society."

"I'm now the chairman of ICWA," he said, "but the decision is not up to me. The institute's website explains the selection process, which is rigorous. I suggest you apply."

After dinner I dropped Joe off at his hotel and headed home. As I lay in bed, I began to realize that I had a great story unfolding in front of me and that it might be worth staying in Syria after all.

On May 11, 2004, President Bush implemented US sanctions on Syria. In a statement to Congress, Bush chose the ban on US exports to Syria and a ban on Syrian flights to the United States. Regime newspapers and pundits immediately declared the sanctions unjust and unjustified.[4] As I made the rounds to the various pundits around Damascus, they all dismissed sanctions as lacking any substance. After all, they reasoned, Syria's trade with the United States was only a few hundred million dollars per year, and the state carrier, Syrian Arab Airlines, didn't fly to the United States anyway.

Nevertheless, a closer look at the Bush administration's implementation of the sanctions, as well as the SAA's implementation, gave hints of how the White House was likely to pressure the Assad regime in the years to come. The order implementing the SAA, Executive Order 13338, first declared a "state of emergency" regarding Syria, and declared it a threat to US national security.[5] This allowed Bush not only to implement the SAA, but to apply other legislation designed to fight the war on terror to Syria. First, Bush announced that the Treasury Department would investigate if Syria's largest state bank, the Commercial Bank of Syria, should be designated by the US government as a money-laundering institution under the USA PATRIOT Act (which stands for Uniting and Strengthening America by Providing Appropriate Tools Required to Intercept and Obstruct Terrorism). For those who understood Syria's economy, this effectively sanctioned the main financial vehicle through which the Syrian government collected the country's oil revenues, which accounted for about half the state budget. Second, Bush announced that Syrian nationals would now be subject to the International Economic Emergency Powers Act (IEEPA), which would allow the US government to seize the assets of those threatening US national security, as outlined under Executive Order 13338.

While the order's announcement was heavy on sticks, there were a few specific carrots, too. Bush issued a letter to Congress stating that waivers would be issued in order to facilitate other aspects of US and Western policy on Syria. "Export licenses" would be issued for certain "discrete categories of exports . . . to support activities of the United States Government and United Nations agencies, to facilitate travel by United States persons, for certain humanitarian purposes, to help maintain aviation safety, and to promote the exchange of information."[6]

After a couple of days chasing Syrian reactions to the sanctions announcement, I returned to MAWRED's office on Thursday, hoping to get some work done before Friday and Saturday, Syria's weekend. But as I stepped through *Syria Today*'s office door and heard Leila screaming into the phone, I knew it was going to be a tough day. In fact, it was the beginning of the worst forty-eight hours of my life.

"What do you mean, do we have the money?" Leila shouted into the phone. While this was hardly the first time my day had started with Leila bellowing into the phone at someone, the look on her face told me that this outburst was prompted by fear, not anger.

"How could the money have been allocated, Dunya?" Leila continued. "We don't have a contract or a term of reference! Are you sure of what you are saying?"

I put down my bag and immediately signaled to Leila to stop the conversation. In all my years in the Arab world, I knew that no conversation dealing with money should be discussed over the phone—especially in Syria. Never one to understand subtlety, Leila immediately parroted, "Please, Dunya, I don't want to discuss this on the phone—talk to you later," and hung up.

"What was that all about?" I asked, hoping Leila was just overreacting to some small incident, which she had a tendency to do from time to time.

"Andrew, Dunya says our proposal to build the Women in Syria website has been approved and that we have received the money. What the hell is she talking about?"

The previous autumn, shortly before the opening of MAWRED, Rola had asked me to put together a proposal to build a web portal dedicated to women in Syria. While I had thought a website dedicated to the needs of women in Syria was a good idea, Rola's request was a little odd from the start. Rola had said an international agency had "a lot of cash" to support media advocacy of development needs in Syria. I knew that starting a conversation by talking about cash was her crude way of getting the usual Pavlovian responses from those who ran projects for her. Stone-faced, I had immediately responded, "Really? What's the subject?"

Rola had then gone on to do what she did best: use the most elaborate words to describe something that had no details and made little sense. Her proposal was simple: make a website about the lives of women in Syria. She said she knew "for a fact" that there was a huge amount of information out there, but much of it needed to be organized, evaluated, translated, and edited. While this had sounded possible, it was when I started asking basic logistical questions that everything became suspect.

"On what do I base the cost estimates?" I asked Rola. "I don't know how much material is available and how many man-hours it will take to locate it. I also have to have some idea of what material needs translated and costs per page."

"Oh, don't worry about that," Rola said.

I cobbled together a proposal as best I could. I had some experiences with websites in terms of content and design, but I had never managed one.

Over the next few weeks, Rola and I played a bit of proposal badminton. I would send Rola a proposal, and she would quickly hit it back to me, claiming the costs were too low. Finally, after five revisions, I submitted the proposal for one hundred eighteen thousand dollars. I made it conditional on confirmation of subject matter, deadlines, and so on. Rola thanked me with a warm, motherly smile, and asked me to provide her with the computer file containing the proposal as well. I complied.

I knew that if Dunya, who was on MAWRED's board, was asking Leila directly about the website project on the telephone, something was amiss. Since it was clear Dunya was not afraid that the conversation might be recorded, that meant she believed she had the country's *mukhabarat* (security agencies) backing her up. Dunya was an old friend of Leila's and mine, but she was also a friend of Mrs. Assad. There were also many rumors of competing political factions in Syria, each with their own agencies. Whatever Syria's true power distribution, and for whatever personal or political reason, Dunya was demanding quick answers.

"Andrew, I don't like the game Rola is playing with us," Leila said bluntly. "Everyone knows Syria is corrupt, but I will have no part of it."

Neither would I. Through my years of work in Syria, I knew that the biggest factor retarding the country's pace of development was its vast web of corruption. This rotten system was tolerated for a simple reason: it bound together members of the country's ethnic and religious sects around a state that, while often loathed, stabilized what was once one of the world's most politically volatile countries. This was perhaps the main reason why Syria's reform efforts were slow and made little sense. As long as the "commissions" kept coming, things went quietly, smoothly—and slowly.

With the president now talking about "reform" and "activation" of Syria, suddenly talk of instability echoed like never before, particularly among the old guard, those resisting Assad's reforms. Since the United States had allowed Israel to bomb a Palestinian "training camp" in Syria in October 2003 and Bush had signed the SAA into law the following December, internal tensions were rumored to be high, and whispers of old-guard resistance had increased.

Leila and I knew that the only way to clarify things was to confront Rola directly but civilly. After all, we had very little information—Dunya had simply said that during a MAWRED board meeting, Rola had reported that the website project was awarded and the money had already been disbursed to Leila.

Leila and I found Rola perched on a rolling chair in her office. After the usual formalities, I asked her about the website and the fact that we had heard the money was allocated to Leila.

"I want to know who told you that," said Rola. "The money has been allocated; it's right here on my desk."

Rola patted a large tan duffel bag sitting to her right. In one smooth motion, she unzipped the bag, showing us a mound of stacked Syrian banknotes. After repeating her question several times, we told her that it was Dunya. Rola's eyes lit up instantly in anger.

"Perhaps it's time we started dealing on paper," Rola said unexpectedly. She handed me a stack of invoices and a bank receipt showing a large transaction in Syrian pounds from the UNFPA. Attached to the top of the stack was a copy of a receipt in the name of Rola's driver—it was roughly the equivalent of one hundred twenty-five thousand US dollars.

Rola seemed to have submitted the project, collected the money from the account without our knowledge, and was now holding the full amount for "safekeeping" in Leila's name, without a term of reference or contract governing and conditioning the use of the funds. It was also strange to be paid in full, in advance.

Leila remained remarkably calm. I was speechless at first, as the nature of the dangerous situation we were in dawned on me. I then asked for copies of the invoices and receipts, thinking that this would stop Rola from going through with it. To my astonishment, she already had copies ready for me.

Leila and I immediately returned to our office—without the money—to talk. After saying nothing for almost five minutes, Leila began sobbing uncontrollably at her desk while smoking a cigarette. I knew it was now up to me to find a solution.

I did not sleep for two days. When you are under intense pressure in an environment where nothing is certain, your mind endlessly runs through scenarios with seemingly logical conclusions—take the money in good faith, believe Mrs. Assad is monitoring MAWRED, carry out the work, and carefully document where it all goes. But what if Mrs. Assad doesn't know about it? And when the *mukhabarat* comes knocking, wouldn't Leila and I get blamed for embezzlement? Did the fact that Dunya was asking aggressively for details mean that she was working for the old guard? Or did she simply want to make Rola look bad in front of Mrs. Assad? Or was Rola trying to set me up? Last, but also important, given all the questions being raised, where was Mrs. Assad anyway? Wasn't she the patron of this "NGO"?

At 2:30 AM on day two of the crisis, I suddenly sat up in bed with the answer at my fingertips. I ran to my laptop and started drafting a letter from Leila to Rola. After thanking Rola for her help over the past year, I worded the letter carefully, avoiding accusing either side of anything:

Registering a company in Syria is a complex process. I have received considerable help from —— and Andrew Tabler to structure my business according to my original business plan. Despite this effort, my company remains unregistered. I hope that the company's incorporation papers can be submitted sometime next month. . . .

I was happy to hear that you have approved the proposal you asked me to submit concerning the creation of a website called Women in Syria. I was also glad to hear the project's funding had been approved.

Mr. ——— has informed me that any money I receive prior to my company's incorporation will be considered income under Syrian law and will be taxable at the top tax rate of 35 percent. Given the fact that my company is not yet established and that I have no way of receiving funds, we will only be able to carry out segments of the proposed Women in Syria website on an invoice basis following my company's registration.

This solution suits the current status of my company as a fledgling business as well as MAWRED's natural desire to make sure it gets the most from its funding. At the same time, I am confident that our involvement in the project will ensure the website is of top quality. With this then out of the way, I look forward to receiving from MAWRED an outline of what it feels is important to be included in the website. The proposal lists a number of general stages and estimated costs to carry out a major web portal on a topic important to Syria. Now it is time for us to work together and establish a clear and detailed plan and time frame to carry out this work.

Immediately after finishing the draft, I returned to bed and fell asleep. My plan seemed the perfect solution for an opaque situation. I had essentially worded it so that Leila said she was happy to help but was unable to receive the funds. Whatever work that was to be carried out would have to be detailed, and the transactions executed from MAWRED's bank account. Finally, the letter implied that an NGO under Asma al-Assad's patronage would, of course, only produce businesses that pay their taxes.

When I entered the office early the next morning, Leila was already sitting at her desk, her face showing the stress of many in Arab countries who fear the secret police and have little faith in justice. I showed her the letter and explained my plan. After studying the letter, Leila added only one thing: a line of cc's at the bottom that included Mrs. Assad, Dunya, and a few others.

I knew that the only way to make sure this did not get out of control was to get it into Mrs. Assad's hands first. In democracies and dictatorships alike, solving problems effectively is all about access to power. In all my months in Syria as an "expert" with FIRDOS, I had had little direct contact with Mrs. Assad. However, I had a way of getting a message to her—through the FIRDOS daily mailbag. On the afternoon of May 18, I sent the letter to the palace via FIRDOS. I attached a note to the first lady telling her that I thought I was being paid for my work by FIRDOS, but Rola indicated that I was being paid by MAWRED as well. I added, "I was hoping you could help Rola straighten this out."

Copies of the letter were also delivered to Rola and Dunya the next morning. At around 9 AM the day after, Rola and Dunya were summoned to Mrs. Assad's office for an urgent meeting. Leila and I, who had reported the problem and knew all of its most intimate details, were not invited to the meeting or ever questioned concerning the contents of the letter.

To this day, my only account of what happened in the meeting is from Dunya and Rola themselves. Dunya said that after asking a series of questions, Mrs. Assad asked Rola why the money was on her desk in cash. When Rola replied that it was because she thought other members of MAWRED would take it, Mrs. Assad reportedly shook her head in disgust.

Rola had a completely different story. She insisted that she had "played her cards very well"—a none-too-subtle reference to the framing of facts in accordance with reported conflicts between various power bases in the country. I imagine that Rola tried to spin Dunya as working with the old guard to take down MAWRED, thus making the Assads' efforts to reform Syria appear insincere.

Around the time that Rola and Dunya received their copies of the letter, I received a phone call from the first lady's secretary, Lina Kinaye. After greeting me and talking a bit, she said, "Oh yes, and by the way, the letters you have sent up through the FIRDOS mailbag? They have been received. Thank you very much for those."

"My pleasure," I said. "I'd like to see the first lady sometime soon to talk about this."

"I'll put in the request," she said. Then she hung up.

I sat at my desk and just stared at the wall in disbelief. What an incredibly strange way to work. No one had actually stolen or misappropriated anything, but it was clear that the system lacked even the most basic of financial controls and checks. I realized that the NGOs were experimental, but wouldn't it just be easier to pass a law governing these institutions? Without laws, the conditions were rife for corruption. But this situation also had an important ancillary benefit for the Assads: they became the only players empowered to investigate malfeasance and arbitrate in disputes between parties. In a rapidly changing society opening up to the outside world, this gave the Assads tremendous power to control society—even more than the political repression that had maintained Bashar's father's grip on Syria.

A few days later, Rola asked me to come to her office. The gloomy and stressed Rola of the past few weeks was gone; color had returned to her cheeks and a smile to her face. She looked me straight in the eyes for at least a minute.

"The first lady would like you to go with us to China," she announced triumphantly.

"What?" I asked, while immediately thinking of the crisis of the previous week. I knew that President Assad was planning a state visit to China soon, but I had no idea when it would occur. Unlike his father, Bashar enjoyed foreign visits and had already traveled to the

United Kingdom, France, Spain, and Turkey in the first four years of his presidency.

"Do you want to go?" Rola said, smiling wryly. No foreign journalist—let alone an American—had ever been permitted to travel with a Syrian president. If Rola was telling the truth, and I actually made it on the trip, I knew that the first lady had approved it. Who else had the authority to clear that through security?

"Yes," I said.

I worked until early evening and then walked over to the British ambassador's residence in Mezze for the Queen's annual birthday celebration. The ambassador's garden was full of Syrian businessmen, almost all of whom were at least fifty pounds overweight. Their wives, covered in jewels to compensate for their fading beauty, stood by their sides. Waiters in black tuxedoes offered guests rich hors d'oeuvres and big crystal glasses brimming with stiff drinks.

Excited by the prospect of going to China with President Assad, and after drinking half a dozen glasses of red wine, I felt optimistic for the first time in months. I chatted with businessmen about US sanctions; I expressed my beliefs that they wouldn't have any effect on the country and that Washington would be better off engaging Syria rather than confronting it.

That night the wine caught up with me, with a sharp pain in my stomach that jolted me out of bed. All the anxieties of my existence in Syria filled my head. Why was the first lady inviting me to China via Rola? Didn't I just diplomatically get Rola in trouble? Why, despite calling the first lady's attention to the irregularities at her NGO, had I still received no contact from her? Last but not least, I worried that I might now be too sick to take such a long flight.

The next thing I knew, I awoke and found myself lying on my back in the hallway leading to my bedroom. The pain in my stomach was gone, and I felt totally at peace with myself. The next morning, when I told Rola what had happened, she took me aside and said, almost in a motherly tone, "This is normal. It's just the stress of being around the Syrian regime. You'll be fine."

One week later I was in Beijing, the first non-Arab foreign correspondent and American to ever travel with a Syrian president on a state visit. Bashar had yet to outline a reform vision for Syria, so a visit to China indicated that the young president would adopt the "China model"—that is, no political reform with comprehensive economic reform. From my hotel room in the Chinese capital, I saw hundreds of construction cranes dotting the city's skyline. Outside, orderly street markets teemed with shoppers sifting through everything from lingerie to MP3 players. As I waded through the market with the members of the Syrian press corps, we all talked about how Syrians and Chinese shared a love for trade. We speculated that Syria could be like this someday soon. All that was needed was some reform.

The following morning, we were herded onto a small bus that would take us to the day's first photo opportunity, the first couple's visit to a section of the Great Wall of China located about an hour outside Beijing. The bus had difficulty keeping up with the fleet of black Audis that made up the official motorcade as the gradient increased the closer we got to the wall. When we finally arrived and saw the president and first lady standing alone atop the ramparts, we hurried out of the bus and up the wall's stairs; standing at the top of the steps and looking down on us were Bashar, Asma, and foreign minister Farouk al-Shara.

As we snapped photos of the lanky six-foot-four Syrian president, it was easy to understand why so many Syrians liked him. His father, Hafez, seldom ventured out in public, preferring to speak through the state-owned newspapers from the confines of the presidential palace overlooking Damascus. Direct contact with a Syrian president was therefore something new, though Syrians' reactions to Bashar's new open ways were clumsy. When Bashar began making state visits in 2001, for example, members of the Syrian press corps didn't know how to react. Because the country had been isolated for so long, they weren't exposed to international norms regarding the handling of VIPs. This led to embarrassing moments. During the photo shoot of Bashar's first state visit to Spain in 2003, members of the Syrian press corps repeatedly shouted out to the Syrian president and King Juan Carlos for personal photos with both leaders—something the king of Spain reportedly found amusing. The palace's press handlers warned us on the bus not to ask for any photos with the president—or to speak to him directly at all.

As the snapping of cameras died down and the photographers got their fill of images, we just stood there, blankly staring at Bashar and his wife, not daring to speak. Reading the situation, he said with a big smile, "Before anyone asks for a photo, let's take one together and get it out of the way." The Syrian journalists laughed with relief and excitedly huddled around the president and first lady. The journalists' faces were filled with glee—in a dictatorship like Syria, a photo with the president wasn't for your scrapbook but for your office wall. Its message was elegantly blunt: "I'm connected—think twice about messing with me."

It wasn't until the bus ride back to Beijing, however, that I realized the degree to which Syria's isolation during Hafez al-Assad's rule made Syrians so suspicious of the outside world. I had not yet had a chance to talk with most of the Syrian journalists, so they didn't know that I spoke any Arabic. I could hear a number of journalists sitting behind me in the bus talking about me. One in easy earshot said that I was "an American spy" and that the "first lady shouldn't trust me." One of them—a Syrian who worked with a wire service—struck up a conversation with me in which he said that he felt all foreign correspondents were spies. As I looked out of the window at the haze hanging above Beijing's burgeoning skyline, I wondered if Joe Battat had to put up with such talk before China's economic engine took off.

The first lady didn't speak to either me or Rola on the entire trip. During a visit to a women's center in Beijing, Rola sat on Asma's right-hand side. When the first lady didn't even look Rola's way, I knew she was out of business as Asma's handler. It was an inauspicious end to a job that Rola never had on paper. I, however, realized that if I was on the trip, I was somehow "OK" with the first lady.

Two days later, the palace's press liaison announced that the president and the first lady would be returning to Syria early and forgoing a scheduled trip to Shanghai. No reason was given. Standing out on the tarmac at Beijing's international airport in front of Assad's Syrian Air 747, members of the press gossiped about the reasons for the early departure. For days, the first lady had been limping badly during official functions. The press handlers told us that Asma had fallen while working out during her first day in Beijing. Most chalked up the early departure to her injury. Lebanese journalists on the delegation, who were being fed news from Beirut, said that Israel's trade minister was also scheduled to visit Shanghai at the same time. Hundreds of Chinese companies were lining up to meet the Israeli minister, which apparently angered the Syrian president.

There were plenty of signs that the Chinese were not taking the Syrians very seriously. For example, only a handful of Chinese companies attended a meeting in Beijing with the Syrian businessmen who were accompanying Bashar. One Syrian businessman told me that the Chinese were not very interested in trade with Syria because its traders had a very bad reputation: many didn't pay their debts, and most bought only irregular goods (seconds) and reconditioned Chinese products.

When I got back to Damascus, the city was abuzz with talk of why Assad had returned early from Beijing. One rumor speculated that there had been a foiled coup attempt. Another, backed up by other rumors in the United States and elsewhere in the region, said that American aircraft based out of Iraq had been violating Syrian airspace in hot pursuit of Baathists and "foreign fighters"—radical Muslims seeking to wage jihad in Iraq against US forces.

Getting confirmation of either report was impossible. However, when the Ministry of Information suddenly organized a supervised trip to take me and a group of journalists to the Syrian-Iraqi border town of Abu Kamal, the government seemed to be trying to undermine US arguments that foreign fighters were flowing across the frontier. At Abu Kamal, workers with heavy machinery were digging a three-foot-wide ditch along the Syrian-Iraqi frontier and piling the dirt in a four-foot-high mound beside it. Border guards dressed in Syrian uniforms, with red and white Bedouin headdresses and skin as rough as leather, followed us everywhere we went. They told us that the berm was designed to flip over fast-moving smugglers' vehicles moving across the border. Standing beside the ditch and berm, it was apparent that a couple of men with shovels could fill in the ditch and breech the wall in thirty minutes or less—it was hardly an effective barrier to those wishing to wage jihad against US forces.

American forces had closed the Abu Kamal border crossing in the days leading up to our arrival. As our bus pulled up to the gate, the driver weaved the bus between 1970s- and 1980s-era GMC vans with raised rear axles, which made them look like hot rods or cars that clowns might jump out of at the circus. One of the Syrian journalists on the bus told us that the vans were used for smuggling fuel from Iraq. Each was equipped with heavy-duty truck suspensions designed to carry much weightier loads. When the vans' extra fuel tanks were full, the rear end lowered, making it look like a van you might see driving around a normal US suburb.

At the guard station adjacent to the gate, Syrian soldiers in drab olive uniforms hid behind cement barriers, seemingly afraid of gunfire from the American side. As we approached the gate and camera operators from Syrian TV began filming, a patrol of US soldiers ran up a watchtower. Two peered through binoculars at us, while another seemed to be speaking incessantly into a radio. Syrian soldiers behind us warned us to take cover, saying, "Sometimes they shoot."

Inside the border post, the commander told us that American forces were shooting indiscriminately across the border, seemingly at anything that moved. A few days before, he told us, a young boy was shot and killed while playing on the rooftop of his house. In the commander's office, he pointed to a bullet hole in the window behind his desk. "This happened just yesterday. It nearly hit my head."

PART II

4

PRESSURE YIELDS RESULTS

The explosion was fifty miles away in Beirut, but the political earthquake it caused could be felt at my desk in Damascus. Television news broadcasts of smoke billowing from a massive blackened crater in the Beirut neighborhood of Ain el-Mreisseh shook me. I had slept that night at my apartment in Beirut, where I spent most weekends. On my way out of town, I asked my driver to stop off at HSBC in Ain el-Mreisseh to use the ATM. Now onscreen I saw that the bank's glass facade was shattered, and rescue workers were pulling bodies out of the rubble nearby. An hour later, the bad news was official: Rafik Hariri and six others had been killed in the blast. I suddenly remembered my dream of being bombed outside Hariri's mansion. I returned to Beirut immediately.

A few days after civil defense forces put out the blaze and recovered all the remains, the "battle of the protests," which would eventually lead to Syria's decision to withdraw from Lebanon, began in earnest. At the first rally on February 18, 2005, several hundred thousand demonstrators poured into Ain el-Mreisseh to survey the damage for themselves. The demonstrators were organized according to sects, with Druze carrying Druze militia flags and Christians carrying Christian banners. But they all had one message: Syria, get out of Lebanon.

For the next ten days, the pro-Syrian Lebanese prime minister, Omar Karami, resisted widespread calls to resign. So the anti-Syrian opposition called for another rally for February 28, parliament's first day back into session following the assassination. Since the Interior Ministry had refused to give permission for the rally, the Lebanese Army cordoned off Beirut's central Martyrs' Square, which had been destroyed during the civil war and was now just covered in gravel. The Lebanese, never a people to take authority too seriously, circled around the long lines of soldiers, searching for ways to sneak through alleyways leading into the square. For my part, I scaled the wall at the back of the French coffee house, called Paul, that was adjacent to Martyrs' Square. So did several of the notoriously beautiful Lebanese women, who did their best to overcome the same obstacle in stiletto heels and skin-tight clothes. The American media described the protests as the "Cedar Revolution," in reference to Lebanon's famous cedar trees, an imprint of which is in the middle of the Lebanese flag. My friends in Damascus sent me text messages saying that it looked more like the "Gucci Revolution" on TV.

The opposition was organized. The party banners of February 18 had been replaced with Lebanese flags and red banners that read INDEPENDENCE '05. To energize the crowd, the Hariri-owned TV channel Al-Mustaqbal (Future) and the Maronite-Christian Lebanese Broadcasting Company (LBC) focused their TV cameras on well-lit, concentrated patches of protestors waving anywhere from two to four Lebanese flags apiece. To a casual viewer wondering whether to defy the government's ban on the protest, it seemed clear that the protests were on and worth attending. People just kept coming.

At the beginning of the parliamentary session discussing the murders, Future and LBC television coverage featured split screens, the right-hand side showing the parliament session and the left showing the gathering protestors. Future set up two large-screen TVs adjacent to the protestors' main podium, which allowed the crowd to react to the heated parliamentary debate.

As deputies took their seats in parliament, even more Lebanese poured into the square. Expecting a long, drawn-out fight, dedicated members of the opposition were pitched in makeshift tents in the town center around the Martyrs' Statue, the recently restored symbol of Lebanon's struggle for independence from France. "We will wait here as long as Syria remains on Lebanese soil," one die-hard protestor screamed. "We are willing to lose our jobs and our lives for this cause."

After intense parliamentary debate, a beleaguered Omar Karami stood and said, "Out of concern that the government does not become an obstacle to the good of the country, I announce the resignation of the government I had the honor to lead."[1] The crowd roared. Chants of "Syria, get out!" and "Freedom, sovereignty, and independence!" rang throughout the crowd.

After the initial shock wore off, pro-Syrian parties struck back. On March 8, the anniversary of the Baathist revolution in Syria, Hezbollah launched a massive counterdemonstration in nearby Riad al-Solh Square to avoid confrontation with the anti-Syrian protestors camped out in Martyrs' Square. Since the estimated headcount surpassed that of the opposition protests of late February, Omar Karami accepted the invitation of the pro-Syrian president, Émile Lahoud, to form a "rescue government" to unite the country.

In response, the anti-Syrian opposition staged a rally on March 14, 2005, the one-month anniversary of Hariri's death. Standing on the bridge atop Martyrs' Square, I and a group of journalists watched as busloads of people from all over Lebanon descended on the Lebanese capital. An estimated one million protestors filled the square—the biggest single protest I had ever witnessed in more than a decade of journalism in the Middle East. A week later, Karami resigned. On April 3, President Assad announced that Syria would withdraw its forces from Lebanon.

The day finally came. On April 27, at a surreal military ceremony at the Riyaq air base in Lebanon's Bekaa Valley, Syrian and Lebanese military top brass and political leaders read out speeches praising Syria's role in stabilizing Lebanon. The chief of Syrian military intelligence in Lebanon, Rustom Ghazaleh, sat pale faced in the grandstand. Under a clear blue sky, squads of Lebanese and Syrian soldiers, dressed in green and red berets, respectively, were assembled in formation in front of French-colonial-era buildings and monuments dedicated to those fallen in the Levant campaigns of World War II. After every major stanza of a speech praising Syria, the Syria soldiers blurted out "*Bi ruh, bi dem, nafdika ya Bashar*" (In spirit, in blood, we will sacrifice ourselves for you, oh Bashar). The Lebanese formations would likewise respond with Lebanese slogans after positive declarations about Lebanon. After they had finished, both formations marched out together. The Syrian troops then piled onto army transports that whisked them back to the motherland. A lone Syrian solider that the caravan had left behind leapt onto the last truck as it snaked its way across the border. Lebanon's twenty-nine-year "Pax Syriana" was over.

The day following Hariri's murder, the United States withdrew its ambassador to Syria, Margaret Scobey. While Hariri's murder was shocking, removing Scobey wasn't surprising, given the quiet tensions in the Levant between the United States and Syria the previous autumn. While Syria and the United States were at odds over Iraq and the Palestinians, they also had divergent views over what should happen when President Lahoud's term was due to expire in September 2004. The United States wanted Lahoud, who was considered Syria's man in Lebanon, replaced. Lahoud had spent the better part of the last two years blocking Hariri's initiatives in the cabinet.

During my last meeting with Hariri in July 2003, he had candidly told me over a cup of tea at Lebanon's Grand Serail that Lahoud's people were sabotaging the government's plans to rebuild the country. "We don't understand where the resistance is coming from," he lamented. "We have toned down our disagreements with him lately at the request of the powers that be. But it's getting worse." "Powers that be" was code for Syria.[2]

After months of watching and waiting, Assad finally played his hand. In late August 2004, Assad used his influence in the Lebanese parliament to extend Lahoud's term an additional three years—half a standard presidential term. In parliament, Hariri, with an empty expression on his face and his arm in a sling, passed the extension through parliament. That evening, pro-Lahoud Lebanese set fireworks off over the port of Beirut.

In response, the United Nations Security Council passed Resolution 1559 on September 2, 2004. The resolution demanded "all foreign forces" withdraw from Lebanon as well as the "disbanding and disarmament of all Lebanese and non-Lebanese militias."[3] In the months leading up to 1559's passage, Hariri liaised with the French president, Jacques Chirac, to draft a UN resolution against an extension of Lahoud's term. Hariri was willing to cut deals on Syria's presence in Lebanon, but Lahoud's extension was a red line. For the United States to support the resolution, it wanted language that called on Hezbollah and Palestinian militias in Lebanon to be disarmed.[4] A month following 1559's passage, a car bomb severely wounded Marwan Hamadeh, an economy and trade minister in Hariri's last government. Hamadeh had been an outspoken critic of Syria's presence in Lebanon.

In the days following Hariri's killing, Washington reiterated its demands that Syria withdraw its troops from Lebanon. In a press release on February 15, 2005, secretary of state Condoleezza Rice condemned Hariri's murder as an act of terrorism, citing that "all those responsible for this terrible crime must be brought to justice immediately."[5] On February 17, shortly before he was scheduled to meet with European leaders, Bush announced in a press conference that Washington's withdrawal of its ambassador to Syria "indicates that the relationship is not moving forward, that Syria is out of step with the progress being made in the Middle East . . . and this is a country that isn't moving with the democratic movement." Concerning Syria's involvement in the murder, Bush said, "I can't tell you that because the investigation is ongoing, so I'm going to withhold judgment until we find out what the facts are. . . . We support an international investigation."[6] However, later that same day, in testimony before the US Senate, Rice said that Syria should be held indirectly responsible for Hariri's murder, "given their continued interference in Lebanese affairs." In response, one senator urged Rice to tighten sanctions on Syria so as to "not let them off the hook."[7]

In Mainz, Germany, on February 24, Bush announced that Syria must withdraw its troops and "secret services" from Lebanon so as to allow Lebanon's upcoming elections to be held freely. "We will see how they respond before there's any further discussions about going back to the United Nations," Bush said during a press conference with German Chancellor Gerhard Schröder, who reportedly supported the statement.[8]

On March 1, in an interview with *Time* magazine, Assad responded with a vague timetable for a pullback of troops that fell short of a commitment to a full withdrawal. "It should be very soon and maybe in the next few months. Not after that," Assad said. "The security situation is much better in Lebanon than before. They have an army, they have a state, they have institutions."[9]

On March 3, Saudi Arabia's King Abdullah visited Damascus and openly called on Syria to withdraw its forces from Lebanon or face Arab isolation. Later that same day, in a press briefing at the Central Intelligence Agency (CIA), Bush turned up the rhetoric against Damascus another notch. "The United States of America strongly supports democracy around the world, including Lebanon," Bush said. "It's time for Syria to get out."[10]

On March 6, the White House branded Syria's gradual withdrawal plan "half measures" and "not enough" and demanded that Damascus withdraw its army and intelligence services "completely and immediately," adding, "the world is watching the situation in Lebanon, particularly Beirut, very closely."[11]

Behind the scenes, while the demonstrations in Lebanon pressured Syria to withdraw, the United States worked with the United Kingdom and France at the Security Council to draft a resolution establishing an international investigation into Hariri's murder. A week after Assad finally agreed on April 3 to withdraw Syrian forces, the council passed Resolution 1595, establishing the United Nations International Independent Investigation Commission (UNIIIC).

With Syria out of Lebanon, the Lebanese cabinet scheduled elections over three successive Sundays in late May and early June. The Hariri-family-led anti-Syrian March 14 bloc captured seventy-two seats, breaking the numerical threshold needed to form a government. As Fouad Siniora, Rafik Hariri's right-hand man in government and former finance minister, struggled to build a coalition, Syria initiated an additional "security procedure" on the Syrian side of the frontier, denying access for cars and trucks departing Lebanon for Syria. Nearly half of all Lebanese commercial trade crossed the Syrian frontier on its way to the richer markets in the Persian Gulf—truckloads of vegetables rotted in the hot summer sun as drivers, stuck with their loads, slept in the shade under the trailers.

While most chalked up the blockade to Syrian spite at having been thrown out of Lebanon, it hurt powerful Syrians, too. Less than a year after President Assad came to power in 2000, his cousin, Rami Makhlouf, had built a massive duty-free store on the Syrian side of the frontier. It sold the cheapest alcohol in the Middle East and housed what was then Syria's only supermarket, where everything from frozen pizzas to Dunkin' Donuts goods could be purchased by the boxful. At Syrian customs, officers had turned a blind eye to anything in a Syrian duty-free bag. With the advent of the blockade, however, customs officials now restricted passengers from bringing in anything other than personal effects and luggage.

In Syria, individual reaction to Hariri's assassination was one of shock and dismay. The country's Sunni population looked to Hariri as someone of their faith who had brought modernity to the Levant. He not only rebuilt Lebanon, he transformed Beirut—a mere two hours' drive from

Damascus—into one of the Arab world's best shopping hubs. His secular Sunni example, transmitted through his Future TV channel in Beirut, dovetailed nicely with secular Syrian Sunnis from the countryside like Leila, as well as Damascus's wealthy businessmen. When asked who they thought did it, most Syrians refused to believe their regime was involved. "It must have been Israel," Leila said shortly after the murder. "We are pulling out of Lebanon. Why would the regime do this?"

After Hezbollah's massive March 8 demonstration in Beirut, the Syrian authorities organized a demonstration the following day. Thousands of students and public-sector workers left work early and were gathered along the Mezze autostrade, part of Damascus's largest modern suburb, for a two-kilometer walk to nearby Malki—the site of President Assad's personal residence, the US embassy, and the diplomatic headquarters of many other Western countries. The area is named after Colonel Adnan Malki, the deputy chief of staff and Baath Party member who was assassinated in 1955 by a sergeant loyal to the Syrian Socialist Nationalist Party (SSNP)—a fascistlike party advocating the creation of "Greater Syria," a political and cultural union of what is today Lebanon, Israel, the Palestinian territories, Jordan, Iraq, Syria, and Cyprus. Following Malki's murder, SSNP leaders were subsequently either imprisoned or had to flee the country, but the party's political influence in the state continued.

This was not the first rally that I had ever witnessed in Syria, but it certainly was the largest. As I walked to the rally, I could hear music and drums up to half a kilometer away. Rounding the first corner onto the Mezze autostrade, I immediately ran into a middle-class Syrian family in modern dress with signs reading NO USA in English dangling around their necks. As I approached the family, their eyes widened in shock. I stopped two feet in front of them and, with an expressionless face, blurted out, "I'm American. I'm angry!"

The father instantly extended me his hand as his children looked clearly frightened. "We don't have anything against the American people, only against the government. Please, don't take it personally!" he said, quite nervously.

I couldn't hold a straight face for more than a second, and I laughed a little as I shook his hand. "But your sign makes it look like you are against the whole United States. What are you protesting against?"

"Bush meddling in our affairs," he said. He shook my hand and walked off.

Until that moment, I'd thought the march was to support pro-Syrian Lebanese "loyalists" such as president Émile Lahoud, prime minister Omar Karami, parliamentary speaker Nabih Berri, and, last but not least, Hezbollah. After all, I thought, this was all about Hariri's assassination, and the Lebanese opposition's attacks on Syria's role in Lebanon.

Instead, the March 9 rally was a march against "foreign interference." As far as the eye could see, protestors marched with signs in English reading NO FOREIGN INTERFERENCE, BOSH [sic]; LEAVE US ALONE; and MR. BUSH, WE DON'T NEED YOUR BLOOD DEMOCRACY. Other Syrian youths carried posters of Bashar al-Assad.

But even to a casual observer, the protests screamed of farce. Most protestors seemed to be just enjoying an afternoon off from work or school. Adding flare to the mob were hundreds of employees of the duty-free company Ramak and the mobile-phone operator Syriatel, both of which are owned by the president's cousin Rami Makhlouf, all dressed in T-shirts with the companies' respective logos. TV cameramen standing in the buckets of boom trucks had to focus on small parts of the crowd to make it seem as if the autostrade was filled with people. When I asked one of the protestors carrying a poster denouncing Bush what his sign said, he looked at me blankly and said, "By God, I don't even know."

Unexpectedly, there wasn't a Baathist flag in sight. Those of us covering the rally thought it was in response to the rallies in neighboring Lebanon, where protesters left their party flags at home in favor of national unity under one banner. Even the statue of the Baathist colonel Adnan Malki, which sits near the presidential residence, was without Baathist decoration. Baathist marching songs were completely replaced by the songs of the famous Lebanese singer Fairouz, who often sings of the natural beauty of Lebanon and Syria.

The only Syrian party flags at the rally were those of the SSNP, which featured a black field adorned with a white circle and a red, swastika-like insignia known as "the tempest." It was not a reference to Nazism, but rather an indication that Syria's Baathist days were dwindling. Baathism itself is a pan-Arab doctrine for Arab political unity in the name of confronting the problems facing the Arab world, most notably, the issue of Israel. For some reason, the government decided that the symbols used seemed to be shifting toward something more limited, more area specific. The SSNP also has a vision for political unity but did not have the authoritarian stigma of Baathism. SSNP doctrine is something Syrians and Lebanese both understand, and some of them support it (though maybe not political union, but something that emphasizes the historical, cultural, and linguistic ties that bind Syria and Lebanon together).

As I walked down from Adnan Malki Square toward the office, I ran into Syrian journalists covering the protest. Most told me about rumors that a Baath Party conference would be held in early June. While many remained pessimistic that the conference would produce anything at all, others said President Assad was about to announce a sweeping round of reforms, called the Jasmine Revolution. They said some public relations agencies were already planting the aromatic flower, native to Syria and Lebanon, all over Damascus in anticipation of the event. The movement was to include, among other things, changes in the constitution to allow for multiparty elections (parties not based on ethnicity or religion, however), as well as the expansion of NGOs and similar other associations. From my work with the first lady, I knew that the latter had been under way for some time. The former, however, had not been seriously discussed in Syria in more than forty years.

Back at the *Syria Today* offices, Leila and I met to decide on how to cover the Lebanon crisis.

"I don't believe Syria would kill Hariri," Leila told me. "But it's going to be the hottest story of the year, and we need to cover it."

"Yeah, but what do we do if the investigation says Syria did it?" I asked. "Can we cover that?"

"I have no idea," Leila said.

My ICWA fellowship was starting in earnest, so Leila hired Hugh Macleod, a British journalist working as an editor for the state-owned *Syria Times*, to edit the magazine. Hugh had just come off a stint at *The Independent*'s foreign desk, so he knew the issues well and gave us an in-house experienced Western perspective that proved to be vital in giving *Syria Today* an edge. Hugh believed in pushing the regime's red lines, and since we had no idea where they now were, we tested them with each edition to see what would happen. As the investigation into Hariri's murder unfolded, we reported on every development—each month we would print the edition and send it to the Ministry of Information's censorship office, and each month it just came back approved with no comments.

Waiting for the state to actually set a date for the Baath Party conference, we then ventured into a realm that I would never have thought possible: opposition politics. Syria's illegal-but-tolerated opposition parties were always hard to take seriously. Not because they hadn't taken their licks from the state over the years, but rather due to the opposition's stale political ideologies, chronic divisiveness, and questionable penetration into society. Marxist parties, for example, which threw around terms used only in North Korea these days, were ironically split along sectarian lines. Sectarian parties, especially Kurds, were divided ideologically. The Muslim Brotherhood, which had waged a terrorist war against the state that culminated in the darkest day of Syrian political life—the state's bombardment of the city of Hama in February 1982—was strictly outlawed, and its leadership was in London. And last but not least, it was hard to point to a single thing that the opposition had done to effectively change political life in Syria for almost four decades.

Nonetheless, in the wake of the Hariri attack, rumors circulated that the opposition was trying to form a central platform for the first time. So we chased down the opposition's leadership to get their story as part of *Syria Today*'s coverage of the conference. What we found, in a Syrian context, was amazing and changed my mind about Syria's domestic opposition.

In the days following Hariri's murder, two unnamed members of the Committee for the Revival of Civil Society flew to Morocco to meet Muslim Brotherhood chief Ali Sadreddin al-Bayanouni to discuss basic principles on which a united opposition front could be formed. The two returned to Syria with agreement on four broad points: democracy, nonviolence, a unified opposition structure, and a commitment to democratic change. Somewhat surprisingly, the two were empowered to negotiate with Syrian parties on behalf of the Muslim Brotherhood to forge an accord. Having direct contact with the Muslim Brotherhood was a risky endeavor for any Syrian, as Law 49 of 1980 made membership in the Muslim Brotherhood punishable by death. The drafting of what would eventually become known as the Damascus Declaration began. Following Assad's promise that the Baath Party conference "will be a leap for development in this country," rumors then circulated that members of the Muslim Brotherhood would be allowed to return to Syria without arrest.

The political base of the declaration started to take shape. Civil-society activists met in the offices of Samir Nashar, leader of the nascent Free National Party and a wealthy Aleppo trader, whose discussion forum was shut down in October 2002 in one of the state's final crackdowns on the Damascus Spring—the period of about two years after Assad's inaugural speech when Syrians met freely and often to discuss the country's problems.

"We met on April 4, 2005, and decided it was time to open dialogue with the Muslim Brotherhood," Nashar told me in an interview in March 2006. "We needed to bring the exiled and domestic opposition together." On April 17, Hassan Abdel-Azim, spokesperson for the opposition's National Democratic Rally—a grouping of five leftist pan-Arab parties—announced that it was ready to talk with the Muslim Brotherhood as well.

Things soon got complicated, however.

"Some of the opposition was afraid to include the Muslim Brotherhood, because they thought it would cause big problems with the authorities," Nashar said. "They didn't know how the regime would react."

It wasn't long before they found out. On May 24, eight members of the Atassi discussion forum—the only group that remained open after the Damascus Spring crackdown—were arrested when civil-society activist Ali al-Abdullah read aloud a statement from the Muslim Brotherhood's Bayanouni. This followed the possibly unrelated disappearance and murder of Kurdish Sheikh Muhammad Mashouk al-Khaznawi, whose tortured body was found on May 11. Nashar claims Khaznawi had an "open dialogue" with the Muslim Brotherhood. The Syrian state denied any culpability in the murder, which has since been attributed to a Sunni Islamic fundamentalist who had earlier branded Khaznawi an apostate. Human rights activists announced on Arab satellite TV that Brotherhood members would be arrested if they returned.

Because of fear of state persecution—or hope that Article 8 of the Syrian constitution, which says that the Baath Party must lead the state and society, would be repealed at the party's conference the following month and a new "parties law" would be introduced that would allow Syria's opposition to officially participate in political life—Abdel-Azim decided not to rush things.

"Our idea was to establish a narrow coalition that could be expanded," Abdel-Azim told me in a March 2006 interview. "We had to talk to a lot of parties. The Muslim Brotherhood was outside Syria as well. So we decided to postpone."

On visits to Beirut, I was always bombarded with questions on "the situation in Syria." I used to be able to answer this authoritatively, citing a specific development or law that had been passed and the impli-cations. In the spring of 2005, however, I had to just throw up my hands and say, "I have no idea."

No one did. The rumor mill in Damascus, always running at full speed, was out of control. Some people talked about tensions between the old guard and the president; others, tensions in the Assad fam-ily itself. As a rule, I always discounted such gossip, but one piece of news put me on edge. A friend with strong connections to the security services stopped by for a drink on my terrace. During the conversa-tion, he paused, deep in thought. When I asked him what was wrong, he looked up and said, "You would never believe what happened to me this morning. Someone from [unnamed Syrian official's] people visited me. The reason? To get my comment on a list of major political figures. It started out with the president's name, and then one word comments or short statements describing their strengths and weak-nesses. Next to the president's name, the descriptions read, 'weak, inept, unable to lead,' things like that. Next was the president's wife Asma, which read 'arrogant, dreamer, etc.' It just went on and on. It was like someone was carrying out a human resources evaluation at a company. When I realized someone was doing just that for Syria, and in such detail, I began to shake. I couldn't believe that anyone in Syria could put such things into print. I was afraid to even touch it."

Syria had always been an enigma, but hearing this story upset me. The way my friend told the story indicated that it had indeed hap-pened. The fact that some kind of human resources evaluation of Syr-ia's leadership was going on indicated to me that Syria was ruled by an oligarchy. And the fact that it was coming from this official—who was supposed to be retired and out of power—was even more shocking. Who was included in this oligarchy remained unknown. It is easy to assume important figures such as President Assad or Vice President Khaddam were involved, but this left out powerful relatives, security chiefs, and associates.

When someone asked me how to describe the political situation in Syria, I simply called it "the blackness." Using the term "fog" would have been out of the question, as fog tends to move or dissipate. The blackness just stayed in place, but it was not without its own dynamics. Rumors of gunfights between rival security services and stories of the house arrest of Vice President Khaddam were indications of the struggle going on inside this black cloud. It was as if suddenly a giant black hand had reached out of the morass and swooped back in, doubtlessly grabbing for some unknown rival obscured in the cloud.

In addition to the opposition's being able to coordinate their activities, security restrictions were also relaxed. This included permitting everything from the establishment of factories, restaurants, shops, and medical practices to allowing embassy staff to visit their citizens in jail or make inquiries about missing nationals in Syria.

The prospects for reform were another matter. In May 2005, for example, Nibras al-Fadel, a special adviser to President Assad on financial affairs, resigned unexpectedly following an interview he gave with the newspaper *Al-Sharq al-Awsat*, in which he outlined the judicial and market reforms necessary for the Syrian economy to avert economic crisis in the near future.[12]

Syrians close to the regime didn't give up hope. One rumor said that the political system would be opened up to allow for independent political parties and that Law 49 of 1980, which made membership in the Muslim Brotherhood punishable by death, would be repealed. Another said that the conference would conclude with a recommendation by the party that Article 8 of the constitution would be amended or repealed. Yet another said that two hundred thousand Kurds without citizenship in Syria, based on the census taken in 1962, would be granted full rights. Some even said that the Baath Party would change its name or even dissolve itself.

But as the conference approached, things didn't look good. In presummit working committees, those advocating substantial changes to the party—concerning democracy or socialism—were marginalized and their ideas shunned. This especially concerned those wanting to abolish Article 8 of the constitution. The buds of the Jasmine Revolution seemed to have withered before bloom.

When my mobile phone rang at 6:40 AM on June 6, I awoke with the realization that the day had finally arrived—the opening of the Tenth Party Conference of the Syrian Baath Party regional command.

"We are just waiting around outside the Ministry of Information for our badges," Hugh told me in an exasperated voice. "There is no schedule, and no one knows if we will have access to the conference center. It's chaos."

I was hardly surprised. In fact, I had purposely ignored the Ministry of Information's instructions to arrive in front of Dar al-Baath, the ministry building, before boarding buses out to the conference. It was not out of laziness but rather based on my experience covering official Syrian events. About a month before, for example, I attended the official visit of Turkish president Ahmet Necdet Sezer to Syria. Arriving at 8 AM as instructed and in a full suit, I waited with the rest of Syria's press corps for two hours for Ministry of Information officials to show up. When they finally arrived, we were simply told a bus would take us to the presidential palace for the arrival ceremony. No schedule was available. We were also told we would be unable to leave the palace until the talks were over. I spent the next nine hours of my life sitting in the hot sun, getting a fabulous tan from the neck up. The wait was punctuated only by a brief press conference with the two leaders; they did not allow questions to be asked.

The wake-up call on June 6, and its message, would characterize my attempts to understand the Baath Party conference, its decisions, and the potential for an authoritarian party to reform itself under increasing foreign pressure.

Returning from my morning workout at the Unity Club, a Baathist sports complex in Damascus, I received another call from Hugh at 8:30 AM.

"There are no badges after all," Hugh said. "We are now sitting on buses that are supposedly going to take us to the conference's media center. The ministry people are not even sure we will have access to the center for Bashar's opening speech. It's a pretty grim scene."

I knew from Hugh's words and subsequent phone calls from a host of other foreign journalists who had turned up in Damascus for the conference that the regime did not want the conference and its proceedings to be understood by the Syrian or international community. It was an old trick that the regime had pulled time and time again: allow journalists to come into the country, greet them kindly at the Ministry of Information, and send them back to their five-star hotels without any clue about the basics—most notably anything resembling a schedule. That's exactly what happened. Finishing my morning coffee, I began to receive more telephone calls from correspondents who had freshly arrived in the country. Like Hugh, they had made the journey out to the conference center with the hope of attending and listening in on President Assad's remarks. Instead, they were herded into a "media center" about two kilometers away—the new Damascus Exhibition Center. The "center" was in fact a room with some chairs and three computers hooked up to a 128K ADSL Internet connection with stand-alone printers. A number of TVs broadcasting Syrian programs were blaring. No food, water, coffee, or tea was available. All this was somehow supposed to sustain about three hundred Arab and foreign correspondents for four days.

When word got out that only cameramen would have access to the opening session, the army of correspondents poured out of the media center and boarded buses back to Damascus. All were disillusioned. As one Arab correspondent told me, "How can I write a story running up to the conference when I know nothing about it?"

I left my house at 9 AM for the short walk to the *Syria Today* offices in the Damascus Free Zone, an area behind the customs house in Damascus where nominally export-oriented businesses escaped Syria's convoluted taxes and tariffs. Upon arrival, I was greeted by Othaina Sahara, a new *Syria Today* staff member who also worked for the state-owned *Syria Times*. "The Ministry of Information says the opening speech will begin at noon. Let's turn on the television and see if there is any news," Othaina said in his usual cheerful voice.

News bulletins on Syria's satellite news channel about the upcoming conference raced across the screen. Listening carefully, I discovered that the opening speech would be aired in only fifteen minutes, at 10 AM. A few minutes later, Hugh and a correspondent for the *Los Angeles Times* arrived, looking haggard.

The time had finally come. We all piled into the office meeting room, readying notebooks and tape recorders for Assad's speech. As Hugh described the appalling inadequacy of the media center, a TV commercial for a local brand of cheese was suddenly blacked out. A few seconds later, a video graphic of Baathist and Syrian flags appeared, complete with triumphal music blaring in the background.

Coverage then cut to a smiling and waving President Assad strolling down the stairway of the Ebla Cham Conference Center. As he took his position at the main podium, everyone in the *Syria Today* office settled into their chairs and got ready for perhaps the most anticipated speech of Bashar al-Assad's presidency—we all hoped that the big reforms that had been anticipated for five years were finally at hand.

Assad began by praising the role of the Baath Party in Syrian life and the concerted efforts the different working committees had made running up to the conference. "The Baath Party remains a vanguard force in the life of our people and our country," Assad said. "Some of the writings and proposals that preceded the congress caught my attention. . . . Whether or not we agree with some of these propositions, and whether they take an upbeat approach to the party or not, and whether they are appreciative or critical of the party, they go to show that the Baath Party is a popular force, central to Syrian life."

Given the fact that reformers had not won in elections of the working committees, I immediately assumed that Assad in fact had opposed some of the more radical reform suggestions concerning changing the constitution. I moved closer to the TV set, making sure I heard every word. Perhaps Assad was going to break free and set a new course for the party himself.

It was wasted effort. Assad surprisingly began his speech with a critique of the communications and IT revolution:

[This] revolution has made room for theories and projects, as well as lifestyles that have overwhelmed Arabs and threatened their existence and cultural identity, and has increased doubts and skepticism in the minds of young Arabs. The forces behind these events have created an illusionary virtual reality that inspires our feelings in a way that drives us in a direction identified by others. . . . This leads in the end to the cultural, political, and moral collapse of the Arab individual and his ultimate defeat, even without a fight.

Strange words from a president who has been hailed as the father of Syria's IT revolution for the past five years.

The speech then went from bad to worse. Assad continued the state's mantra that economic reform in the country was progressing but was simply hamstrung by personnel problems. According to Assad, there was nothing wrong with the Baath Party or its ideology—rather, "individuals" were responsible for its failings. A new initiative to combat the country's rampant corruption problems was then given lip service by the president.

In conclusion, the president seemed to fire a warning shot over the heads of those who might cooperate with the United States in its efforts to promote "reform" in the region.

I call upon you to exercise your role in a courageous and responsible manner by pointing out both our limitations and our achievements, by addressing the shortcomings we suffer from as well as the successes we enjoy, and by being as honest as possible in your discussions and proposals about the concerns and aspirations of the public, bearing in mind that every decision you take and every recommendation you make should express only our internal needs, regardless of any consideration which aims at pushing us in directions which harm our national interests and threaten our stability.

Much more interesting than the speech was what was going on around me in the *Syria Today* meeting room. Hugh and the *Los Angeles Times* correspondent understood less Arabic, so they relied on the translation services of Syrians in the room. As the speech continued, a sort of struggle emerged between Hugh and the Syrians present that spoke volumes about the speech's content. One of them began translating the speech word for word, which Hugh and the *Times* correspondent wrote down studiously. After only a few moments, they stopped their attempt at simultaneous translation and went silent, switching to summaries of a few words following what seemed like each of the speech's main sections.

"Why aren't you translating?" Hugh asked, visibly annoyed. "This is a major address by the president."

The Syrians did not immediately answer, continuing their brief summaries. At a certain point, one staff member stopped and looked at another staff member, who in turn began translating word for word. After a few moments, another Syrian began to summarize as well. Hugh, even more annoyed, asked both of them why they were not simultaneously translating the speech.

"There is nothing of substance to translate," one of them said, clearly disappointed. "There is nothing."

Assad's address was followed by speeches from the heads of each of the parties of the National Progressive Front (NPF), the body of ten loyalist "opposition" parties formed in 1972 under the umbrella of the Baath Party. As each leader delivered their speech, praising the Baath Party and its role in society, we speculated on the outcome of the conference.

"There is not going to be much," I said. "Political reform will be limited, outside pressures do not affect internal reforms, and individuals are the problem and not the Baath Party. He didn't even mention trade."

"See?" one of the staff said. "Nothing."

That evening, I invited a group of correspondents to dinner at the Damascus Journalists' Club, an institution sponsored and supported by the Journalists' Syndicate of the Baath Party. It is a place with cheap beers, good mezze (oriental salads), and grilled meat and chicken—the staple main course in Damascus. Sitting around the table were three correspondents from the *New York Times* and one each from *The Economist*, the *Christian Science Monitor*, the Associated Press, and Reuters.

After only one day of covering the conference, all were at a loss as to what kinds of stories they would be able to write with such little information. They had filed stories that day, outlining Assad's speech but describing it as falling short of expectations.

Throwing back whiskeys and Barada beer (Syria's staple brew, which is reminiscent of *weissbier*, or wheat beer), the group shared their frustration about not understanding exactly what the conference was all about. A few hours and many more drinks later, we decided to head home. The bill for food and drink for eight people came to a whopping one thousand Syrian pounds (nineteen US dollars)—while we might not have understood the Baath Party, we sure enjoyed some of its subsidies.

I awoke at 7 AM the following morning, June 7, wondering how we would be informed of what was going on in the conference's different working committees. I hurried to my desk and tried to connect to the Internet about a dozen times before it finally hooked up. I visited the website of the state information service, Syrian Arab News Agency (SANA)—born during Syria's Soviet-leaning Cold War years—in search of news on what to expect. Only an English-language translation of Assad's speech was available. I made a few early morning phone calls to Arab journalist friends who might have information on press conferences and possible conference-access times. Not a single one answered. Not a good sign, I thought.

I then tuned into Syria's satellite TV station. The 9 AM newscast talked extensively about the president's "important and historic" speech, with numerous snippets from the address. The newscaster simply said that the various working committees would begin their deliberations that day. No mention of press conferences. I turned to BBC World Service, hoping to find out what was going on elsewhere in the world. Suddenly I saw a still of Syrian vice president Abdel Halim Khaddam, under which appeared a box reading RESIGNATION. That got my attention. The BBC gave no details, only reporting that Khaddam had resigned from "all party and government affairs."

After a brisk walk to the *Syria Today* offices, I was greeted at the door by Othaina.

"Khaddam resigned," I said.

"Really?" Othaina answered. "There's nothing in the Syrian media about it. But remember, all members of the regional command resign on the first day of the conference. Maybe it's just a rumor and he's staying."

I checked the website of the newspaper *Al Hayat* for details. Ibrahim Hamidi reported that Khaddam had indeed resigned on the first day of the conference.

"Some people were saying yesterday there will be a 2:30 PM and 9:30 PM press conference each day," Othaina said. "Maybe we will get some details then. Bouthaina Shaaban will apparently head each one."

Perhaps more than any other person, Bouthaina Shaaban was the best-known international spokesperson for the Syrian regime. A former translator for late president Hafez al-Assad, Shaaban was a member of Syria's ruling Alawi sect. With a doctorate from the University of Exeter, complete with a Fulbright fellowship, Shaaban had a friendly but proud manner that made her the favorite of international journalists around the time of the US invasion of Iraq in March 2003.

As the spokesperson for the Syrian Ministry of Foreign Affairs at the time, Shaaban landed telephone interviews on CNN, the BBC, and other major English-language news services due to her excellent English and ties to the regime.

Following a rumored fallout with foreign minister Farouk al-Shara, Shaaban was "kicked upstairs" by the president and made the country's first "minister of expatriates." She was charged with bringing talented Syrians back to their homeland, and her ministry building was set up in the Damascus satellite city of Dummar, about a thirty-minute trip from the center of the capital. She has been traveling the world ever since, the human face for Syria's estimated fifteen million diaspora community.

In the world of Baath Party politics, however, Shaaban still carried weight as a member of the party's fifty-member central committee—the body immediately under the party's ruling "regional command" ("regional" in this case meaning Syria, since Baathist pan-Arab ideology considers Syria only a "region" of the "Arab nation"). Given her experience and position, it was no surprise to me that Shaaban was appointed as the party's official spokeswoman for the conference.

I called the public relations office of the Ministry of Information for clarification of the press-conference times. The office assistant confirmed the rumor about the times for the conferences. After I hung up, I looked at Othaina.

"Now we wait," I said.

And we did just that. As the morning dragged on, I combed newspapers in search of details about Khaddam's resignation and information on the conference agenda. The three state-owned daily newspapers carried only excerpts of the president's speech, along with a full spread of photos. No other information was available, other than the names of the four working committees.

Around 2:30 PM, I switched on the TV and tuned into the Syrian satellite channel. The transmission quickly cut to reporters greeting Shaaban as she sat down at the head table. She's on the short side, so the forty or so microphones positioned in front of her nearly eclipsed her face. Speaking in Arabic, Shaaban outlined some of the points from the president's speech the previous day. She also informed the audience that the president had ordered that some of the proceedings of the working committees would be broadcast on national TV stations. When one Syrian journalist asked which committees would be broadcast and when, Shaaban simply replied, "It will be announced."

Shaaban went on to announce in a loud voice, "The conference will discuss everything of importance to the Syrian citizen. The slogan of this conference is flexibility and steadfastness." Foreign journalists attending the press conference were already lost, due largely to the fact that no simultaneous translation services were available. Those from major media relied on their "fixers," or local helpers, to translate all questions and answers. After a few more questions, a foreign journalist asked if translation services could be made available for the press conference, given the number of non-Arabic speakers.

"Today, if the question is in English, I will answer in English," Shaaban said. "In the next press conference, translations services will be available."

Shaaban was then asked about Khaddam's resignation and if it was indeed permanent. Laughing, Shaaban replied, "Well, yesterday at the conference, Khaddam spoke for one hour. When he was asked why his speech took so long, while each person was only allotted five minutes, he replied, 'Because I am a member in the regional command of the Baath Party.' So I believe he is still in the party."

With that strange answer, the ten-minute press conference was over. What did her answer about Khaddam mean? We might have something at 9:30 PM, I guessed. About thirty minutes later, Othaina called me to his desk, excited.

"The all4syria.com news service says there was a fight between Khaddam and Foreign Minister Shara yesterday," Othaina said. Sure enough, on the screen in front of us were details of the "hour-long speech" Shaaban spoke of. Apparently, Khaddam declared that what Syria needs now is "democracy" and went on for some length about how opening the political system was the best way to confront the country's problems. Shara, openly miffed at Khaddam's out-of-turn statements, asked the vice president to submit his criticisms to the political committee for consideration.

But that was not all. After Khaddam's speech, a member of the political committee, journalist Ali Jamalo, stood up and asked Khaddam some tough questions. "You are calling for democracy," Jamalo reportedly said. "You were in power for almost forty years. . . . What did you do for democracy when you were in power? You complain about Syria's handling of the Lebanon crisis. But you were the one who established Syria's presence in Lebanon. We want this free market for the economy. Why didn't you do anything about it? When you call for democracy, it is we, the young blood, that demand democracy. What did you do for forty years? Don't bring us your faults and frustrations."

That afternoon, calls continued to come in from foreign correspondents wanting to know about the possibility of meeting or having dinner. Most added the caveat that they would need either to attend or monitor the press conference at 9:30 PM. So I left most appointments open and made plans to be at home to tune into the press conference myself.

In the meantime, I turned on the TV to see which committee proceedings were being broadcast. None was featured; Channel One was running a segment on pets.

At 9:30 PM, Syria satellite TV cut its transmission to cover the press conference. Shaaban began by giving small briefs about the workings of each committee. The economic committee, for example, discussed tourism projects, how to better deal with expatriates, and efforts to combat corruption. Shaaban added that loss-making state companies would be privatized, which was in line with the recommendations of the State Planning Commission. Shaaban went on to say that the political committee was trying to find "a formula for national participation in the framework of national unity" for new political parties. No parties would be tolerated based on religion, sect, or ethnicity.

She then added that the political committee had discussed a new media law that would help "change Syria's image" abroad. The private sector would be allowed to set up satellite TV and radio stations, Internet services, and other electronic media. Last but not least, Shaaban said the name of the Baath Party would stay the same.

After making her statements, Shaaban was bombarded with questions about Khaddam's resignation as well as basic questions on what she'd said in her statement.

"My words from earlier today were clear about the VP," she said. "You will get answers to all your questions. On the final day, we will tell you everything."

That event was essentially the last major happening until the final press conference on June 9, following the closing ceremony. It did not seem so at the time, so I continued to monitor Syrian TV around 2:30 PM and 9:30 PM each day. The much-promised broadcasts of committee sessions were in fact only ten-minute excerpts and were not worth following, and the first press conference that day was canceled. On June 8, the 9:30 PM press conference was not convened. Those conferences that were held featured no major announcements, other than the creation of the Higher Media Council to help promote media expansion and modernization through greater private-sector participation. And the promised simultaneous translation services at press conferences never appeared.

The net effect of the lack of coherent information coming out of the conference was the inability of any of the army of foreign correspondents to produce stories. In fact, by the end of day two, most didn't even go to the center. Wire services such as Reuters ran small stories on the decision to privatize loss-making companies, but major newspapers like the *New York Times* failed to cover the conference.

It was, as one correspondent told me, a "missed event." After all, as most of them argued, how can you write about something you cannot understand?

Cut to 3:30 PM on Thursday, June 9, the conference's final day. My mobile rang.

"Ministry of Information says the conference ends today," Othaina said, referring to speculation that the event might drag on until Saturday. "The press conference is scheduled for 7 PM."

Finally, I thought. Then I engaged in an internal debate about whether to actually attend the conference or not. After a few hours of wavering, I decided not to make the trip out to the media center. I knew very well that the chances the press conference would be delayed, or not held at all, were high. I had a number of journalist friends working for wire services for whom attendance was mandatory, so I asked one of them to call me if something happened. That evening, I sat in my living room reading about the recently returned Lebanese leader Michel Aoun.

I fell asleep around 10:30 PM, papers scattered around me. Around 11:15 PM, my mobile rang. It was my friend—the much-awaited press conference was about to finally happen. I tuned in.

Bouthaina Shaaban strolled out to the press conference table, smiling and greeting people as she sat down. By the look on her face, I could tell the message was going to be short and sweet.

"We have so much ground to cover, it is impossible for me to give you everything now," Shaaban told those in attendance. So much for her promises all week that everything would be crystal clear at the end.

"These recommendations cover all the life domains," Shaaban said. "The economic committee took a long time in its deliberations and decided Syria would have a social-market economy. We will have an independent commission to combat corruption in order to attract more Arab and international investment. Women will play a greater role in decisions, and we will form an independent judiciary."

Shaaban's statements continued, broad and vague. A new parties law would be issued, but it would be based on "national unity" and would not permit parties based on religion, sect, or ethnicity. Article 8 of the constitution, which says the Baath Party leads the state, was not touched. The emergency law—in place since the Baath Party took power in 1963 (and installed Hafez al-Assad, then a military attaché at Syria's embassy in Argentina, as chairman of a national council)—would be reviewed with the idea of limiting certain issues to "state security." Also under review would be the fact that the Kurds in the country were not citizens; thus most of their rights would be granted.

Concerning the party's powerful "regional command," the positions of prime minister and speaker of parliament would be held by party members. In the past, only individuals were appointed to the regional command. This, Shaaban said, would "enhance relations between the party and the government." The Higher Media Council would be established to help "correct Syria's distorted image" abroad. Last but not least, Shaaban said the president was pleased with the conference's outcome.

Her statements lasted a mere ten minutes. She entertained a few questions from reporters, to which she provided vague answers or said that they would be outlined at a later time. And that was it. I sighed in disgust, switched off the TV, and went to bed. They don't want to be understood, I thought.

Shaaban's slogan of "flexibility and steadfastness" in many ways was the correct way to describe the Tenth Baath Party Conference. The Baath Party was not making a great leap forward, as the president seemed to indicate on the eve of Syria's withdrawal from Lebanon, but was rather simply stretching its boundaries a bit. Since Article 8 of the constitution had not been touched, and whatever political project that was on the way would not be permitted along sectarian, ethnic, or religious lines, the party was standing fast to its principle that Syrians are first and foremost Arabs and would therefore manage things politically as such as long as the Assad regime was in power.

The dreaded emergency law—which justifies anything the state wants to do, including detaining Syrians without charge—would be reviewed, but many questions remained about what "national security" meant in today's Syria. The definition of "national security" would still remain in the hands of the leadership. Syria's media sector would continue to be opened up, but all in the name of improving the country's image. Could such a formula really cultivate a properly functioning fourth estate? Making the prime minister and speaker of parliament members of the regional command seemed significant—or did this move simply guarantee the Baath Party's hold over the state, even in the event of having an independent prime minister, which was something that has been promised for years?

This was strange behavior for a regime under intense international pressure, which always complained that it was misunderstood. Although perhaps it was not so odd after all, given the situation in Syria. The most important outcome of the conference—the retirement of major political figures—was not emphasized in any way by the regime and in turn was ignored by the Syrian and foreign media.

In many ways, the conference signaled the end of a five-year transition period for the Baath Party, marked by a struggle between the old guard of the late president Hafez al-Assad (commonly referred to as "Bashar's uncles") and the "new generation" of the current president. During the transition, the old guard was blamed for hindering President Bashar's reform efforts, largely through "loyalist networks" that had been formed throughout the senior Assad's three decades in power. These figures included two vice presidents, Abdel Halim Khaddam and Muhammad Zuheir Masharqa; two longtime regional-command members, Abdullah al-Ahmar and Suleiman Qaddah; former parliamentary speaker Abdul Kader Kaddoura; and former defense minister Mustafa Tlass. Their exit from party life at the conference seemed to have strengthened Bashar al-Assad's grip on power and the new generation's ability to carry out reform in the country. The aging foreign minister, Farouk al-Shara, was still around, however, and reportedly he would be appointed vice president soon.

In fact, just as the final conclusions of the conference were finally published in the state daily newspapers five days after the event, the president appointed lead reformer and state planning commission chief Abdullah Dardari as deputy prime minister for economic affairs. A day later, he quietly removed Bahjat Suleiman, head of the powerful general security department. While the Baath Party conference might have been a nonevent itself, something was happening in the darkness behind the scenes of Syrian politics. Perhaps "flexibility and steadfast-ness" was less a slogan for the conference and more a coded reference to the president's quiet efforts to wrestle greater control of the regime from the old guard.

Disappointed that the Baath Party conference failed to produce any reforms, the Syrian opposition continued work on the Damascus Dec-laration. In the summer and early autumn of 2005, negotiations began with Syria's eight Kurdish parties and the tribal-based Future Party led by Sheikh Nawaf al-Bashir, as well as some of Syria's most prominent independent opposition figures, including the outspoken Riad Seif, who was in prison at that point.

"Hassan [Abdel-Azim] came to visit in September," Seif told me in a March 2006 interview. "He is my lawyer, and it was easy for him to see me. We needed to unite the opposition, and he gave me a full pic-ture of the Damascus Declaration. I accepted immediately."

On October 5 and 6, negotiations with the last group that was holding out on signing the declaration—the ethnically based Assyr-ian Democratic Organization (ADO)—foundered on the declaration's references to Islam as the "religion and ideology of the majority" and its mention of the Kurds as the only ethnic "issue" in Syria.

"We were convinced that they mentioned Islam in the document. simply to attract Islamists," said Bashir Ishaq Saadi, secretary-general of the ADO, told me in a February 2006 interview. "Second, we said, 'Hey, you mentioned Kurdish rights. What about Assyrians?'"

Time was running out, however. In neighboring Lebanon, Detlev Mehlis, the chief UN investigator into the Hariri assassination, was due to give his first report on October 19. Sources quoted in the Lebanese press said the investigation was pointing fingers of blame toward Damascus. "We wanted to announce the declaration before the Mehlis report," Samir Nashar said. "We didn't want people to say we were taking advantage."

To avoid the same kind of leaks that were undermining Mehlis's investigation, Abdel-Azim kept the only signed copy of the declaration in his pocket. In the end, five parties and eight opposition figures came onboard.[13] On October 16, Abdel-Azim held a small press conference in his office to announce the declaration.

"*Mukhabarat* [intelligence services] showed up," said Abdel-Azim. "I tried to call the Ministry of Information, but the minister was not in. We had invited the satellite TV channels to cover the event. So I went upstairs and announced it to the world."

Two hours after the declaration's announcement, the Muslim Brotherhood—which had been party to the negotiations from the beginning—became the first to sign on to the accord. While Abdel-Azim was unclear with me as to motive, a number of opposition figures told me that he had arranged the timing of the Muslim Brotherhood's signature so that the Syrian authorities could not say the declaration was spawned by the Brotherhood and therefore subject to the state's strict ban on the organization.

"Apparently the report [into Hariri's murder] is going to name names," my flatmate, Katherine Zoepf, said over coffee on the morning of October 20. Katherine was then in Damascus as a freelance journalist for the *New York Times*. "We've got to talk to some people about this."

We headed over to the office of Sami Moubayed, a Damascus-based historian educated at the American University in Beirut. While Sami had published a number of books in English on Syrian history, he had also become an analyst on Syrian and regional politics.

When Katherine told him that word out of New York was that the report would finger high-level members of the Syrian regime, Sami looked down and sighed. "This contradicts everything we have been hearing over the past few days. . . . What we've been hearing from sources close to the government is basically that the regime is innocent, but that it will be incriminated nonetheless. Naming the regime as a whole is still much less embarrassing than saying that a particular person is responsible. This changes everything," Sami said. "The regime's best-case scenario was going to be that the regime as a whole would be held responsible. Now they are going to be told to hand over Assef Shawkat, and I don't know if they can actually do that. Assef Shawkat is a very strong man, and it's not just about the love story between him and Bushra al-Assad [Bashar's sister]. Shawkat was hated by Hafez and hated by Basel [Bashar's brother, who died in 1994], and he's overcome that. He's very, very strong. No one ever sees Assef Shawkat. He's my neighbor, and I've only seen him once in my entire life."

Katherine and I just looked at each other. It was very rare that Syrians, especially analysts, spoke so openly about members of the regime. However, there were plenty of signs of trouble in the Assad family. In the days leading up to the investigation announcement, former Syrian intelligence chief in Lebanon Ghazi Kanaan and the current interior minister had committed "suicide" in his office. As the de facto viceroy of Lebanon for years, many suspected his involvement in Hariri's murder, and most I met doubted that he had committed suicide.

"With Ghazi Kanaan and Assef Shawkwat gone, this completely breaks the power of the Alawi community in Syria," Sami continued. "They will never arrest Assef. Syria will have to simply say that this report is political and that we are innocent. This is going to be really terrible. If Syria does not respond, there could be more sanctions. There's no telling what might happen. When you've got someone like Assef Shawkat who is so powerful in his own right, you can't arrest him."[14]

As Katherine filed her quotes to New York, I jumped on the Internet to see if a soft copy of the report was available. After two hours of searching, I gave up looking and helped Katherine prepare dinner for a party we were hosting that evening for Hugh and Joshua Landis, an American professor from Oklahoma University on a Fulbright in Syria to turn his dissertation into a book. Joshua was particularly attuned to the thinking of the Alawite sect via his marriage to the daughter of an Alawite admiral in the Syrian Navy. Joshua spent most of his time working on his blog, Syria Comment. Several times a week, he would blog on things he was hearing around Damascus—everything from the Hariri investigation to reform.

Over several glasses of Lebanese wine and oriental salads, all of us speculated about what would happen and what the final text of the report might say. In an interview the previous week, Joshua had expressed what we were all thinking. "Obviously, this is going to lead to the Syrian government," he told the Council on Foreign Relations. "How far up the line is [the investigation] going to go? . . . Will Mehlis implicate someone in the president's family[?] . . . If it was somebody in the immediate family, it would be a real crisis."[15]

As soon as I awoke the next morning, I ran to my computer to see if the report's text was available. A colleague in Beirut, The Times' correspondent Nicholas Blanford, had sent me the report electronically. As soon as I opened it, Hugh called.

"Did you see it? Did you see it?" he yelled into the phone. When I asked him what he was talking about, he said, "The report. Hit 'View Changes' in Microsoft Word. Someone at the United Nations removed Assef Shawkat and Maher al-Assad's names right before the report was published."

Sure enough, in paragraph ninety-six, the report said, "One witness of Syrian origin but resident in Lebanon, who claims to have worked for the Syrian intelligence services in Lebanon, has stated that approximately two weeks after the adoption of Security Council Resolution 1559, senior Lebanese and Syrian officials decided to assassinate Rafik Hariri." The "Track Changes" version, however, showed that the names "Maher al-Assad, Assef Shawkat, Hassan Khalil, Bahjat Suleiman and Jamil al-Sayyed" in the original draft had been removed and replaced with "senior Lebanese and Syrian officials." The tracked changes showed that the text had been removed at midday on October 20 by "special rep"—presumably Terje Roed-Larsen, UN special representative for the implementation of Security Council Resolution 1559.

I just stared at the screen in disbelief. Assef Shawkat? Maher Assad? Until then, the only place where you might see their names associated with any crime—the Hariri assassination or anything else—would be on far-right Lebanese websites or that of the exiled Reform Party of Syria in the United States. At *Syria Today*, we didn't dare write their names, which was out of fear, but also out of lack of evidence. This report seemed to change all that.

I called my friend Ibrahim Hamidi at his office in the *Al Hayat* newspaper bureau. When I asked him if he had heard about the changes, he had no idea what I was talking about. After a few minutes of trying unsuccessfully to explain how "Track Changes" in Microsoft Word worked, I jumped in a taxi and went over to his office. At his terminal, I showed him the text. He didn't say a word and just stared at the screen, expressionless, in shock.

At the United Nations, Syria's foreign minister, Farouk al-Shara, faced tough questioning over the investigation. Shara responded to a line of the report stating that "there is probable cause to believe that the decision to assassinate former prime minister Rafik Hariri could not have been taken without the approval of top-ranked Syrian security officials" by turning the statement around and saying that, by the same definition, the United States, Spain, and the United Kingdom must therefore be responsible for the recent terrorist attacks on their own countries. Immediately, the United Kingdom's foreign secretary, Jack Straw, issued a strong rebuttal, describing Shara's comparison of Syria's situation in Lebanon to that of the United States, United Kingdom, and Spain as "grotesque and insensitive." He also reiterated Mehlis's position regarding Syria's lack of cooperation with the investigation, which he hoped Syria would rectify. "But I have to say, after what I have heard, that I am not holding my breath," Straw said.[16]

The panic started immediately. In open-market currency trading in Lebanon, the Syrian pound lost nearly 25 percent of its value overnight. At *Syria Today*, staff members were stunned by the news. "My family and I stayed up all night watching television coverage of the report," one staff member told me. Another said that he never "dreamed of a day when he would see high-level Syrians atop a United Nations report."

In private, Hugh and I discussed the investigation in depth and how it would impact *Syria Today*'s coverage. We both understood that the day's events would have a profound impact on what the magazine could and could not print. However, we also recognized, based on our conversations with trusted sources, that things at the top of the Assad regime seemed chaotic and that it was a distinct possibility that the regime could topple, resulting in some kind of palace coup or an Alawite military officer seizing power. The Syrian opposition, historically hapless, had managed to agree on the Damascus Declaration. More impressive than the declaration's text were the political skills shown by Syria's most well-known opposition leader, Michel Kilo, who had managed to draft the declaration quietly. The Muslim Brotherhood had also jumped onboard. Perhaps some sort of democratic transition was possible in Syria—but the chances seemed remote.

Concerning *Syria Today*, we decided to go ahead with our coverage of the Hariri investigation but also to push red lines to see where things stood. In December 2005, *Syria Today*'s cover story, "When Exception Becomes the Rule," probed Syria's use of security courts to try civilians and examined the Hariri evidence in detail. To our surprise, the edition came back from censorship approved. We were relieved, not only for the edition's clearance, but because in the days leading up to the magazine's publication, rumors had spread throughout the Syrian capital that our former patron, Asma al-Assad, had fled to London to live with her family. Her NGOs remained open, but reports from friends said that no one was showing up for work.

On December 15, 2005, the Security Council met to discuss Mehlis's findings since his first report. After extensive deliberation, they passed Resolution 1644, which demanded that Syria respond "unambiguously and immediately" to the commission investigating the terrorist attack that had killed former Lebanese prime minister Rafik Hariri, and they extended the investigation another six months. The resolution also demanded that Syria implement "without delay" any future request of the United Nations International Independent Investigation Commission. The resolution was passed under Chapter VII of the UN Charter, meaning Syrian noncompliance would be a "threat to peace," allowing the United Nations to use sanctions or military force to enforce the measure.[17]

As 2005 drew to a close, many predicted that the Assad regime would soon fall. On December 30, former vice president Abdel Halim Khaddam gave a lengthy interview on the Saudi-owned pan-Arab satellite television station Al Arabiya. He said that Assad's advisers were putting the country on the path to ruin, forcing Khaddam to choose between the regime and his country. He did not directly criticize Assad, but descriptions of how easily he had been duped by the former Syrian security chief in Lebanon, Rustom Ghazaleh, and Farouk al-Shara made the president appear naïve.

While Khaddam had polite words for the president, his comments on the Hariri assassination grabbed international headlines. He said that if Hariri's murder was carried out by Syrian intelligence, "they would not make such a decision alone . . . this is not possible"—indicating Assad would have certainly known about the murder. Khaddam added that Assad had threatened Hariri during their last meeting in Damascus. Khaddam said that he and other Syrian officials heard Assad say "very, very, very hard" things to Hariri and that "he will crush anyone who tries to get out of our decision. I cannot recall the exact words. But they were very harsh words."[18]

5

THE ENEMY OF MY ENEMY IS MY FRIEND

For ten days after Mehlis announced his findings, the presidential palace in Damascus was silent. Rumors spread throughout the Syrian capital that President Assad had suffered a nervous breakdown, as Syria now faced even greater diplomatic isolation and the specter of UN sanctions should the regime fail to comply with the investigation. Many in Damascus talked of a possible palace coup, in which Bashar would be replaced by his brother Maher or his brother-in-law, chief of military intelligence Assef Shawkat—both names in the tracked changes of Mehlis's first report. Others predicted that Assad would try and build up popular support by implementing the reforms promised at the Baath Party conference, most notably a new political parties law.

At 7 AM on November 10, a mobile-phone text message—sent in Arabic and English to all subscribers of Syriatel, the mobile network owned by Assad's cousin and business tycoon Rami Makhlouf—broke the silence. It asked Syrians to attend a rally that day near Damascus University demonstrating "love of country and the rejection of external pressures." By midday, thousands gathered out in front of the main hall of Damascus University. Pumping their fists into the air, the crowd chanted, "In spirit, in blood, we will sacrifice for you, oh Bashar"—the same mantra that Syrian soldiers had chanted at that airbase in the Bekaa the day Syrian forces pulled out of Lebanon.[1]

When President Assad took the podium inside the university's main hall, he seemed ill at ease. Obviously under pressure, Assad started in a way that his father never did: he made it personal.

> Before I start this speech, I would like to say that I was asked several times last week why I look pale, and whether it was because of the pressures. I said no. In fact I was a little ill. I am saying this so that I do not get asked the same question again. Political circumstances make us more united, and when we get united we become stronger and livelier. This speech was scheduled for next week, but because of the fast pace of developments, I decided to make it today.

With that, Assad slipped back into standard "regime speak," urging his people to remain strong in the face of "cultural and psychological warfare." Instead of addressing the points raised in the UN investigation, Assad framed the crisis as a US or Israeli conspiracy against Syria. "We must be steadfast in facing this foreign attack," Assad said. "We don't want to name names, but you know who I am talking about." The audience erupted in laughter.

Concerning Syria's domestic scene, Assad added that the regime would extend citizenship to hundreds of thousands of Kurds in Syria whose citizenship had been stripped away in the 1960s—a key point discussed at the Baath Party conference the previous June. In a clear warning to the Syrian opposition, Assad said, "If someone in Syria raises his voice in tandem with foreigners, he is being controlled by foreigners."

In the final lines of the speech, Assad hinted at his plan for rolling back the pressures bearing down on his regime. "This region has two options: chaos or resistance," Assad said. "In the end, we are going to win, one way or another, even if it lasts a long time. Syria is protected by God."[2]

As I watched Assad receive a standing ovation, I thought about the speech and what it all meant. Directly and indirectly, Assad had told Syrians that the Hariri investigation in Lebanon was "politicized" and part of a plot against Syria by foreign powers. He was also clearly warning the opposition not to work with "foreigners"—that is, Americans or Westerners trying to help the Syrian opposition. But what was with "Syria is protected by God"? The Assad regime never made references to God, in keeping with the Baath Party's distinctly secular language. And what did he mean by "resistance"? Resistance to the pressures bearing down on Syria? Or resistance to Israel? When I asked the *Syria Today* staff what they thought it all meant, they just shrugged their shoulders.

We didn't have to wait long for an answer. In the days following the speech, Iranian foreign minister Manouchehr Mottaki arrived in Damascus for talks with Assad. After a long set of meetings with the Syrian president, Mottaki also consulted with "resistance" groups based in Syria and Lebanon, including Hezbollah leader Hassan Nasrallah, Hamas leader Khaled Meshaal, Popular Front for the Liberation of Palestine–General Command (PFLP-GC) chief Ahmed Jabril, and a representative of Palestinian Islamic Jihad. A week later on November 21, Hezbollah launched an attempted kidnapping in Ghajar, a border village disputed between Lebanon and the Israeli-occupied Golan Heights. The raid marked the largest attack on Israel since the withdrawal of its forces from Lebanon in May 2000.

On January 19, the hard-line Iranian president, Mahmoud Ahmadinejad, made his first state visit to Damascus. The two leaders announced a bilateral alliance to confront "foreign pressures," and President Assad publicly declared Syria's support for Iran's efforts to acquire nuclear technology. High-level delegations accompanying Ahmadinejad signed a number of protocols pushing economic, educational, and cultural cooperation between the two countries to unprecedented levels, followed up by scores of visits by Iranian officials. By June, Damascus and Tehran concluded their first mutual defense pact. "Syria's security is considered as part of the security and national interests of Iran," Iranian defense minister Mostafa Mohammad Najjar said after the June 2006 signing ceremony in Tehran. "We find ourselves bound to defend it."

While Syria's deepening relationship with Iran made international headlines, the regime began to reorient its rhetoric and propaganda toward Islam. At first, the symbolism was largely political. On the streets of Damascus, posters with images of Assad, Ahmadinejad, and Nasrallah, all surrounded by roses, began appearing on shop facades and car rear windows. Larger banners with SYRIA IS PROTECTED BY GOD were strewn throughout the Syrian capital. Syrian flags, with the slogan written into the middle white band alongside two stars—reminiscent of Saddam Hussein's addition of "*Allahu akbar*" (God is great) to the Iraqi flag after his forces were driven out of Kuwait in 1991—hung from buildings. State-owned radio and TV repeated the slogan so many times that it quickly turned into a mantra.

By January 2006, however, there were real signs that the regime was reorienting itself away from its secular past and toward Islam. In September 2005, the Danish newspaper *Jyllands-Posten* published twelve caricatures of the Prophet Muhammad. States throughout the Arab world demanded that the Danish government apologize for the incident. Danish prime minister Anders Fogh Rasmussen's refusal to do so, because his government "does not control the media," as it would violate "freedom of speech," fell well short of most Syrians' expectations.

On the morning of February 4, banner-wielding protesters began gathering near Rouda Square in Damascus for what would be the biggest diplomatic incident since the storming of the American ambassador's residence in 2000 in response to US-coalition air strikes on Iraq.

Around 3 PM, demonstrators marched toward the Danish embassy located in the adjacent neighborhood of Abou Roumaneh, where Leila and I were sitting in that neighborhood's local Kentucky

Fried Chicken—Syria's first Western fast-food restaurant. As I tucked into my three-piece-chicken combo meal, I noticed a swelling crowd through the restaurant's front windows. When the demonstrations first started, uniformed security services patrolled the streets and traffic policemen directed cars across the district's main thorough-fare. Soon, however, the waves of protesters could not be controlled. Leila and I rushed out of the door to see what was going on. The crowd was angry but not unruly. Uniformed security agents were gathered at the far end of the boulevard, where a perpendicular street led to the three-story villa housing the Danish, Swedish, and Chilean embassies.

As I rounded the corner of Abou Roumaneh Street, pushing my way through security forces dressed in olive green, I began to hear something that sounded like popcorn popping. About thirty yards down the street, protesters were stoning the Danish embassy. I stopped in my tracks and took a photo.

As I got closer to the embassy, I heard calls of *"Allahu akbar"* punc-tuated by sounds of shattering glass. Around a thousand protesters were pushing hard toward the embassies, packed into an area the size of half a football field. Flags of Hamas, Hezbollah, and Islamic Jihad fluttered in the air. Banners with enigmatic slogans in English, such as WE ARE READY printed in blood-red ink, dotted the crowd. I was a bit surprised, since Syrian protest banners are usually handmade, full of horrible English spelling and grammar mistakes. What happened next helped me understand just what that slogan meant, a little about where it was coming from, and who was behind it.

The front gate of a church adjacent to the embassy complex was open, with no signs of forced entry. Half a dozen Syrian men, between the ages of fifteen and fifty, were trying to scale the wall of the embassy from the church garden. As the crowd cheered the climbers, I began to notice that more than fifteen uniformed state security agents were assembled in front of the church—smoking cigarettes. Not a single officer lifted a finger to stop the rioters or looked at all nervous.

A number of protesters had already climbed onto apartment-block balconies across from the embassy—a perfect pitcher's mound for the rock barrage that was still under way. A banner reading IT'S NOT FREE-DOM THAT YOU MEAN, BUT INCITEMENT WHAT [sic] YOU MEAN was draped over one terrace railing. Where the stones came from was anyone's guess, but their brown, earthen color indicated that they did not come from the immediate surrounding area, which was completely paved or covered in asphalt.

One of the climbers, a Syrian man in his early thirties with long black hair and a shortly cropped beard, finally made it onto the terrace of the embassy complex's second floor, which was home to the Swedish embassy. He immediately began tugging at the Danish coat of arms, a colorful metal plate under the flagpole a floor above. Breaking it loose, he lifted it above his head and slammed it to the earth. Momentarily silenced by the spectacle, the crowd then roared approval, as chants of "*Allahu akbar*" echoed again. Unable to reach the Danish embassy on the third floor, the bearded man hoisted the green banner of Islam—on which was written LA ALLAH ILLA ALLAH, WA MUHAMMAD AR-RUSUL ALLAH (There is no God but Allah, and Muhammad is the prophet of God)—up the Swedish embassy's flagpole. The crowd roared again.

Protesters were excited but not full of the kind of hate that might justify their stoning a building. While my light-brown hair, blue eyes, and northern European features (a Danish friend once told me that I look a bit Scandinavian) would have seemed to scream "hit me," I noticed not so much as a dirty look. I was sporting a short-cropped beard, which could have been taken as a sign of Muslim piety. Every time Leila called me on my mobile phone, I made sure I spoke in Arabic. When a few English words slipped out of my mouth, a number of protesters looked my way, but not too hard.

Things soon turned sour. Protesters began throwing office paraphernalia from the Danish embassy into the crowd. Suddenly, black smoke began billowing, as the protesters set the Chilean embassy on the first floor ablaze. I immediately looked at the security forces gathered in front of the church. They were still standing around, still only smoking cigarettes. More flames shot out of the embassy, and the crowd erupted in approval. I tried to push my way toward Leila, who was in front of the church beside the security services. I spotted something square and flat resembling a pizza box sailing through the air—it looked as if it might hit me. As I ducked, the object hit a number of protesters. They tore the package apart, only to find a plastic raincoat with a company logo on the breast. People tried to rip it apart, found it too tough, stepped on it, and just let it lie on the ground.

The mob rage didn't seem too convincing. In fact, people seemed to be just enjoying the spectacle. It was hard to move through the dense crowd, but a simple pat on the back and a murmured "*afwan*" (sorry) allowed me to pass. Few, at least so it seemed, gave me a second look. When they did, they gave a little smile when I started taking photos. They want me to see this, I thought.

After about ten more minutes of struggling and frantic phone calls, I finally reached Leila and some friends in front of the church.

"What's with them?" I asked.

"Come on, Andrew, *mukhabarat* is controlling everything," one of her friends said with a patronizing look on her face.

I hadn't dared talk to anyone in the crowd, but now with Leila at my side, we could play Local Reporter, Foreign Journalist without much trouble. Leila began asking people questions, and I started taking photos.

"*Inti ajnabiya?*" (Are you a foreigner?), a group of male protesters asked Leila. Her physical features are very Syrian, including olive-brown skin; brown, curly hair; and brown eyes to match. Leila was wearing jeans and a jacket but was hardly the only one in the crowd in Western-style clothing. Why are they asking her if she is foreign? I thought.

"*Ana arabiya*" (I am an Arab), Leila replied. In Syrian speak, this means "I am first an Arab, then a Syrian, then a Muslim." They then glanced at me and looked down before starting what seemed a rehearsed tirade.

"America is behind this [cartoon]," said one of the group, a forty-year-old man named Mohammed. "We are here to express our anger." He then looked at me a bit sheepishly. I snapped a photo.

"But Denmark is in Europe. The European Union helps Syrian reform. What do you think of that?" Leila said.

"The government has its policy," Mohammed said. "The people are here to defend the Prophet and express their anger."

Pretty lame, I thought, but interesting. Mohammed was making a distinction between the state and religion. In the past, acting publicly on behalf of religious sentiments could have got you thrown in jail. In 1982, it also could have got you killed or "disappeared" during the state's battle with the Muslim Brotherhood.

Moving on, we stopped three other middle-aged men—including one wearing a green Islamic headband—to ask what brought them out into the street.

"Down with the Baath Party!" the men exclaimed. Leila raised her eyebrows; here in the land of the Assad family's Baath Party, I knew that she hadn't heard that shouted before in public. They didn't seem nervous at all, and they let me take their photos. When Leila asked them their names, they just continued shouting, "Down with the Baath Party!" and walked off.

Islamic protesters openly calling for destruction of the Baath Party? I thought. Contemplation of the deeper meaning of what I had just heard was interrupted when fire trucks turned up—much too late to save the Danish embassy. They rolled through the crowd so lazily that they eventually coasted to a stop. No firemen were in sight. Protesters just used the trucks as observation decks for the spectacle. A red station wagon arrived—one of the well-known "protocol" cars that direct traffic for President Assad in the Syrian capital. It blew its siren once, half-heartedly. The crowd quickly parted, then broke up. The fire trucks moved in, their hoses shooting water at the flames. Street gutters flowed with water like small streams. Everyone who remained stood calmly and watched the firemen do their duty.

As we walked away from the protest, we ran into Tarek, Leila's friend. He was smiling, joking with several men in black leather jackets and expensive, well-polished shoes. After watching them for a few minutes, I realized that Tarek was talking to intelligence officers. Men around them with black handheld radios were barking orders; all held wooden batons.

"So what did you think?" Tarek asked me.

"I think it was quite a show," I said. "People are angry, but the security services don't seem to be doing much."

"Yep," Tarek said with a grin on his face. "People are under a lot of pressure. We have the Hariri problem, and the government just raised petrol prices by 20 percent. They [the regime] are just letting off the pressure." Tarek moved his hand as if turning a valve.

On the surface, Syria seems a secular society. Minority rights, religious or ethnic, are guaranteed by the state, which is dominated by the Alawites—an offshoot of Shiite Islam from which the Assad family hails. The Baath Party is a secular, pan-Arab party. The other political parties aligned with the Baath in the National Progressive Front are secular as well.

In the half decade leading up to the Danish protests, increased signs of Islamic sentiment in Syria had appeared. At first it showed up in terms of Islamic dress, then mosque attendance grew, as did Islamic study centers. In the midst of this trend was a female religious leader, Munira al-Qubaisi, who runs an organization Syrians call "Qubaisiaat" in her name. The influence of the group had spread rapidly under Bashar al-Assad's rule.

As we walked away from the demonstration toward Tarek's office for coffee and chitchat, he pointed toward a new *musali* (prayer room) constructed beside an ancient domed shrine, which housed the body of a notable who had once donated the land to build an Islamic school; the school was razed long ago, but the tomb remains.

"I renovated this," Tarek said. I knew he was a practicing Muslim; Leila had told me so. But on the surface, Tarek looked like a wealthy, Westernized Syrian who had spent time in the United States—which he also happened to be. I took off my shoes and stepped inside. Tarek took me through the carpeted room to the shrine, opened the door, and showed me the sarcophagus. "By building it next to this tomb, I get around the permits," Tarek said. After a few words with the prayer room's sheikh, I returned to the front door and recovered my shoes from a locker. Tarek remained to pray, saying he would join us later in his office.

For a secular state that arrested people for praying in public in the 1980s, tolerance of this Islamic trend raised eyebrows. What was pushing a nonreligious state, dominated by Alawites, to openly accept growing Sunni Islamic movements? The short answer: external pressures and the complex internal tensions they created.

Standards of living were eroding in Syria. The reasons behind this slide were pretty clear: a general lack of investment, due largely to an extremely corrupt legal and regulatory environment, was not creating enough jobs. Exacerbating this trend was the fact that, when political tensions bubbled over in the 1980s, Syria endured one of the highest birthrates in the world. That massive demographic wave was now hitting the Syrian market with full force.

At the same time, the secular state and the ruling Baath Party continued to hold up socialism as an economic ideal. The public sector's ability to create enough jobs to absorb labor-market entrants was rapidly declining, however, due to decreasing oil production. Public-sector salaries were also much lower than those in the private sector. Pure and simple, the state was running out of ways to buy off its population and keep them complacent.

Enter the external pressures. Since the US invasion of Iraq in 2003, relations between Syria and the United States had deteriorated rapidly. Because of Syrian support for the Iraqi insurgency as well as for radical Palestinian groups based in Damascus, Washington had tightened sanctions on Syria in 2004. Washington was also talking about spreading democracy in the Middle East—something Syrians do not necessarily oppose. However, television images of US forces waging a bloody war on insurgents in Iraq also turned Syrian popular opinion against the United States and its "democracy agenda." After all, the majority of Iraqi insurgents were Sunni Muslims—a minority in Iraq, but a majority in Syria.

Syria's rapid withdrawal from Lebanon following the assassination of Rafik Hariri as well as the subsequent investigation into his death put the Syrian regime under tremendous international pressure. Trade, both formal and informal, between Syria and Lebanon had been drastically interrupted, impacting the livelihood of an unknown number of Syrians and Lebanese.

As the investigation into Hariri's death focused its attention on Damascus, the Syrian regime hunkered down, preparing for a siege—including possible UN sanctions. So instead of sharing some of the wealth generated by record-high oil revenues over the last year, the state increased salaries by only 5 percent that January—far short of the 20-percent increases in 2004 and 2002 respectively. Gasoline subsidies had also recently been slashed, which caused a 20-percent increase in prices at the pump. Inflation ran at an estimated 15 percent. Syrians were feeling the economic pinch of reform and external pressure at the same time.

When we met Tarek in his office after his prayer, he looked relaxed and at ease. We had a glass of tea, talked over a bit of business, and went on our merry way.

However, the fun was not over. We soon learned that the demonstrators had moved on to the Norwegian embassy and burned it down as well, since two of that country's newspapers had reprinted the

Jyllands-Posten cartoons. A couple of phone calls confirmed what we feared—the riot was now moving to the French embassy, as the French newspaper *France Soir* had also run the caricatures.

It was dark when we arrived in Afif, the Damascus neighborhood that is home to the French embassy. Security forces had finally assembled themselves in force. Leila continued to shout "*sahafa*" (journalism) as we approached the uniformed security agents. They let us through without batting an eye. When some plain-clothed security agents tried to stop us, she just repeated "*sahafa*," and they moved away.

At the French embassy, the situation was far from tense. Police and soldiers mixed freely before the embassy's stone walls, joking and smoking cigarettes. Two fire trucks were out front, this time complete with firemen in full uniform. They were adjusting the water cannons and firing up the trucks' compressors. Out in front of the fire engines, about twenty yards down the street, a wall of uniformed security agents donned what looked like old green football helmets and grasped clear Plexiglas riot shields.

I took photos for a few minutes before the police told me to step back. Water shot out of the lead cannon for about thirty seconds, filling the air with a heavy mist. When the firemen turned the cannon briefly to the left, I was caught in the jet stream. I hid behind a tree to dry off and braced myself for another soaking. It never came, however. The "Muslims on a rampage" gave up without much of a fight. Leila and I walked back to the main street and headed to the nearby Damascus Journalists' Club for oriental salads and good stiff drinks.

But the wheels inside my head were already spinning. Why would Syria's security apparatus—which, as one civil rights activist once told a journalist friend, "sends ten agents for every protester at a human rights march"—stand back and do little to stop the burning of a number of European embassies? The answer seemed simple: the Bush administration's Middle East "democracy agenda" had run into unexpected problems, and the Syrian regime knew it. The Muslim Brotherhood scored well in Egypt's autumn 2005 elections (and probably would have done better without widespread government vote rigging), Shiite parties had dominated Iraq's December 2005 poll, Hamas had upset Fatah in January's Palestinian legislative elections, and Hezbollah remained part of the Lebanese government.

Direct regime involvement in the incidents at the embassies was hard to determine. The state did issue a permit for a peaceful demonstration. According to student activists in Islamic centers in Damascus—which are not owned by the state—they received instructions from the centers' sheikhs to organize protests against the cartoons as well as Denmark in general on February 3. The call to protest, like the call to support President Assad's November speech at Damascus University, was publicized by text message.

The following afternoon, as much more violent protests raged outside Denmark's embassy in Beirut, the Syrian state news agency released a statement confirming that one armed Islamist had been killed in a security raid outside Damascus that lasted ninety minutes.

At cocktail receptions the next week, Western diplomats in Damascus were asking everyone the same question: What is the strength of political Islam in Syria? Their reason for asking was apparent: policy makers in Washington and Europe were wondering if the very pressures they were currently orchestrating would push Syria into the hands of political Islam—from which support for Islamic terrorist groups was highly suspected—or into sectarian political chaos, like that in nearby Iraq.

Answers to this question varied. Everyone noted increased Islamic sentiments, but it was unclear how much this trend had entered the political sphere. Religious parties were banned and 1980's Law 49 made membership of the Muslim Brotherhood punishable by death. Gauging Brotherhood strength was difficult. The organization's leaders remained in exile, and members inside Syria had moved underground long ago. By and large, however, many Syrians, including Sunni Muslims (the religious base of the Brotherhood), shunned the organization due to its bloody history in Syria.

Evidence of armed Islamic groups in Syria had been growing since April 2004, when authorities foiled an attack on an abandoned UN building in Mezze, a modern district of Damascus. According to a January 2006 report by Ibrahim Hamidi in *Al Hayat*, three of the four assailants involved had gone to Iraq to fight US forces in the days before Saddam's fall. Many observers (including me) and diplomats doubted the authenticity of the attacks, since they happened while Washington was making a decision on how to apply the Syria Accountability and Lebanese Sovereignty Restoration Act (SAA). If Syria seemed on the edge of the abyss, perhaps Washington wouldn't strictly implement the sanctions.

Then, in May 2005, the authorities announced that they had broken up a "terrorist cell" in the Damascus neighborhood of Daf al-Shawq. As Syrian TV showed footage of the cell's arms depot, the state announced that the cell was part of a larger organization, the Munazama jund al-sham l'wahda wa jihad (the Soldiers of Damascus Organization for Unity and Jihad). Subsequent reports indicated that the group was well organized and was distributing propaganda throughout Syria. According to Hamidi's analysis of the group's pamphlets, the group sought to "establish an 'Islamic Emirate' or 'caliphate' in Syria, Jordan, Lebanon and Iraq."

The following December, security forces attacked a "*takfiri* cell"—a group that unilaterally declares other Muslims apostates. Members of such groups have been known to inflict their punishment by, among other things, strapping on explosive belts and walking into Western hotels in the region. While the attack got some play in the Syrian media, a Syrian journalist friend told me at the time that the attack was the first instance where the authorities used helicopters against civilians in Syria since the state's bombardment of Hama in 1982. In his subsequent article, the journalist cited "informed sources" who said that when the security forces surrounded the cell's hideout, its members refused to give up prior to the government's air raid. They also accused the security forces of being "infidels."

To get a handle on this Islamic trend, I visited the offices of Mohammed Habash, a supposedly independent parliamentarian and founder of the Damascus Islamic Studies Center. Unlike most religious figures in Syria, Habash openly spoke about Islam in Syrian political life. The interview was strange from the start. Interviews with prominent Syrians are usually well-managed affairs: office calls are diverted and strong tea or coffee is served to help get people in the mood for candid conversation. It is one of the best things about Syria under Bashar al-Assad: people talk quite openly behind closed doors. So when an unexpected guest showed up for my interview with Habash, it couldn't be chalked up to mere coincidence.

As I walked into the center's main salon, a man followed on my heels, shook my hand, and sat down at Habash's side. The man was well dressed, sported a five-o'clock shadow, and wore a smile from ear to ear. Somewhat unnervingly, he did not say a word. Thirty minutes later, when I asked Habash about his thoughts on the relationship between authoritarianism in the Arab world and the spread of Islamic extremism, I was finally introduced to the mystery guest.

"I have no desire to justify terrorism, but I would like to explain it," said Habash, who preaches a tolerant version of Islam that he dubs "renewal." "I agree with you that radical movements began before the invasion of Iraq, but not the occupation of Palestine. Look at Musa here. I have only known him for about a month. He traveled to Iraq with two hundred and ninety others to wage jihad. He was the only one who survived."

My eyes opened wide. Could Musa really be one of the jihadists that the government denied were crossing from Syria into Iraq in support of that country's insurgency? Musa then spoke in broken English about "traveling to Iraq to attack occupation," fighting "two hundred kilometers from Baghdad," and about "some people in that city being very bad." When I told him to speak in Arabic, he said the same thing. Musa was one of the Syrians who I had watched out of the US embassy window climb onto the buses outside the Iraqi embassy on the eve of the 2003 US invasion. I glanced back at Habash, who appeared ill at ease.

"Why did this young man with an open mind and future plans decide to attack the US in Iraq?" Habash blurted out. "*Mukhabarat* didn't order him to; he decided to go on his own. You can find hundreds like him. Why? Because the Bush administration does not understand our people."

Other powerful Americans were apparently asking for Habash's help in trying to do just that, however. At the end of the interview, Habash casually quizzed me about the National Prayer Breakfast, a forum held every February in Washington for political, social, and business leaders of the world to break bread together and talk about problems. I gave him my best account of what it was.

"Hillary Clinton invited me this year, but I apologized," Habash said. "I tried to travel to New York last year, but US security didn't let me in."

To my surprise, Musa was leaving at the same time I was. After bidding Habash good-bye, Musa and I walked into the street. Still smiling, he gave me his mobile number, shook my hand, and went on his way.

My unsolicited introduction to Musa was so bizarre that I could not resist asking to meet him again. In an on-the-record, hour-long interview two days later, Musa gave me a blow-by-blow account of waging jihad against US troops during the invasion of Iraq and fleeing back to Syria. His story made little sense and seemed tailor-made to suit the regime's red lines on this issue. Since he had gone to Iraq in the waning days of Saddam Hussein and returned only a few weeks later, he was technically not one of the famed "Arab fighters" that Damascus denied was crossing the Syrian frontier into Iraq. He certainly was an Islamist, however, and had just joined the new private sector and

Islamic-leaning Sham TV as a newscaster. The very fact he was talking about his experience publicly to a foreigner was something new in Syria. And to make matters more bizarre, halfway through the interview, I had a sudden bout of déjà vu that I could not readily explain.

As diplomats and journalists combed the streets of Damascus chasing the "Islamic genie" that had appeared out of Syria's secular Baathist bottle, the regime of Bashar al-Assad busily reached out to Islam in subtle and unprecedented ways. And it was hard to know what to make of any of it.

Two days in April 2006 epitomized the regime's efforts to connect with Islam. In Syria, April 7 is Baath Day—the anniversary of the party's first congress in 1947. Since the Baath Party seized power in 1963, April 7 has been a day of speeches, marches, and banner-filled streets hailing the party's accomplishments. This time, celebrations were small, few marches were held, and Baath Party flags were hard to find. Party offices held small receptions, serving only cake and soft drinks.

Instead, the Syrian regime waited until April 10—the prophet Muhammad's birthday—to celebrate. Colorful banners hailing the Prophet's virtues lined the major thoroughfares of Damascus, people filled the streets, and President Assad prayed with the Baath Party leadership in Damascus's Hasseby Mosque beside the new Grand Mufti of the Republic, Ahmad Badr al-Din Hassoun—all very strange for a secular state famously carved out of a virtual civil war with the Muslim Brotherhood in the early 1980s. The regime's first step to engage these rising Islamic sentiments had come on September 1, 2004, with the death of Hassoun's predecessor, Ahmad Kuftaro. For forty years, Kuftaro served as the ceremonial head of Islam in Syria, staying out of the spotlight in keeping with Syria's secular orientation. Instead of holding the customary Majlis al-Aala (consultative council) to elect a new mufti from among Syria's Islamic clergy, the regime waited for eleven months before appointing Hassoun—by presidential decree.

Hassoun began breaking with tradition and pushing Islam back into public life. He met frequently with community leaders, preaching "interfaith dialogue" and the tolerance of Islam. Following the burning of the Danish embassy, Hassoun met and communicated regularly with representatives from the Vatican and Europe. He also prayed often and publicly with President Assad in the grand mosques of Damascus and Aleppo. All of Hassoun's activities were covered in detail by SANA—the state's primary propaganda machine.

Regime efforts to engage rising Islamic sentiments accelerated substantially after the "defection" of Syrian vice president Abdel Halim Khaddam to the opposition on December 30. In a speech to the Arab Parties General Conference in Damascus on March 4, President Assad said that the Arabs derive their strength from "Islam, which is strongly connected with Arabism." He later said that Islam and Arabism were mutually interdependent and that any political party that ignores either is bound to fail—echoing the words of one of the Baath Party's founders, Michel Aflaq, and even turning them on their head.

On March 13, Syria held its first competition for reading the Koran in the auditorium of Damascus University—a venue traditionally reserved for Baath Party occasions and presidential speeches. Two weeks later, a ban on mosques that opened between prayer times was lifted to allow for Islamic instruction. A week after that, Aleppo was named the Islamic cultural capital of 2006 amidst great fanfare and, more importantly, open presidential patronage. The city then underwent a major renaissance project, which was funded by donations from pious businessmen.

Then, on April 1, the Syrian military shocked the country when it announced that Islamic clergy would be allowed to enter barracks to talk to soldiers about religion for the first time in forty-three years. Defense minister General Hassan Tourkmani reportedly announced at a conference that the decision was in response to "the thirst for God in the barracks." Brokering the agreement were none other than Habash and Hassoun.

On April 5, President Assad issued a decree establishing an Islamic college in Aleppo—the center of the Muslim Brotherhood's uprising in Syria in the 1980s. Two days after Assad prayed with the Baath Party regional command on the prophet Muhammad's birthday on April 10, Habash was invited to deliver a lecture on Islamic morals and values to a gathering of the state-dominated National Union of Syrian Students (NUSS).

As journalists and diplomats continued to file stories and cables about the regime's slide toward Islam, many questions remained concerning the actual makeup of this Islamic wave. Strangely enough, the only people who seemed to have any answers—and would talk about them to foreigners—came via Mohammed Habash.

"Muslims in Syria are certainly becoming more religiously conservative," Habash had told me during my interview. "Conservatives believe that there is only one way to God and paradise, and others are false . . . but this doesn't mean that they have any desire to use violence against others."

It was hard to know where the line between conservatives and radicals lay, however. Reports of security clashes with *takfiri* groups—militants who declare other Muslims to be apostates and therefore legitimate targets of terrorism—continued to make their way into the media. All reports originated from "security sources," who approached local journalists with accounts of state raids on the Soldiers of Damascus Organization for Unity and Jihad. There was considerable speculation that the clashes could have been fabricated for external consumption so as to persuade the United States and Europe to ease pressure on the Syrian regime.

"The groups that traveled to the US and carried out the September 11 attacks were not conservatives; they were radicals," Habash said. "In Syria, such people are less than 1 percent. Syria has a population of seventeen million, which means that we have one hundred seventy thousand radicals running around. Any injustice they see, they will use violence. You don't have to ask why they are here—we are in the eye of the storm between the occupations of Iraq and Palestine. They believe the Syrian army should go to Iraq to attack Americans. They have a problem with this regime."

To counter this trend, Habash advocated what he called "renewal Islam." "Renewal believes that there is one way to God, but his names are many," Habash said. "Spirituality is one, but religions are many. There should be no monopoly on salvation, paradise, religion, and the day of judgment."

While this might have seemed all well and good to the regime, the strange thing is that Habash himself admitted that his interpretation had little following in society. "Only about 20 percent of Muslims in Syria are renewal," Habash said. "The rest are conservative, and their numbers are growing."

Although seemingly well fitted to the political situation, Habash had no time for the regime's nemesis, the Muslim Brotherhood. "There is an upsurge of Islam in Syria, but that does not mean people support the Muslim Brotherhood," Habash said. "They have no chance in Syria because there is a bloody memory from the 1980s. If they find a way back into Syria, they will have to change their name."

Habash was also rather forthcoming about his ambitions to form a political party under the new parties law—whenever it would be issued of course. "This is my secret; why are you asking me?" Habash said. "I am looking to participate fully in political life. I am not looking for an Islamic party—this would not be beneficial for our country. We don't need a theocracy, as we cannot achieve real development this way. At the same time, I am looking for some party with an Islamic affiliation. Like the [ruling] Justice and Development Party in Turkey."

And what about Musa, the mystery guest at Habash's office? When I listened to the interview tape later a couple of times, I still made no sense of his tale of waging jihad in Iraq (and will waste no time explaining it here). Much more interesting, however, were Musa's surprisingly moderate views concerning a number of recent political issues—for a man that not long ago says he fired a rocket-propelled grenade at a US Army Humvee.

"These Muslims were being stupid when they burned the Danish embassy," Musa said of the February 4 attacks on the Danish, Swedish, and Chilean embassies in Damascus. He had a relaxed smile and a twinkle in his eye that could give any diplomat or foreign correspondent some glimmer of hope that the Islamic tide sweeping Syria was nothing to worry so much about as to intervene in an Arab country's internal affairs. "I was among the demonstrators. It was peaceful, but a few people got out of control. The Prophet for Muslims is not the same for Christians. Denmark doesn't understand that."

At that moment, I realized it wasn't déjà vu after all. During my years of working in Egypt in the 1990s, I had often interviewed a prominent researcher and professor at the American University in Cairo named Saad Eddin Ibrahim, then a confidant of Egyptian president Hosni Mubarak and now one of his most outspoken opponents. Ibrahim used to run a foreign-funded program rehabilitating Islamic "terrorists" captured by the state in upper Egypt and around major Western tourist sites. After swearing off violence, former combatants were released from prison and given seed money and soft loans to open small businesses such as cigarette kiosks and sandwich counters. Foreign journalists in search of the story of Islamic fundamentalism in Egypt flocked to Ibrahim, who would boast about the program and arrange interviews with beneficiaries. A few days later, a story would appear in the Western press outlining how the Egyptian government and society recognized its "Islamist problem" and had matters under control.

After fifteen editions of *Syria Today*, and about a week after the riots, it finally happened: security agents showed up in our office. When Syrian security comes to investigate foreigners, they don't have a face-to-face meeting with you. Instead, they talk with your Syrian friends about you, which in turn scares your friends to death. Although Leila didn't say that she had been questioned, her behavior told me all I needed to know.

"Andrew, we have to watch what we are writing," Leila told me as I walked into her office. She was nervously trying to light a cigarette. "We are responsible for everything anyone writes from here, be it for *Syria Today* or outside newspapers."

From day one, we knew that our publication had to make it past the Syrian censors, so we were as careful as we could be concerning red lines. Both Hugh and I could get away with a lot more when we published in the international press.

"What do you mean 'we are responsible'?" I said.

"I mean things are bad, and anything anyone from *Syria Today* publishes can be used against us," Leila said, with a twinge of nervous anger in her voice. "They could close us down."

The reason to be cautious would become apparent a little later that day, when Hugh, Othaina, and I headed down to the old justice palace to cover an opposition rally. It was March 9, 2006, the forty-third anniversary of the declaration of emergency law in Syria. For the second year in a row, members of the National Union of Syrian Students (NUSS) were busy beating up and chasing off opposition figures that were staging a sit-in in front of the old Ministry of Justice—a stone's throw away from the radio station where martial law had been declared in 1963, the morning after the Baath Party seized power in a military coup. Multiparty politics in Syria had been suspended that day, all in the name of bringing to an end the raging political instability that had plagued the country since independence in 1946.

A man with gray hair broke from the crowd of demonstrators, arms waving overhead. Scores of student-union protestors were on him like a swarm of bees, shouting "traitor" while beating him with wooden sticks adorned with Syrian flags. As I took a photo of the melee, Hugh and Othaina sized up the situation, notebooks in hand.

"Come on, let's go talk to that guy!" Hugh said.

Othaina and I looked at each other. Without saying a word, we understood that the worst thing that could happen to this brave man at that moment would be for two foreigners to ask him how he felt about being abused and beaten up. We probably knew the answer anyway.

"That's the story!" Hugh shouted, eyes wide.

In an ideal sense, he was right. But in a country where nationalist sentiments were high due to US and UN pressure, it was often hard to know what to do. If the man wanted to talk to foreigners—and put his neck on the line—that was his choice. But if we approached him, it could be seen as the very treasonous activity of which he was being accused, possibly leading to dire circumstances that could prevent him from enjoying the permanent freedom he sought.

We did not have time to mull it over, however, since the students quickly converged on another target—me.

"We are here to support Syria and President Bashar against the traitors!" one protestor shouted, as the crowd closed in around us. "The West just wants our oil!" I could hear someone whispering the word "American" behind me. Suddenly, a sweaty young man with wild blue eyes, short-cropped hair, and a Syrian-flag bandanna appeared.

"So, an American!" he boomed, strutting like a rooster. The crowd roared. Someone started tugging on the belt of my raincoat, which admittedly would have been more appropriate on Washington's Dupont Circle than the edge of Damascus's Old City. I went silent, as did Hugh. Othaina shouted back, "We are journalists for a Syrian magazine!" and whipped out a few copies of *Syria Today*. The protestors, most with confused expressions, stared at the magazines' covers.

Not to be cowed, the blue-eyed man raised his arms above his head. "America—fuck America!" he screamed, throwing his arms down. The crowd roared again.

Suddenly a young man appeared, wearing a white baseball cap on which was printed I LOVE SYRIA in English.

"It's OK," he said, smiling at me. "Please, this way."

He made a single motion with his hand, like Moses parting the Red Sea, and the crowd quickly obeyed. We were escorted to the side, and the mob turned its attention toward its next victim.

We decided to visit the nearby office of Damascus Declaration spokesman Hassan Abdel-Azim. It was bustling with activity, packed full of Damascus Declaration members, whom I had interviewed over the last two months; they were all sipping cups of strong tea to calm their nerves. I hardly recognized Abdel-Azim, despite the fact that I had interviewed him recently.

"I can't see you very well. They smashed my glasses," Abdel-Azim said, shaking my hand. "They weren't students who beat us; they were just parrots. They don't even know what our declaration stands for."

After the declaration's announcement the previous October, members of the Syrian opposition slowly came onboard as the Assad regime weathered the heavy political storm of the Hariri investigation. External international pressure, combined with the regime's lack of a political-reform plan, had old foes putting differences aside and overcoming deep-rooted suspicions.

"If you look at the names who signed the Damascus Declaration, all but one is a Sunni Muslim," said Fateh Jammous, leader of the Communist Labor Party and an Alawite—the same sect from which the Syrian leadership hails—who signed in the days following the declaration's announcement. "We don't accuse them of being sectarian, but we objected at first to the declaration's references to Islam. . . . The Syrian bureaucracy is corrupted and cannot be reformed. We don't need slow reform—we need a rescue operation."

It was the declaration's appeal to moderate Islamists in an increasingly Islamized environment that seemed to be giving it staying power. "We have liberal Islamists, political Islamists, and fundamentalist Islamists in Syria," said Samir Nashar, the spokesperson for the Syrian Free National Party and a member of Syria's Committee for the Revival of Civil Society. "The difference between them is difficult to distinguish. We need to gather the first two together, as the fundamentalists cannot live with others. They see only in terms of black and white, believers and apostates."

And with bloodshed in neighboring Iraq filling TV news reports every day, a more liberal-based opposition lacked major appeal. "We tried to organize a parallel liberal rally alongside the Damascus Declaration in November and December," said the Assyrian Democratic Organization's Bashir Ishaq Saadi, who finally signed the declaration in February 2006. "Liberal parties in Syria are now very weak. Some of the Kurdish parties were demanding 'self-determination' as well. We couldn't support that."

After lying low for a few months as the Hariri investigation blew over and the Assad regime vented its fury over former vice president Abdel Halim Khaddam's dramatic "defection" to the opposition on December 30, the declaration's leadership began to organize. On January 18, a twenty-member transitional committee was formed, including thirteen domestic and seven exiled opposition groups. On January 29 and 30, Samir Nashar and other members of the transitional committee attended a Syrian opposition conference in Washington, DC, sponsored by the Syrian National Council in the United States and the Syrian Democratic Assembly of Canada. Farid Ghadry, the head of the Bush-administration-supported Reform Party of Syria (RPS), was not invited. Receiving foreign funding emerged as a fault line in the opposition. The day following the conference, the Damascus Declaration issued its first follow-up statement, which rejected foreign pressure on Syria, declared Syria to be part of the Arab nation, and clarified that the declaration's references to Islam were not limited to Sunni interpretation.

"More people signed after that," Abdel-Azim said. "The demands came from declaration signatories. They said to be silent on Iraq and that Palestine was dangerous. We certainly don't want the Iraqi or even the Lebanese scenarios in Syria. We need democratic change to strengthen nationalist forces to face external pressure."

On February 18, the transitional committee began work on the formation of a fifty-member national council, with representatives from all of Syria's fourteen governorates. Its members were scheduled to be announced on April 6.

Both the Syrian government and Washington responded to the Damascus Declaration selectively. The regime gave Abdel-Azim considerable leeway in carrying out the accord's activities, despite the fact that the regime's nemesis, the Muslim Brotherhood, was one of the declaration's primary supporters. Drafts of a new parties law that made their way around Damascus indicated that the regime was not making much space for opposition parties. Syrian political commentator Sami Moubayed, who had seen drafts of the law, reported that while the parties law would be issued within the month, it would not accept parties whose "behavior is opposed to the Revolution of March 8 [the day the Baath took power]." Parties that were "chaotic, terrorist, fascist, theocratic, religious, ethnic, sectarian, tribal, etc." would be denied license—leaving little room for many of Syria's opposition parties, including the Muslim Brotherhood and the Kurds, to formally join political life. Not surprisingly, foreign funding was strictly forbidden as well.[3]

The regime then began going after outspoken declaration members to force the opposition to toe the nationalist line. Riad Seif, who was released from prison on January 18—the very day that the transitional committee on which he now sits was formed—bore the brunt of regime harassment.

"On February 14 [the first anniversary of Hariri's assassination], there was a decision to contain all the Syrian opposition," Seif said. "I am one of the primary names on the Damascus Declaration, so they arrested me again."

He was released the next day. On March 12, during a rally supporting Kurdish rights, the same thing happened. "If they arrest and hold me, I will be a hero, and they don't want that. They cannot get rid of me other ways, because that would be costly. So they try to scare me so that I am unable to think," said Seif, whose son disappeared under mysterious circumstances in 1996. "They warned me not to talk to foreigners or diplomats. They follow me everywhere. They tell my neighbors not to talk to me. I was less isolated in jail."

The problem, according to Abdel-Azim, was a stark contradiction between the leadership's words and the regime's actions. "In his last two speeches, the president said the national opposition that doesn't take foreign funding should be respected," Abdel-Azim said. "But on the street, two days later, they call us traitors and beat us."

Washington struggled to find ways to handle the Damascus Declaration as well, especially in light of the rising Syrian nationalist sentiments resulting from the US occupation of Iraq, Washington's strong alliance with Israel, and the Hariri investigation.

"I told the Americans that they will get more credibility if they focus on corruption and the regime's crimes in the 1980s," Nashar said, following his return from the Washington conference. "On these issues the regime cannot defend itself. . . . The human rights associations have a lot of files [on corruption and human rights abuses]. If America concentrates on this, Syrians will emerge from fear. Look at what happened in Lebanon. Do you think that a million Lebanese could have protested on March 14, 2005, [demanding Syria's withdrawal from Lebanon] without international cover?"

Perhaps with Nashar's nuanced advice in mind, on February 18, the same day that work on the declaration's national council began, Washington announced that five million dollars from the State Department's Middle East Partnership Initiative (MEPI) would be earmarked "to accelerate the work of reformers," including "build[ing] up Syrian civil society and support[ing] organizations promoting democratic practices such as the rule of law; government accountability; access to independent sources of information; freedom of association and speech; and free, fair, and competitive elections."

A week later, the Damascus Declaration's leadership predictably, but kindly, turned Washington down. "The Damascus Declaration refuses foreign funding, including the $5 million from the US State Department for the Syrian opposition," read the group's statement a week later. In a follow-up report by Reuters, Abdel-Azim said that while "support by international powers for democratic change in Syria is welcome," financing was out of the question. "It means subordination to the funding country," Abdel-Azim said. "Our project is [for] nationalist, independent democratic change in Syria, not through occupation or economic pressure, as we see the United States doing."

Making things more complicated, former vice president Abdel Halim Khaddam and the Muslim Brotherhood's Bayanouni announced in Brussels on March 17 the formation of a National Salvation Front, a group of seventeen exiled opposition parties that called for "democracy" to replace the regime of Bashar al-Assad. Another opposition meeting, sponsored by the Aspen Institute (officially dubbed a "small and informal meeting with oppositionists from Syria" on the sidelines of a conference called Civil Society and Democracy in the Greater Middle East), was held in Doha, Qatar, on March 22. A few days later, as Khaddam reportedly met with the virulently anti-Assad Lebanese politician Walid Jumblatt, Bayanouni announced that his organization had in fact had contact with Khaddam since 2003—some two years before the former vice president left office.

"The Damascus Declaration has no value without the Muslim Brotherhood. I am a liberal, and I am responsible for my words," said Nashar, who was arrested and then released three weeks after my interview. "I saw them in Washington. They have a democratic awareness—perhaps more than the Syrian intelligentsia." While Abdel-Azim said that the new front had "nothing to do with the Damascus Declaration," Riad al-Turk, a member of the Syrian Democratic People's Party, one of the five parties included in Abdel-Azim's National Democratic Rally, blamed him for dividing the opposition.

"The formation of the [National Salvation] Front is because of the backwardness, slowness, and hesitation of the Damascus Declaration's leadership," Turk said in an interview with the pan-Arab daily *Al Hayat* on March 20. "The basic conflict is now between external opposition representing America and the domestic opposition repre-

senting the regime. The hope is that there is a liberation front that will support a general political line calling for democratic change and preserving national independence while not falling into a severe crisis like in Iraq."

To try and understand where the Damascus Declaration was heading, I visited the home of Michel Kilo for a long interview.[4] Greeting me at the door in a brown corduroy suit and slippers, he escorted me into his office: a small desk in the corner of a guest bedroom. Despite the ongoing crackdown on dissidents, Kilo seemed eager to talk.

"The Syrian opposition didn't leave the country—especially true democrats," Kilo said. "In the past we had only one block: the regime. Now we have two blocks: the regime and its parties, and the opposition and its parties."

When I asked Kilo why he was picking a time when the regime was under pressure to launch the declaration, his answers were surprisingly nationalistic.

"We are not calling for changing the regime or a revolution—we are calling on reform," Kilo said. "It's not right to ask for foreign assistance. We are not part of the American pressures. We are not toys in the West's hands. We will make a democratic state in this country no matter the cost."

I then asked Kilo if the regime had asked the opposition what they would like to see in a political parties law.

"For five and a half years, Abdel Halim Khaddam said that the parties law was coming after one month. Nothing happened," Kilo said. "There is a draft law. It forbids ethnic and religious parties and all parties have to recognize Article 8 of the constitution and commit to the goals of the Baathist March 8 revolution. This is not a political parties law—it's a law to prevent political parties."

As much as Kilo was critical of the Assad regime, he was equally critical of the Bush administration's foreign policy. Kilo insisted tha

the opposition could not work according to "an American under-standing" but "our own understanding" and that Washington's inten-tions were to "Americanize the region," not democratize it. "We want to discuss Arab unity and that we will not accept doing nothing about the Palestinians."

When I asked him if he would have thought differently had the US occupation of Iraq not broken out into sectarian warfare, Kilo nearly leapt out of his seat. "Of course! There is no democracy without a state."

Last but not least, Kilo rejected accepting any money from the Bush administration for Damascus Declaration members. "No one will enter the Damascus Declaration if they take money from the US administration." As Kilo shook my hand cordially in farewell, I won-dered what his next move might be.

On May 12, Kilo helped engineer the Beirut-Damascus/Damas-cus-Beirut Declaration, another manifesto urging Syria and Lebanon to establish full diplomatic relations between the two countries and demarcate the long ill-defined Syrian-Lebanese frontier. Two days later, Syrian security forces arrested Kilo at his home.[5] The Security Council reiterated these demands on May 17 in Resolution 1680, which called on Damascus to demarcate the Syrian-Lebanese frontier—a key element in ending the dispute between Syria, Lebanon, and Israel over the territorial status of the Shebaa Farms—on which Hezbollah legiti-mizes the retention of its weapons. Anwar al-Bunni, an opposition figure working with Kilo and head of a closed EU-supported civil-society center, was arrested the same day. The next day, Washington issued Executive Order 13399, freezing assets of "anyone involved in the Hariri murder" and subsequent bombings in Lebanon.

6

NO VOICE LOUDER THAN
THE CRY OF BATTLE

A little after 8 AM on July 12, 2006, Hezbollah fighters fired *katusha* rockets from Lebanon into Israel. Simultaneously, a squad of Hezbollah fighters crossed the "blue line" from Lebanon to Israel to attack two Israeli Humvees patrolling the frontier near the town of Zar'it. Three Israelis soldiers were killed, and two were wounded and were taken by Hezbollah back over the frontier into Lebanon. Following a failed rescue attempt, Israeli prime minister Ehud Olmert declared the soldiers' capture an "act of war" and ordered the Israeli air force to begin striking targets throughout Lebanon. The war between Israel and Hezbollah that analysts had been predicting for half a decade had finally broken out.

People across the Syrian capital crowded around television sets and tuned in their radios to get the latest news. After three days of bombing, Al Jazeera television reported that Israel had bombed a Syrian military installation near the Lebanese-Syrian frontier. In Damascus, people openly speculated whether Syria's old enemy, Israel, was approaching the gates.

"Did you see the report?" Leila asked me as soon as I answered her call on my mobile. I could sense from the tone of her voice that she was panicking. "Do you think they will hit us as well?" she asked.

I didn't know what to say. Syrians and Lebanese are socially and economically joined at the hip, but following the forced withdrawal of the Syrian Army from Lebanon in April 2005, formal political relations were more distinct than at any time in the last thirty years. When it came to a Hezbollah attack on Israel, however, it all came down to what Israel considered to be the "return address." Given Hezbollah's strong support from both Damascus and Tehran, it was anyone's guess who Israel would hold responsible—and when.

It wasn't clear that Assad knew the answer either. Syria's state-dominated media reported the Israeli attacks without official comment for the first two days, instead using statements by Russian president Vladimir Putin and random Italian communist party officials condemning the violence. On July 15, Syrian information minister Mohsen Bilal responded to the border strike with a warning: "Any Israeli aggression against Syria will be met with a firm and direct response whose timing and methods are unlimited." Iran quickly backed Syria up, warning Israel of "unimaginable losses" if it struck Syria. Tehran added that it was only offering "spiritual and humanitarian" support to Hezbollah. The Iranian regime denied, like Syria, that Tehran supplied Hezbollah with weapons.

President Bush thought otherwise. On July 17, as Putin openly teased Bush about Washington's "democracy agenda" at that week's G8 Summit in Moscow, a microphone that was inadvertently left on recorded a muffled and candid conversation between Bush and British prime minister Tony Blair that would shed light on Washington's idea of how to end the crisis. "What they need to do is to get Syria to get Hezbollah to stop doing this shit," Bush blurted out to Blair over the lunch table.[1] The question was how.

As journalists in the West transcribed the candid Bush-Blair lunch exchange, the US embassy in Damascus held a leaving party for deputy chief of mission Stephen Seche, the de facto ambassador to Syria after Margaret Scobey was withdrawn following Hariri's murder. When I arrived at the US ambassador's residence—the recent remodeling of which was a bit ironic, given the historically low relations between Damascus and Washington—Seche greeted me at the garden's entrance along with Bill Roebuck, the embassy's political officer. After about five minutes of discussion, arms folded, looking down at the ground, I said how, despite their hard-line rhetoric, I thought that I heard some conciliatory gestures in Hezbollah leader Hassan Nasrallah's TV address as well as in Israeli prime minister Ehud Olmert's hard-line speech from earlier in the day. Perhaps the situation would calm down soon, I added.

"Are you kidding?" one of the diplomats said. "*We* wrote that hard-line speech!" And with that, he turned away to greet the garden's next visitor. Seche's message toed the diplomatic line on US support for Israel—but there was something about the way he spoke that told me that something big was up and that he wasn't totally happy about it.

That "something" turned out to be the proxy war in Lebanon between Israel and its regional nemesis, the nuclear-hungry Islamic Republic of Iran. From the first days of the 2006 Lebanon War, stories reported how Israeli generals had, before the war, briefed US officials about a military response to an expected Hezbollah attempt to capture an Israeli soldier. These expectations were based on the fact that Hezbollah had attempted to capture two Israeli soldiers the previous January. Hamas, the Islamic resistance organization with a parliamentary majority in the Palestinian Authority, did successfully capture Israeli soldier Gilad Shalit in June, leading to an Israeli military rescue attempt.

So when Hezbollah used a tunnel under the "blue line"—the cease-fire line of 1949 that demarcates the southern border of Lebanon—to kill four Israeli soldiers and abduct two others on July 12, it was no surprise that Israel struck back with a massive military response.

What was unexpected, however, was Hezbollah's ability to fight back. A week after the beginning of the bombardment, which included strikes on civilian targets that Israel claimed Hezbollah was using as "human shields," diplomats attending the garden party were expressing surprise that Hezbollah continued to fire hundreds of rockets into northern Israel every day. Syrians seemed surprised as well, but pleasantly so. Day by day, more Hezbollah flags appeared across the Syrian capital, and young people lined up at shops to buy yellow Nasrallah T-shirts. Homemade decals showing busts of Assad, Nasrallah, and Ahmadinejad arranged together suddenly appeared on professionally printed posters in shop windows.

Over the next few days, the Syrian media's pro-Hezbollah propaganda campaign made it hard to determine the depth of popular support for "the resistance." State-owned Syrian television's morning and evening news programs—the only two that most Syrians now watch (besides soap operas) in an era of pan-Arab TV satellite stations—led in with video footage of women and children being pulled from the rubble in Lebanon. Marching music played in the background, complete with war drums. The ruckus suddenly stopped, only to be followed by an audio recording of US secretary of state Condoleezza Rice's statement of July 21 that the war in Lebanon was part of the "birth pangs of a new Middle East." The linkage between Washington's democracy agenda, Israel, and death and destruction was clear. Rice's dictum was repeated every day on Syrian television for weeks, and many Syrians parroted it back to me with the addendum, "a new Sykes-Picot"—referring to the secret 1916 agreement between Britain and France that led to the division of the Ottoman empire into the Arab states we know today.

In many ways, history seemed to be repeating itself in Bashar al-Assad's Syria in the summer of 2006. The late Egyptian president Gamal Abdel Nasser was famous internationally for turning his country's military defeat into a "diplomatic victory" over Israel, Britain, and France in the 1956 Suez Crisis and defiantly shifting Egypt into the Soviet camp during the Cold War. However, in the Arab world, Nasser is better known for his subsequent embrace of authoritarian socialism and its export during the pan-Arab revolution across the region. The domestic political reforms Nasser and his "free officers" promised when they seized power in 1952 were postponed until Arab "dignity" was restored by Israel's defeat. The policy, which dramatically ended when Israel routed the Arabs in the Six-Day War of June 1967, was encapsulated in the slogan "No voice louder than the cry of battle."

The question remained whether Syrians would buy into the regime's version of "the plot." After six years of Syria's "reform process," most Syrians were unhappy with the way they were ruled. A host of European countries had stepped forward to support Bashar al-Assad when he assumed the presidency in July 2000 following the death of his father, Hafez. The primary reason for engaging the son was political: Syria bordered Israel and controlled Lebanon, and Hafez al-Assad had nearly signed a peace agreement with Israel only three months before his death. The secondary, but nevertheless related, reason was to reform one of the most corrupt and authoritarian systems in the Arab world, to bring it into a Western orbit, and to arrange for a smooth transition toward democracy. Overly centralized decision making, combined with Syria's continued socialist ideals a decade after the Soviet Union's collapse, weighed heavily on Syrians. Their innate Levantine entrepreneurial spirit ensured that the private sector survived, however distorted it was by triple bookkeeping and a system of bribes that substituted for taxation.

What held the Syrian people back in the autumn of 2005 from rioting in the streets and demanding the downfall of the Damascus regime at perhaps its weakest point in the last forty years? Fear of arrest by the security services, for sure, but also serious doubts over Washington's intentions for a post-Assad Syria. The Hariri investigation coincided with a rapid increase in the bloodshed in neighboring Iraq. If television news footage of the slaughter of civilians was not enough to raise questions in Syrians' minds about Bush's agenda, waves of Iraqi refugees flooding into Syria certainly was. Some brought suitcases full of money, but most did not. The Syrian government offered Iraqis basic support, but budgets ran out in early 2006. Charities and international relief agencies tried to fill the gap.

The "chaos" raging next door in Iraq was no accident, Syrians told me again and again. They said it was part of an Israeli-inspired plan, forged with neoconservatives prominent in the Bush administration, to smash Arab societies through military action, create sectarian strife, and cause civil war. While I argued back that the Levant was full of crazy conspiracy theories, Syrians would reply, "Do you think what is happening in Iraq for the past three years is just a mistake? No, it's policy."

The Syrian regime exploited the Iraq fiasco by issuing daily statements attributing the region's problems to the "Zionist-American" conspiracy and implicated the Syrian opposition with a wave of arrests following the signature of the Beirut-Damascus Declaration. The regime also made Washington's worst nightmare come true: the permitted burning of the Danish embassy in Damascus in response to caricatures of the prophet Muhammad published in a Danish newspaper, along with news reports of radical *takfiri* Islamic groups carrying out operations in Syria (with American weapons), fit in nicely with the regime's newly strengthened alliance with Iran.

When Hezbollah and Israel went to war, therefore, it was a perfect regime safety valve for releasing popular aggression toward its enemies. Hezbollah is a Shiite Islamic movement, so Syria's majority Sunni population, and its supporters in the Muslim Brotherhood, could not control it. It also helped people to feel that they were fighting the Western powers that supported Israel and were overseeing the carnage in Iraq. Last but not least, because the Israeli and American threat to Syria turned to violence in Lebanon, it allowed the regime to put off reform until the "enemy" was defeated and "dignity" restored.

The first government-organized demonstration for "the resistance" on July 17, 2006, indicated that popular support for Hezbollah was lukewarm. When I called Syrian friends and journalists that morning to ask if they were going to the rally, most were still in bed shortly before it kicked off at 10 AM. Only a few thousand state workers, who had been given two hours' leave, attended.

The giant television-camera booms I had first seen at the pro-Syrian demonstrations in Damascus in March 2005 were back in action. TV cameras used close-up images of the crowd to exaggerate its true size. This technique was repeated at several Damascus rallies over the next week.

The demonstration was so uninspiring that a group of journalist colleagues and I decided to visit the nearby Rouda Café—an opposition hangout adjacent to parliament. As they sucked down cups of tea to wake up, a Syrian colleague leaned over the table and whispered in my ear to look behind me. Sitting only three feet away was Hussam Taher Hussam, the thirty-year-old witness cited in the first report of the Hariri investigation who had recanted his testimony against the Syrian regime the previous November. There was a brief but comical moment of excitement when I snapped a photo of Hussam stealthily over my shoulder. Meanwhile, the café's patrons were extremely laid back, seemingly unconcerned about the war raging next door.

As civilian casualties increased, however, Syrians got behind the resistance. For weeks, I noticed that my friends' cell phones had ringtones featuring excerpts from Nasrallah's speeches. Some even bothered to play longer clips for me; they traded these among friends. As the war dragged on, my Syrian friends began including me in mass e-mails showing photos of dead women and children being pulled from bombed-out buildings in Lebanon and in the occupied territories. Some were even arranged into PowerPoint presentations, though they were badly made, with photo captions that had bad English and Arabic spelling and grammar mistakes. They were genuine expressions of popular concerns, however, and were a far cry from the state's clumsy propaganda. Such sentiments grew after Lebanese refugees began flooding into Syria in the war's second week.

"See, like Iraqis," Othaina said to me as our car approached the swarm of Lebanese cars piling across the Syrian border crossing at Al-Jdeida. Iraqis continued to stream into Syria from Iraq every day too. The fact that Othaina made the connection helped me realize that popular sentiments and the regime's official line were quickly merging.

This notion was reinforced by the genuine hospitality extended by Syrian society to the Lebanese refugees upon arrival. While semiofficial organizations like the Syrian Arab Red Crescent passed out water and food, it was the private sector that delivered truckloads of supplies. A phone booth set up by the mobile-phone operator Syriatel, owned by President Assad's cousin Rami Makhlouf, offered free calls to anywhere in Syria and Lebanon. As Lebanese waited to pass immigration procedures, young activists from the Lawyers' Syndicate—the equivalent of the Syrian Bar Association—and the Syrian Public Relations Association (led by Nizar Mayhoub, the Ministry of Information official responsible for foreign journalists) canvassed arriving cars and trucks, asking passengers if they had a place to stay in Damascus. Those in need of food and shelter were put in touch with Syrian families who had placed their names with the canvassers. "We have so many names!" one of them told me, pointing to a clipboard stuffed with papers in her hand.

All in all, more than 230,000 Lebanese refugees found shelter in Syria. Around 80 percent of those were housed in private Syrian homes. In many cases, sons moved back in with parents to make room for the war's displaced. As I walked among the throng of vehicles making their way into Syria, I reflected on the soft power of Syrians' generosity. I also sadly realized that the United States—the world's superpower and the champion of globalization—had absolutely nothing to offer as a counterweight. "Assad is sitting pretty now," a friend said to me later that evening. If a regime's legitimacy doesn't come from its people, the next best way to obtain it is by responding to an external threat.

At the offices of *Syria Today*, the magazine's staff had put up Syrian flags and banners on the walls and affixed prints of photos showing children killed and wounded from Israeli bombs. Every day that the civilian death toll climbed, the staff became more nationalistic, including wearing pins with I LOVE SYRIA on the lapels of their jackets. Others wore Hezbollah T-shirts.

High civilian casualties seemed to be helping the regime's case, even among the opposition. "We denounce the Israeli aggression against Lebanese civilians," Hassan Abdel-Azim told us a few days later. "Israel cannot attack Lebanon without an approval and support from the United States. We call on the Syrian leadership to strengthen the national unity through more opening to the Syrian opposition to make Syria stronger to face the Israeli threats."

Meshal Tammo, the secretary-general of the Kurdish Future Party, said they drew the line at violence against civilians as well. "We as a Kurdish people condemn all kinds of aggression and violence against the Lebanese civilians," Tammo said. "We sympathize with Lebanese because our people [Kurds] face the massacres and killing [of] civilians. The war in Lebanon is a regional war between Syrian, Iranian, and Lebanese Hezbollah front and the United States, Israel, and some Arab states which follow the American orders. The war aims to change the game rules in the Middle East."

Even Riad al-Turk, one of Syria's most outspoken opposition leaders, toed the nationalist line, though ever so critically. "Lebanon is a yard for the world to fight in," Turk said. "Lebanon is a part of the Arab-Israeli conflict. Israel and the US used the capturing of two Israeli soldiers as a pretext to wage a war against Lebanon. The Syrian stance to open the border to Lebanese civilians and humanitarian aid is acceptable. Syria should support the Lebanese by using its army. In this regard, the Syrian official stance is very weak."

The US State Department soon leaked a plan in the *New York Times* that a new US policy was being formulated to drive a "wedge" between Syria and Iran, but it didn't get anywhere.[2] According to another *Times* report a few weeks later, Secretary of State Rice sent Deputy Chief of Mission Seche over to meet Syrian foreign minister Walid al-Moallem and see if Syria was willing to negotiate. While the meeting took place, the report said that Moallem "gave no indication that [the Syrian regime] would be moderately constructive."

So with Washington defying Damascus and Tehran and vice versa, the conflict dragged on for weeks. As the United States and France argued over ceasefire texts in the Security Council, Syrians (and later Lebanese) said to me over and over again that Washington was simply giving Israel more time to finish the job, at the expense of more Lebanese civilian lives.

Those specialists of "positive pressure," the Europeans, then stepped in to give diplomacy a chance. On August 3, 2006, Spanish foreign minister Miguel Ángel Moratinos arrived in Damascus for talks with Assad. His arrival seemed promising, as his last trip to Damascus on February 14, 2005—the day of Hariri's murder—marked the last time a European official had set foot in Syria. Moratinos told reporters after the meeting that Assad was willing to use his influence to rein in Hezbollah—a statement that was quickly denied by the state news agency. European newspapers reported that certain EU countries—led by Germany, the primary supporter of Syrian reform—were preparing a package of incentives for Syria to cut off arms supplies to Hezbollah. Among these "carrots" was reportedly a German-led effort to push the member countries of the European Union to sign its long-delayed "association agreement" with Syria. Once ratified, the agreement would lock Syria into a schedule of reform steps aimed at liberalizing trade, promoting investment, and bolstering respect for human rights.

Finally, on August 11—one month to the day after the conflict began—the Security Council passed Resolution 1701, which called for a ceasefire and the deployment of an international force in south Lebanon. The ceasefire, to which Hezbollah and Israel consented, was to take effect forty-eight hours from the resolution's passage.

In a clumsy attempt at a public relations coup de grâce, Israel quickly launched its "largest airborne operation since the 1973 war" throughout south Lebanon. They were hoping to capture what would be the war's great surprise: Hezbollah's extensive network of tunnels and concrete-reinforced bunkers—some only one hundred meters from the Israeli frontier—from where daily rocket barrages were launched during the conflict. Their construction in hard limestone had gone completely undetected by Israel, the UNIFIL force (United Nations Interim Force in Lebanon) in southern Lebanon, and the Lebanese government. One UN commander told a friend that Hezbollah "must have been bringing the cement in by the spoonful."

Eager to talk with Lebanese about the war, I passed through the only crossing point from Syria to Lebanon that had not been destroyed by Israeli bombing the minute the ceasefire took effect on the morning of August 14. The usual two-hour journey from Damascus to Beirut took a little more than six due to Israeli strikes on roads and bridges. When I arrived, I quickly rented a car and went for a drive around Beirut, including the Hezbollah headquarters in the southern neighborhood of Haret Hreik.

Israel's "precision bombing" was impressive, as Israelis were able to destroy a sole building with very little if any damage to adjacent structures. Their intelligence information on targets seemed to have been less successful, however: nearly one thousand Lebanese civilians died from Israeli strikes during the war. In the south, Israel used so many cluster bombs that unexploded ordnance has since claimed the lives of almost fifty children and wounded more than one hundred.

Hezbollah hung huge banners off buildings in the southern suburbs to make their point. One banner hanging in Haret Harek read EXTREMELY ACCURATE TARGETS and was adorned with a photo of a bandaged child missing a limb. It was footnoted by the slogan "The Divine Victory."

That afternoon, *The New Yorker* magazine posted an article on its website by veteran journalist Seymour Hersh, which stated that Washington had indeed planned Israel's response to the Hezbollah kidnapping well in advance. The reason? To destroy Hezbollah's ability to hit Israel during possible future US preemptive strikes on Iran, which had a UN deadline of August 31 to stop enriching uranium. As much of Iran's program was literally underground, Hersh said that the United States wanted to understand the effectiveness of its weapons in Israel's arsenal against such targets. The report also said that the Bush administration hoped that the raid would further democracy by strengthening the government of Lebanese premier Fouad Siniora "so that it could assert its authority over the south of the country, much of which is controlled by Hezbollah."[3]

The next day, President Assad finally broke his silence in an address to a Syrian journalists' conference in Damascus. The fire-and-brimstone speech, which featured the word "conspiracy" scores of times, dashed hopes for peace anytime soon.

"The more elusive the realization of peace becomes, the more important and necessary other ways and methods become," Assad said. "The whole world only got interested in the Middle East after the 1973 War . . . [the West] only moves when Israel is in pain." Resistance, Assad added, "is necessary for the achievement of peace." While Assad's pro-Hezbollah rhetoric was not unexpected, his open swipe at Europe, which supported Syrian reform efforts, was unprecedented. "The countries concerned with the peace process—and they are mostly European—are responsible for what is happening. We might wonder what motivates some officials in these countries to send messages about a sick prisoner [in a Syrian jail]. . . . What nobility! What humanity! What greatness! We might ask as well, where are these same officials concerning the massacres perpetrated in Lebanon?"

Assad had a few words for his fellow Arab leaders as well. "One of the other positive sides to this war is that it has completely uncovered the Arab situation. If we asked any Arab citizen about the Arab situation before this war, they will say it is bad—which is true. Arabs used to see our situation under makeup, now they see it as it is in reality. This war prevented the use of such cosmetics as it classified positions in a clear way. There was no room for half-solutions in such a war where it unveiled half-men, or people with half-positions . . . i.e., those who were waiting to see where the scales would tip have fallen along with their positions. This is one of the very important outcomes of this battle."

Less than an hour after Assad's speech, German foreign minister Frank-Walter Steinmeier canceled a trip to Damascus scheduled for later that day. He dubbed it a "negative contribution that is not in any way justified in view of the current challenges and opportunities in the Middle East."

A few days later, in an interview with Dubai TV's Hamdi Kandeel, Assad tried to mend fences with Arab leaders, nearly all of whom were refusing to speak with the Syrian president. Assad insisted that Iran had a strong role to play in the region.

"Iran is a country that has existed in the region for centuries," Assad said. "It is the Arabs who are absent from the political arena, whether in decision making or in shaping the region's future. . . . If strong countries play a just and positive role, this would serve stability in the region. . . . Iran says it wants its nuclear project for peaceful means. There is nothing to fear from Iran."

Kandeel then asked Assad about concerns that the Islamic Republic's influence would feed an already "growing religious current" that could undermine the regime's pan-Arab ideological bedrock. The president responded that he could handle it. "Syria is a secular country, and has no problem cooperating with Iran. If one looks to what is happening in Iraq, it's easy to see that the Western powers, which are propagating secularism, are working to consolidate the nonreligious radical current in the Arab world as well."

When Kandeel asked Assad point-blank if Syria would adopt the resistance model that it was now championing in the region, Assad mapped out a Saddam Hussein–like insurgency strategy in the event of war. "We know there is a semi-siege imposed on Syria, and we know that the US backs up Israel one-hundred percent," Assad said. "So we have changed the army's duties and are preparing, at least in the first phase, to defend our territory. Israel is an expansionist state, and if peace is not achieved, war is the natural future in the region. . . . The resistance is a public process, not a state resolution, and people may overtake their governments to carry it out."

While Syrians were now free to resist Israel, Assad, like Nasser, was clear that political reform would remain on the back burner until the enemy was defeated and dignity restored. "We have made steps [toward greater freedoms], and we have a vision," Assad said. "But we don't want freedoms that are exploited from the outside, which is happening. . . . [We do not want to] enter into the framework of chaos or dependency and cheat our domestic situation. Loyalty to the country means not accepting foreign interference from any embassy. . . . Work continues on a new parties law, but we must have more room to accomplish it under the circumstances."

After two weeks of surveying Israel's destruction in Lebanon, I took the Damascus Road over the Lebanon mountains and across the Bekaa Valley back to Syria's Al-Jdeida border crossing. A Syrian border guard whom I knew smiled when he took my passport, sat down at his computer terminal, and typed in my name and passport number. I had made the crossing hundreds of times, so stamping in and out was a formality.

He suddenly frowned and repeatedly hit a key on the keyboard, like he was scrolling down my file. Then he stood up, threw back his shoulders, and thrust my passport back at me. "You are forbidden from entry," he said. When I tried to ask him what the computer said or what the problem was, he just brushed me aside with his hand.

"You will never get back into Syria."

While Leila tried to sort out what was behind my ban and figure out how to get me back in the country (which eventually did happen), events in Washington and Beirut did not bode well for the Bush administra-

tion's Syria policy. With sectarian violence spiraling in Iraq throughout 2006 and no end to the war in sight, Republicans and Democrats
began openly questioning President Bush's Iraq policy. The Iraq Study
Group (ISG)—a bipartisan commission established in March 2006
to assess the situation in Iraq—had spent the better part of the year
evaluating the Bush administration's Iraq policy, with the goal of pro-
posing a way out of the chaos. Its co-chairs, former secretary of state
James Baker and former US representative Lee H. Hamilton, promised
that, in order to keep the report nonpartisan, its findings would not be
released until after the US general election on November 4.

In reaction to the Iraq chaos as well as the summer war in Lebanon,
Americans voted en masse for Democratic Party candidates, wresting
the House of Representatives and the Senate away from Republican
control. The following day, President Bush announced the resignation
of secretary of defense Donald Rumsfeld. In the days that followed, the
international media reported that the ISG report would recommend
engaging Syria and Iran over Iraq and the Middle East. Baker began
appearing on national television openly advocating "hard-nosed"
engagement with Damascus, based on his experience negotiating with
Hafez al-Assad to get Syria to attend the 1991 peace conference in
Madrid.

A few days later, on November 11, 2006, one day before a key vote in
the Lebanese cabinet concerning the establishment of an international
tribunal into the assassination of Rafik Hariri, Shiite ministers, led
by Hezbollah, plus a Christian ally, walked out of the cabinet. While
Lebanese premier Fouad Siniora technically had enough ministers to
continue to hold cabinet sessions, the Hezbollah-led pullout from the
cabinet left it with no representatives from the country's Shiite community, essentially breaking the long-standing practice of communal
shared participation in government. The opposition claimed Siniora's
rump cabinet was illegal, making its decisions nonbinding.

In response, Hezbollah followers, as well as their Christian allies, took to the streets of downtown Beirut. The protestors surrounded the Grand Serail, Siniora's administrative offices, and erected a tent city, essentially occupying the center of the Lebanese capital. The state's internal security forces erected a barbed-wire barricade between the protestors and the Grand Serail, which divided the downtown area in two. Hezbollah and its allies opened hospitality tents for visitors and foreign journalists. Their message was simple: the tribunal into Hariri's murder is a US-Israeli plot to destroy Lebanon.

7

PLAYING WITH FIRE IN EASTERN SYRIA

Turning on the television the morning of January 11, 2007, I flicked through the local channels to catch the news, eager to get the Syrian reaction to President Bush's much-anticipated policy announcement on Iraq the previous evening. Syrian TV Channel One reported on the spiraling violence in Iraq as well as criticisms by the new US Democratic House and Senate leaders of Bush's speech. Eager to hear what the president said and with only a dial-up Internet connection at home, I headed for the *Syria Today* office, where one of the country's relatively few DSL connections made video streaming possible.

My Internet browser chugged for several minutes to load the file. Finally, President Bush's face filled up my laptop screen. Wearing a blue tie and standing before a bookshelf in the White House library, he looked older than I remembered him, with graying hair and a puffy face. As he started the first few lines of what would become one of the most important policy speeches of his administration, he breathed deeply between each sentence.

"Tonight in Iraq, the Armed Forces of the United States are engaged in a struggle that will determine the direction of the global war on terror—and our safety here at home," Bush said, his voice slightly shaky.

"The new strategy I outline tonight will change America's course in Iraq and help us succeed in the fight against terror."[1]

Bush went on to say that almost a year earlier, twelve million Iraqis had cast their ballots "for a unified and democratic nation." However, spiraling violence following al-Qaeda's bombing of the Shiite Golden Mosque of Sammara in February 2006 had overwhelmed the election's political gains. Calling the situation "unacceptable to the American people" as well as himself, Bush, in a rare mea culpa, admitted "mistakes have been made" and that "the responsibility rests with me."

What Iraqis needed most was security, Bush said. With 80 percent of sectarian violence taking place within thirty miles of the Iraqi capital, Baghdad, Bush announced that he was ordering a twenty-thousand-person increase in force levels that would assist Iraqi security services and the army to clear neighborhoods, protect the population, and, unlike in the past, hold areas under coalition control. In another new step, Bush announced that coalition forces would now have a "green light" to go into all neighborhoods. He said that past "political and sectarian interference" had prevented US forces from going after those fueling the violence, a situation Iraqi prime minister Nouri al-Maliki now promised would "not be tolerated."

Ten minutes into the speech, Bush turned his attention to Anbar Province, an area adjacent to Syria which al-Qaeda now used as a home base. Describing Anbar as "the most violent area outside the capital," Bush cited a captured al-Qaeda document "describing the terrorists' plan to infiltrate and seize control" of the province. Bush claimed that this would "bring al-Qaeda closer to its goals of taking down Iraq's democracy, building a radical Islamic empire, and launching new attacks on the United States at home and abroad." Bush said the situation was not without hope, as "local tribal leaders had begun to show their willingness to take on al-Qaeda," a situation that US commanders believed provided "an opportunity to deal a serious blow to the terrorists." To do that, Bush announced that he was ordering four thousand more troops to Anbar Province.

Bush blamed the Iranian and Syrian regimes for allowing "terrorists and insurgents" to use their territory to move in and out of Iraq. In a stark warning to both countries, Bush announced that US forces would "interrupt the flow of support from Iran and Syria" and "destroy the networks providing advanced weaponry and training to our enemies in Iraq." Framing Iraq in ominous terms, Bush described the conflict there as part of "the decisive ideological struggle of our time." He portrayed the struggle as one between "those who believe in freedom and moderation" and "extremists who kill the innocent and have declared their intention to destroy our way of life." The best way to protect the American people was to "provide a hopeful alternative to the hateful ideology of the enemy by advancing liberty across a troubled region."

In concluding the speech, Bush struck a firm but conciliatory line with his critics from the Democratic Party. He said, "It is fair to hold our views up to scrutiny" but that "all involved have the responsibility to explain how the path they propose would be more likely to succeed." In a rhetorical jab intended for those advocating a quick withdrawal from Iraq, Bush went on: "It can be tempting to think that America can put aside the burdens of freedom," but "throughout our history, Americans have always defied the pessimists and seen our faith in freedom redeemed."

In Damascus, Syrians close to the regime were triumphant about what they viewed as their victory over Bush's attempt to transform the region. One analyst told me in an interview that the United States was now in a "trap of its own making" in Iraq and predicted that it would withdraw soon. While such bravado was standard in Damascus, for the first time in nearly two years, the United States was listening to what Syrians had to say.

In the final days of the 2006 Lebanon War, Washington replaced its top diplomat, Stephen Seche, with Michael Corbin, a seasoned diplomat who previously served in the US embassy in Cairo. Almost immediately after his arrival in August, Corbin began reaching out to Syrian businessmen and media figures, holding small gatherings at his residence in West Mezze. During the Muslim month of Ramadan in October, the embassy hosted an *iftar* (the breaking of the fast) celebration attended by Damascus's rich and famous. The US Cultural Center in Damascus also began reaching out as well.

This was a far cry from the depths of Washington's isolation of Syria the year before, when the embassy refused to hold even a Fourth of July celebration. Some said that it was because the embassy feared regime pressure would keep Syrians from showing up, but more than one person had pointed out the irony of how a US administration pushing "liberty" in Syria was incapable of celebrating its own—if for no one else than other foreign diplomats.

Damascus's early response to these overtures did not bode well for the prospects of US engagement with Syria. On September 12, 2007, a group of militants attacked the US embassy in Damascus, wounding fourteen. Washington expressed appreciation for efforts by Syrian security guards to stop the attackers; following the incident, however, the Syrian government refused to share any intelligence gathered from the attackers.

In late November, the regime ordered the closure of the Damascus offices of AMIDEAST, an American nongovernmental association dedicated to fostering better communication and educational links with the Arab world. What made this particularly ironic was that the president and CEO of AMIDEAST was Theodore Kattouf, an American of Lebanese origin and former ambassador to Syria during the early days of the Bush administration who was known for his criticism of Washington's isolation policy. The Syrian regime also stopped cooperating with the embassy's Fulbright program, which had sent scores of Syrian students to the United States over the years to study in a variety of professional fields. American Fulbright students also began to encounter problems acquiring visas to Syria or renewing their residency permits if they were already in Damascus. It was almost as if the Syrian regime preferred isolation to engagement.

Damascus prepared to put its best face forward though. In late 2004, Syrian historian Sami Moubayed and Abdulsalam Haykal, a Syrian businessman with close links to the Syrian regime, had founded *Forward*, an English-language magazine that, according to its website, looked at "the bright side of things." While the magazine most definitely targeted the international community, the fact that *Forward* was the name of America's most popular Jewish-American magazine showed that—despite the fact both publishers had graduated from the American University in Beirut—both remained markedly out of touch with the outside world. More worrying, however, was the magazine's content. In its first few editions, the magazine ran essays on how Syria was the "key" to the Middle East. A regular contributor to the magazine was the Syrian ambassador to the United States, Imad Moustapha, who wrote articles that were intensely critical of the Bush administration's foreign policy. While *Forward* was nominally a competitor of *Syria Today*, its approach was more about public relations than actual journalism.

Rumors of an Iranian "takeover" in Damascus filled the cafés and bars of Beirut and Amman. Some referred to reports that Israeli and UN forces in southern Lebanon had uncovered extensive evidence that Damascus had openly supplied Hezbollah with antitank weapons, including RPG-29s, AT-5s, AT-13s, and AT-14s, which had been extremely effective at knocking out Israeli armor. The weapons were also used to destroy buildings in southern Lebanon that Israeli soldiers used for command and control. Other rumors of spreading Iranian influence were based on announcements in the Syrian and Iranian press of millions of dollars of Iranian investments pouring into Syria. One report from Iran's national news agency reported that Iranian investments in Syria had topped four hundred million dollars in 2006, representing 66 percent of the total Arab investment in the country.[2]

To understand just how close Iran and Syria had become, I attended the Iranian embassy's twenty-eighth anniversary celebration of the Islamic Revolution on February 8, 2007. After a quick check of our passports, Andrew Butters, correspondent for *Time* magazine, and I entered the embassy compound, which was decorated with beautiful cobalt-blue tiles with vine patterns.[3] A press conference was under way between Syrian journalists and the Iranian ambassador to Syria Mohammad Hassan Akhtari, whose long beard, flowing robes, and white turban seemed to make him an archetypal ayatollah of the Islamic Republic. As he answered questions, I noticed that he spoke beautiful classical Arabic—something the journalists respected, if for no other reason than they didn't have to dub the television or radio footage. Akhtari spoke about the strong relationship between Iran and Syria and boasted about the millions of dollars in projects being planned for the country. He looked keenly into the eyes of the journalists as he spoke, exuding a kind of self-confidence reminiscent of Hezbollah leader Hassan Nasrallah. The Syrian journalists ate it up, scribbling nearly every word he said into their notebooks.

Suddenly the door to the room swung open, revealing a ruckus outside. In strutted Syrian minister of information Mohsen Bilal, the former ambassador to Spain and Syria's chief spokesperson during the Israel-Hezbollah war. Sporting a mane of white hair and looking a bit like a retired rock star, Bilal walked over to Akhtari and shook his hand in front of the cameras. The ambassador motioned us to a square of tables, draped with bright yellow cloths reminiscent of the Hezbollah flag and heaving with platters of yellow rice and roasted chicken with pistachios.

Akhtari graciously welcomed us to the celebration as we took our seats, and he urged us to dig in. Akhtari began a long, eloquent speech about the history of the Islamic Revolution and its significance in the Muslim world. While he didn't look like a Westerner, Akhtari's words indicated that he had a worldly intelligence and understood how to gauge an audience of journalists. He explained in very matter-of-fact terms that the Islamic Revolution was a product of the late Shah Mohammad Reza Pahlavi's iron grip on his people and his alliance with America. While I didn't agree with everything he said, I noticed that Akhtari didn't take the opportunity to bash Bush or the United States. The audience clapped when he had finished, and Akhtari then motioned with his hand for the information minister to begin.

On the surface, Bilal looked like any wealthy Westernized Arab, the cuffs of his fitted shirt flaring ever so slightly out of the sleeves of his expensive Italian suit. However, as he spoke, Bilal betrayed a deep distain for the West. He told the audience that the West had sat on their hands as Israel bombed Lebanon, killing untold numbers of civilian Lebanese. As the journalists struggled to jot down Bilal's comments, he seemed to really get into his stride, his chest puffed out proudly like a rooster calling his mate. "You know, an Arab diplomat once asked me while I served in Paris, 'Hey, how can a guy like you not like the United States?'" Bilal said, pausing to add a bit of suspense. "Do you know what I told him? 'I can't name one good thing about the United States!'"

Suddenly the journalists stopped writing and looked over to the corner table where Andrew and I sat. Akhtari looked as well, a sorry look spreading across his face as he could tell from my grimace that I understood the ambassador's words. My friend Ibrahim Hamidi, *Al Hayat*'s correspondent in Damascus, leaned over and said, "I don't think he knows you are here."

After a few more bombastic lines, Bilal concluded his talk, shook Akhtari's hand, and exited the room. As I gathered my things, I thought how ironic it was that Bilal—a man who dressed like a Westerner, spoke several foreign languages, and had lived in a number of European countries—used vitriolic language that most Americans would more readily expect from an Iranian official. The Iranian ambassador, however, spoke carefully and seemed a person from a culture and country that was confident enough in itself to allow the faculty of reason to flourish. As I shook Akhtari's hand good-bye, I saw in his eye that he was the kind of person who thought things through. While his clothes looked nothing like mine, he seemed a reasonable diplomat, and his self-assurance reminded me of many American officials I had met over the years.

Such ceremonies demonstrated that Syrian-Iranian ties were moving from strength to strength, but trying to assess to what degree Iranian influence was spreading in Syria was difficult. Throughout the spring, there were increasing reports of conversions of Syrian Sunnis to Shiite Islam—an issue particularly sensitive to Syria's majority Sunni population and Washington's Sunni allies. I had first come across the rumors on a trip the previous September to the Jazeera—the section of eastern Syria between the Euphrates and Tigris Rivers. A local notable there told me in a hushed voice over dinner that Iranian Shiite clerics were converting poor Sunnis in the dry riverbeds of eastern Syria to Shiite Islam in return for money or "a few bags of macaroni."[4]

When I started asking around about Iranian-sponsored Shiitization upon my return to Damascus, I immediately ran into some kind of imaginary barrier and a great deal of obfuscation. First, Othaina took me to see Syrian parliamentarian Mohammed Habash, the head of Damascus's Islamic Studies Center whom I had interviewed the previous year on Islam in Syria. Habash said that talk of conversions was "Wahhabi propaganda"—a reference to the conservative version of Sunni Islam practiced in Saudi Arabia, Iran's regional rival and America's chief ally. A little later in the interview, however, Habash added that Shiitization was a "phenomena, especially in the Jazeera." Instead of converting, Habash said that they were, in fact, returning to their Shiite roots.

It was a story many journalists knew well, but without the geographical context. The previous month, Shiites had celebrated Ashura, the commemoration of the slaying of the prophet Muhammad's grandson Imam Hussein in 680 CE at Karbala, situated in present-day Iraq, by forces that were loyal to the Damascus-based Umayyad caliphate. Its leader, Yazid I, a traditional Sunni from outside Muhammad's family, ordered Hussein's decapitation, mounted his head on a pike, and paraded it alongside surviving members of his family throughout the empire. After brief stops in Kufa and Mosul, the procession headed through the Jazeera to Aleppo, then south toward the Syrian cities of Idlib and Homs before ending the journey in Damascus.

The spectacle backfired, however, turning Hussein's cause into a local crusade. Small Shiite communities sprouted up along the procession's route and were later joined by Sunni tribes from southern Iraq who were familiar with Shiite customs. Some built *maqaam*, or shrines; other Shiite communities in Syria gathered around the tombs of Ahl al-Bayt (the family of the prophet Muhammad). During the Ottoman caliphate (1415–1918), which was overwhelmingly Sunni, many Shiites in these communities converted to the dominant Sunni Islam to avoid harassment and discrimination. Now, according to Habash, they were converting back.

I asked Habash if he could introduce me to a few converts. Looking flustered, Habash said that he "met some a few years ago, but [he] didn't know where they were." When I asked him if he knew of any converts in the aftermath of the Israel-Hezbollah War, Habash looked out of the window over my shoulder and said no.

Still confused, I asked Leila and Othaina to arrange an interview with Syria's grand mufti, Ahmad Badr al-Din Hassoun. A few minutes into the interview, I asked him if reports of Shiitization were true. Hassoun, smiling from ear to ear, said that there were no conversions, as there were in fact no differences between Muslims in Syria. Reading the puzzled look on my face, Hassoun added that there were only different schools of thought. Traditionally, Syrians followed either Hanafi or Shafi'i schools of Islamic jurisprudence, but Syria's small Shiite population, which was estimated to account for less than 1 percent of the population, followed the Ja'afari school—the same one followed in Iran. Hassoun estimated that around 7 to 8 percent of Syrians now adhered to the Ja'afari school. When I asked him if this included the country's ruling Alawite minority—an obscure offshoot of Shiite Islam—Hassoun replied, "No," followed by a big smile.[5]

Othaina next took me to see Imam Ja'afar as-Sadiq, the leader of a *hawza* (a Shiite school) near the shrine of Sayyida Zaynab outside Damascus. After two cups of coffee and a pleasant chat, Sadiq told me that most of his students were originally Shiites from Iraq who follow Ayatollah Ali al-Sistani, based in Najaf. As for converts, Sadiq said that he could not allow interviews with them for fear of their safety. "There are a lot of Salafists in this country who might kill them." Instead, Sadiq referred me to the newly built *hawza* of Iran's supreme leader, Ayatollah Ali Khamenei.

A few days later, Othaina told me that he had tried to contact the Khamenei school many times, but to no avail. I began to worry: without an interview with at least one convert, the magazine would likely kill the story. I also knew that if I did not come up with answers from "on the ground," other, more alarmist reports of Shiitization were likely to continue, beating the war drums for a strike against Syria at a time when US forces were at a turning point in dealing with the insurgency.

After a few more days, Othaina entered my office and announced, "We have hit a dead end."

"I know how to find a convert," said Samah, a thirty-year-old woman from the mountains overlooking the Syrian city of Homs, who worked at *Syria Today*. "My husband is Shiite, and his best friend just converted."

Othaina suddenly looked uncomfortable and began fidgeting in his seat. Sensing that he thought he would lose his eight-hundred-dollar fee if he failed to find a convert himself, I assured him that he would be my translator. This statement helped, but it didn't resolve whatever was on his mind. Despite his unease, the next day we met the Syrian, Bilal—a thirty-four-year-old recent convert to Shiite Islam. Bilal said that he had converted to obtain spiritual freedom through the practice of *ijtihad*—individual interpretation of the Koran and the sayings of the prophet Muhammad. But at the same time, Bilal said that he had converted shortly after Hezbollah's summer war with Israel. When I asked him if the timing had anything to do with the conflict, he didn't indicate one way or the other.[6]

Whether for his own reasons or the fact that Othaina—a Syrian he didn't know—was beside me, his vagueness made it clear to me that the Syrian regime preferred some kind of tactical ambiguity on this story. It also helped me understand the limits of reporting in Syria. While I had great access to the country (and could therefore sell stories to the outside world), this was mitigated by Syrians' reticence to fully explain their relationship with Iran. While Syria was seemingly accepting of Iran's spreading influence, it didn't want anyone to measure it.

The Democratic Party leadership, which was now in full control of the US House and Senate, rejected Bush's Iraq plan. Prominent Democratic politicians, including Ted Kennedy and Harry Reid, rejected the surge proposal almost immediately, while a number of White House hopefuls, including the then favored senator Hillary Clinton, as well as Barack Obama and Joe Biden, voiced opposition to the plan.

Obama, in a televised interview at the Capitol, said, "I am not persuaded that an additional twenty thousand troops will solve the situation there. In fact it could do the reverse, as it takes pressure off the Iraqi parties to arrive at the political solution every observer believes is the solution to the problems we face there."[7]

The alternative, as outlined the previous August in what became known as the "Biden Plan," advocated "maintaining a unified Iraq by decentralizing it and giving Kurds, Shiites, and Sunnis their own regions." While this solution would be underpinned by guaranteeing minority Sunnis a share of Iraq's oil revenue, promoting a jobs program, and convening an international conference that would produce a "regional non-aggression pact," the plan's cornerstone was the rapid withdrawal of US forces by the end of 2007. The plan intended to tap into a groundswell of opposition to the war, as poll numbers at the time indicated that up to 60 percent of Americans opposed the surge and an even higher percentage opposed the war. As a rapid withdrawal from Iraq would require cutting a political deal with Syria and Iran, Democratic Party White House hopefuls advocated engagement with Damascus and Tehran without preconditions.[8]

Finally, on March 31, the new House Speaker, Nancy Pelosi, dropped the diplomatic bombshell that Syria was waiting for. When she arrived in Jerusalem on the first leg of a tour of the region, Pelosi's office released a statement saying, "As recommended by the Iraq Study Group, a bipartisan delegation led by Speaker Pelosi intends to discuss a wide range of security issues affecting the United States and the Middle East with representatives of governments in the region, including Syria."[9] The delegation included a number of senior House officials, including Democratic representative Tom Lantos, the chairman of the House Foreign Affairs Committee; Henry Waxman of California; Louise Slaughter of New York; Nick Rahall of West Virginia; Keith Ellison of Minnesota; and Republican representative David Hobson of Ohio. The Bush administration immediately dubbed the announcement "a really bad idea."[10]

In Damascus, however, Syrians began to prepare for the first of what they hoped would be many visits by US officials to break Syria out of its diplomatic isolation. Imad Moustapha, dubbed the "loneliest ambassador in Washington" due to his isolation at the Syrian embassy on Wyoming Street in Washington's northwest quarter, returned to Damascus to prep Assad for Pelosi's arrival.

At the offices of *Syria Today*, the staff was elated. Only a little over a year before, Damascenes had whispered about power struggles at the top and Bashar's possible fall from power as the chaos following the Hariri murder swept the country's political scene. Pelosi's visit, combined with America's failing prospects in Iraq and the 2006 Lebanon War, strengthened the idea in Syria that Bashar was once again a political horse worth betting on. When an invitation to the US embassy showed up at *Syria Today* for the delegation's reception, Leila slapped the invitation against the palm of her hand, looked at me, and said, "The Americans are coming!"

The next day, the streets of Damascus were blocked off as Pelosi's motorcade whizzed along the main route to Damascus's Souk al-Hamidiyya, the main covered market where Syrians had peddled their wares for centuries. Syrian television showed Pelosi, along with the rest of the delegation, browsing through the market stands, smiling and meeting Syrian shop owners. It also showed clips of Pelosi meeting with President Assad at the Republican Palace overlooking the Syrian capital.

What exactly transpired in the talks was open to interpretation. Pelosi told reporters after the meeting that she had brought a message from Prime Minister Olmert that he was "ready to engage in peace talks" with Syria and that the delegation expressed its "interest in using our good offices in promoting peace between Israel and Syria." In a *New York Times* article, Pelosi and her delegation were quoted as urging Assad to stop his support for militants, including Hezbollah, Hamas, and jihadi fighters to Iraq. The House Committee on Foreign Affairs chairman Tom Lantos—long a critic of Syria and a chief backer of tightening sanctions on Syria—said that he asked Assad how a man "of his intelligence and knowledge of the world could have common cause with President Ahmadinejad of Iran, who has denied the Holocaust and calls for the elimination of Israel." Pelosi added that "we came in friendship, hope, and determined that the road to Damascus is a road to peace."

Pelosi's statements immediately drew criticism from Bush himself. "Sending delegations hasn't worked," he said. "It's just simply been counterproductive." A little later, National Security Council spokesman Gordon Johndroe was more blunt: "Unfortunately, that road [to Damascus] is lined with victims of Hamas and Hezbollah, and the victims of terrorists who cross from Syria into Iraq. It's lined with the victims in Lebanon, who are trying to fight for democracy there. It's lined with human rights activists trying for freedom and democracy in Syria."[11]

Pelosi's statements also drew qualified criticism from Israel as well. Olmert's office issued a statement almost immediately after Pelosi's press conference saying that "although Israel is interested in peace with Syria, that country continues to be part of the axis of evil and a force that encourages terror in the entire Middle East."

At a reception that night at the US ambassador's residence in Abou Roumaneh, Damascus's elite rubbed shoulders with the delegation, whose members whispered to the diplomats about the possibility of lifting US sanctions on Syria and the need for more delegations. It was a far cry from the tense atmosphere a year earlier, when Syrians invited to US embassy functions received calls from Syrian security officers ordering them not to attend, which was an apparent attempt at revenge for US isolation of the Syrian embassy in Washington.

The next morning, the lead editorial of the *Washington Post*, entitled "Pratfall in Damascus," attacked Pelosi—it accused Pelosi of falling for Assad's "propaganda" by quoting a statement from Olmert's office that said, "A number of Senate and House members who recently visited Damascus received the impression that despite the declarations of Bashar Assad, there is no change in the position of his country regarding a possible peace process with Israel." The op-ed added that "thanks to the speaker's freelancing, Mr. Assad was getting mixed messages from the United States. . . . Mr. Assad is a corrupt thug whose overriding priority at the moment is not peace with Israel but heading off UN charges that he orchestrated the murder of former Lebanese prime minister [Rafik Hariri]." Finally, the *Washington Post* accused Pelosi of "attempting to introduce a new Middle East policy that directly conflicts with that of the president. We have found much to criticize in Mr. Bush's military strategy and regional diplomacy. But Ms. Pelosi's attempt to establish a shadow presidency is not only counterproductive, it is foolish."[12]

However, it wasn't just Democrats who sought engagement with Syria. The Iraq Study Group had recommended engaging Syria and Iran in order to stabilize Iraq. While the Bush administration was clearly reticent to publicly embrace Syria as Pelosi had, the White House decided to honor the ISG's recommendations by engaging Syria solely on the issue of Iraq. Secretary of State Rice broke the Bush administration's two-year isolation policy on May 4, 2007, when she met Syrian foreign minister Walid al-Moallem on the sidelines of a fifty-nation summit in Sharm el-Sheikh dedicated to Iraqi reconstruction. The details of the meeting have not been made public, but the main American issue concerned the movement of foreign fighters into Iraq from Syria. According to interviews with US diplomats, Moallem's main request concerned securing parts to repair Syria's aging fleet of Boeing and Airbus commercial aircraft that had been blocked by US sanctions.[13]

This marked the first of many signals from the Assad regime that US sanctions were having a deeper impact than first thought. Both diplomats described the meeting as positive, with Rice calling the discussion "professional" and "businesslike," and Moallem "frank" and "constructive." Rice later told CNN, "We have no desire to have bad relations with Syria. Of course, we want to have better relations with Syria."[14] Whatever was agreed, a few days later US military spokesman Major General William Caldwell told reporters that Syria had acted recently against the flow of foreign fighters.[15] What that actually meant was anyone's guess.

As American diplomats waited to see what Syria might do regarding Iraq, the regime of Bashar al-Assad consolidated its authoritarian grip on power at home. On April 25, Anwar al-Bunni—the Syrian civil-society activist who was arrested a mere thirty minutes after the UN Security Council approved Resolution 1680 on demarcating the Lebanese border—was sentenced to five years on charges of "spreading false information."

Activists saw this as a signal to Europe, as al-Bunni had tried to open a civil-society-awareness center with EU funding, only to see the center shut down a few days after its public opening (which had been attended by the EU's representative to Syria). On May 11, 2007, Kamal Labwani—a civil-society activist and dissident who had been arrested on November 8, 2005, upon his arrival at Damascus's international airport—was sentenced to twelve years' hard labor. More than anyone, Labwani was associated with the Bush administration's plans to topple the Syrian regime because of his meeting with officials from the White House the day after the announcement of the first Mehlis report into the murder of Rafik Hariri.

Finally, on May 13, the regime sentenced perhaps the country's most prominent dissident and architect of the Damascus Declaration, Michel Kilo, to three years in prison on charges of "spreading false news, weakening national feeling, and inciting sectarian sentiments."[16] For years, Kilo had been tolerated by the Assad regime because he was a Christian from Latakia, the capital of the Alawite-dominated coast. His connections, combined with his insights on the regime's problems and Syrian civil society, had made him a key resource for most foreign diplomats.

The sentences angered diplomats and journalists in Damascus. In the year leading up to them, the Syrian regime had virtually paraded the dissidents before foreign diplomats attending their trials in the Old Justice Palace next to the Souk al-Hamidiyya, the main market in Damascus's Old City. I had attended Kilo's last trial earlier that spring. After making a mix of journalists and diplomats wait for over three hours, courtroom officials opened the doors—specifically for foreigners only. Inside, Kilo was kept in a large cage in front of the judge. After a few minutes of deliberation, the judge announced that the case could not be tried in that court and referred the case to another judge. As the doors to the courtroom swung open again and we were escorted out by uniformed security officers, each of us shook Kilo's hand through the bars of the cage. Kilo, who had grown a thick mustache since I had last interviewed him a month before his arrest, smiled widely and thanked us. We never met again.

With President Assad's opponents in jail and the United States once again engaging Damascus, the way was clear for the regime to prepare for Assad's reelection to a second seven-year term as president. Syria's constitution stated that parliament must approve a candidate for president, who then in turn must be approved in a national referendum. In the last referendum in July 2000—a year after the death of his father, Hafez—Bashar had won the referendum with an approval rate of more than 97 percent of ballots cast.

In the weeks leading up to the new referendum, scheduled for May 27, posters with a stylized black-and-white photo of Assad began appearing on bus stops and billboards throughout the Syrian capital. The poster's background featured a thumbprint—the mark that voters had to make on each ballot in the "Yes" or "No" box. The thumbprint's ink was red, white, and black and adorned with two green stars—a replica of the Syrian flag. Below the image, in big red Arabic script, read the word "*Mnhibak*," which roughly translates from the Syrian Arabic dialect as "You are our beloved." As the posters multiplied, my Syrian friends mentioned under their breath that Iraqi refugees in Syria found the posters confusing, as "*Mnhibak*" in Iraqi dialect means "We don't like you."

I headed from my apartment down Shahbandar Street to an Assad rally in front of the Central Bank on Damascus's central Sabeh Bahrat (Seven Seas) Square; "*Mnhibak*" posters were taped to nearly every tree and signpost. Russian-made Syrian military helicopters, with missiles attached and towing streamers reading "*Mnhibak*," circled over the square. A hot-air balloon hovered over the square, also carrying a giant "*Mnhibak*" poster. Everywhere thousands of Syrians with "*Mnhibak*" T-shirts, baseball caps, and signs filled the streets. Everything was regimented—young boys and men stood in lines facing rows of girls and women.

As I passed by, I could tell from their appearance and dialects that they were from eastern Syria—the part of Syria's Sunni community that Bashar's father had co-opted by bringing them to the Syrian capital to work in the regime's bureaucracy. As I walked along, groups of young Druze from the southern Syrian town of Swaida and Alawites from the Syrian coast clustered around the square's central fountain. These young Druze and Alawite men carried posters showing photos of President Assad with logos of Syriatel, the cell-phone provider owned by Assad's cousin, Rami Makhlouf. A few of the women wore Islamic veils, but most were dressed in tight-fitting jeans and paraphernalia, like biker chicks. On a terrace above the columns at the front of the Central Bank stood all the regime's main players—Bashar, his wife, Assad family members, ministers—who waved to the crowd below. If anyone needed a snapshot of Bashar's minority-dominated regime and its pecking order, this was it.

Taking out my notebook and speaking in Arabic with a few of the attendees caused scores of people to flock around. One man from Damascus said they supported Bashar because he was "open-minded and just—everything in Syria is good." A seventy-year-old man from Muhajreen, the neighborhood occupying the slopes of Qassioun Mountain above Assad's apartment in Abou Roumaneh, said, "Syria was once a place of sand—now it is a castle." Another man said, "Syria is protected by God!"—the line from Assad's speech following the first Mehlis report into Hariri's death, which outlined Bashar's plan to push back against the United States.

When I asked them about the rampant corruption that everyone seemed to talk about, one man said, "Who did this corruption? It wasn't Bashar!" Another said, "Bashar is the best leader in the Arab world." When I asked them how many Syrians supported Bashar, one man shouted, "Ninety-nine percent!" Another blurted out, "We want him to be president forever!" Beside me I could hear someone whispering to a wild-eyed man from the security services, "He's an American journalist."

Suddenly Bilal, a good Syrian journalist friend, appeared through the crowd to my left. Bilal was an Alawite from the Syrian coast. He looked annoyed and kind of tired. "I have to get out of this place," he said. Thinking he meant the rally, I suggested he just go back to the office or his home. "I mean this country!" he said.

I stopped in my tracks and stared at him. I knew Bilal was a critical thinker and the best writer I had ever trained in Syria. However, he was also an Alawite and, like many of his sect, historically pro-Assad. "I just don't understand why all this is necessary," he added. I suddenly realized that, for all the economic and social changes that had taken place in Syria—not to mention technological—very little had changed politically from the day that Bashar had taken over.

When the poll took place on May 27, 2007, Assad secured 97.62 percent of the vote, a slight improvement over the 97.24 percent he obtained in 2000. The answer to Bilal's prescient question was an extra 0.38 percent.[17]

From Washington, Ammar Abdulhamid—my one-time colleague at MAWRED and director of the Tharwa project—covered the Syrian elections via his website, Syrian Elector. Ammar was a recipient of funds from Washington's Middle East Partnership Initiative (MEPI), the controversial program established by the Bush administration to spread democracy in Arab countries. While funding well-meaning projects, MEPI was criticized as part and parcel of the Bush administration's "democracy agenda" in the Middle East. Funding was distributed to US NGOs such as the International Republican Institute (IRI) and the National Democratic Institute (NDI), who in turn issued grants to civil-society activists in Syria. The initiative was also harshly criticized for funding the exiled Syrian opposition, though the criticism varied, because many saw the exiled group as deeply divided, ineffective, and lacking the street credibility of the Damascus Declaration and other domestic opposition.[18]

Syrian Elector covered the election in detail; reports came from all over Syria. The website reported on voting fraud and other kinds of regime manipulation of the ballot. While it was an interesting window for foreigners into the Syrian referendum, it was unclear how many Syrians used the site to track the referendum—a referendum that had very predictable results, as Assad was the only name on the ballot—or whether they learned via the site why their vote mattered. Nonetheless, in a Syrian context, the site was unprecedented.

The other big change that day was Leila's departure to study in the United States. For over three years, she had struggled to keep the magazine afloat, even going without her salary for well over two years. The Damascene businessman who had invested in the project, Nazeer, thought it would motivate her to work harder—instead it wore her out. With a scholarship to the University of Maryland to study broadcast journalism, Leila saw her chance to escape and took it. While I was happy for her, I suddenly realized that I was on my own in Damascus for the first time. I had never navigated the Syrian regime without her. So I asked a friend and wealthy businessman, Abdul Ghani Attar, to invest in *Syria Today* and give it the financial and business backing that the magazine would need to survive. Abdul Ghani, son of wealthy businessman Abdul Rahman Attar, agreed to do so, as long as I stayed long enough to make some changes at the magazine and get it on a successful path. While I agreed to his terms, I had no idea how to balance that work with my growing journalistic and analytical work for international publications and think tanks.

To take my mind off the spectacle surrounding Bashar's reelection, I focused on doing the only thing I knew to help the situation and, in a small way, promote America's long-term interests—I offered journalism training through *Syria Today*. While the world focused its attention on the dramatic political changes in Syria and Lebanon following Hariri's assassination and the 2006 Lebanon War, few noticed the economic changes that Syria's withdrawal from Lebanon caused on the Syrian economy.

During the years of Syrian occupation of Lebanon, Syrian officials used the institutions in Lebanon's free-market economy—most notably its banks and insurance companies—to finance imported goods into Syria. These imports were mostly smuggled into Syria, which still maintained import restrictions to heavily protect the Syrian economy in line with the country's socialist goals. Syrian and Lebanese traders paid bribes to the Syrian army and security officers who controlled Lebanon and Lebanese customs, forming large networks of corruption on both sides of the border.

When Syria was forced to withdraw from Lebanon in April 2005, these networks were suddenly broken up, as importing goods through an independent and perceivably hostile Lebanon threatened the black market that underpinned Bashar's opening to the outside world. By necessity, the regime was forced to liberalize import restrictions and allow private banks in Syria—which had formally opened for the first time in 2004—to expand to finance Syria's new economy.

This was in line with the recommendations of the five-year plan drawn up by Abdullah Dardari—then minister of planning, now deputy prime minister for economic affairs—the German-drafted blueprint for bringing Syria from a socialist system to a "social market economy" and the same model actually used by Germany. Throughout 2005 and 2006, the regime issued licenses for a handful of private banks and private insurance companies in Syria. These institutions issued letters of credit to fuel a boom in imports through Syria. As more boutiques and shopping centers opened throughout the capital, Syrians enjoyed the fruits of globalization—designer shoes and clothes, modern appliances, modern technology—like never before.

Instead of seeing the boom as the product of Syria's forced withdrawal from Lebanon, most attributed it to Bashar's vision for a more open Syria—despite the fact that most, if not all, of the state's five-year plan had yet to be implemented. Washington's isolation policy, combined with US sanctions, kept the United States from using its influence in this rapidly changing part of Syrian society that was, in many ways, the direct result of Washington's effort to push Syria out of Lebanon. Instead, Iran took advantage of this power vacuum and announced a slew of investments in Syria to help fuel the boom.

To see Iran spreading its tentacles into Syria and taking advantage of the reform that I had advocated for so many years was like icing on a bitter cake. During the 2006 war in Lebanon, I had written an op-ed for the *New York Times* advocating the expansion of the Bush administration's promotion of democracy to include Syrian reform. As it was clear that direct engagement between the two governments was out of the question, my article advocated reaching out to Syria's private sector through the American embassy in Damascus instead. The article's bottom line was that supporting Syria's private sector would help the United States compete with spreading Iranian influence in Syria and ultimately help the country move toward a peace agreement with Israel.[19]

A few days after the article's publication, I received a phone call from the US embassy's public-diplomacy department asking for an appointment. When we eventually met, the embassy official—who knew I had helped carry out journalism training in Syria in the past— encouraged me to carry out journalism training through *Syria Today*. This seemed like a great idea—not only did I have the chance to engage directly with Syrians and promote American values, but it was a chance to test my theory as well. Could the United States reach out to the Syrian people directly and effectively?

After putting an ad in the daily Arabic papers for the training, we were swamped with applications. I and some of the other *Syria Today* staff weeded out the applications to a final list of twenty-five interviewees. Following the interviews, we narrowed down the list to five finalists. Leila hired them on a small salary to, in her words, "ensure their loyalty." We then arranged to have secondary training with existing *Syria Today* writers as well. I taught the course, along with a few American journalist friends from Beirut, using the basic textbook used at Columbia's journalism school.

In many ways, teaching Syrians who had never studied writing, or never worked for state-dominated newspapers, was a treat. "Going to the tree"—finding people uncontaminated by these influences—for recruits allowed us to attract a number of Syrians who proved intelligent and well-meaning. It was frustrating as well, though—the Syrian educational system had not taught them the basics of composition, let alone to distinguish between basic concepts. For example, the students did not know the difference between the subject of a story and a theme. The idea that the opening of a story should introduce the reader to the subject was completely foreign to them. This was largely the product of the writing style of Arabic newspapers, which tended to "bury the lead" or soften the point of stories in order not to offend influential people. Many of the students not only didn't do the home-work—a common occurrence in any school—but when they did, they failed to grasp the basic concepts of the assignment. Many used their writing not to construct a rational or compelling argument but simply as an opportunity to vent their spleen against whatever angered them that day.

In the end, two writers joined *Syria Today* magazine. Eager to get more writers and build on our relative success, I opened another train-ing session. This time, however, *Syria Today* didn't have the funds to pay the trainees, which forced me to offer the course for free. Like the previous class, I advertised in the local newspapers, vetted candidates, and selected a dozen new students for a course that met once a week. But with each passing week, more students dropped out of the course. Some had other commitments; others just stopped showing up. A core of six students remained, but they showed up intermittently. Few did their homework, and those that did cobbled it together on the way to class. Each worked two or three jobs to keep up with the rising cost of living in the country. While the same number of students finished the course as the first time, only one continued writing. I realized that reaching out to the Syrian private sector would take considerably more effort than one-off, small-scale projects—it needed institutional support in order to make an impact.

During the two months following Bashar's "reelection," Syria experienced a massive heat wave, which transformed the Syrian capital into a polluted oven. During the height of the crisis in Lebanon, Bashar had cut the high tariffs on cars from more than 200 percent to less than 40 percent. Syrians who had been saving for decades to buy a car could finally afford to do so—the results were traffic jams in Syria's major cities and rapidly declining air quality.

From atop Qassioun Mountain overlooking Damascus, a lead-colored smog cloud hovered over the world's oldest most continuously inhabited city. To escape the heat and bad air, Syrians purchased air conditioners, which were also suddenly available at affordable prices due to the cuts in import tariffs.

Sitting at my desk, I could hear a deep humming noise outside our office. I assumed the noise was from welders working next door, a building which had been under continuous construction since the day we moved into office in 2005. The humming got louder and began to pulse, which reminded me of the sound you might hear in a sci-fi film like *The War of the Worlds* when a spacecraft is about to attack.

Suddenly, a trainee in the magazine's writing program came running into my office. "Evacuate the building!" he screamed.

Running out of the office, the acrid smell of burning plastic filling the air, I immediately saw the problem as I got out of the door: smoke was billowing from the Free Zone's transformer building, located next door to the *Syria Today* offices. When the staff reached the other side of the street and joined employees of other local businesses fleeing the chaos, I could see flames and smoke coming from different electricity-transmission boxes along the main thoroughfare. Instead of blowing some fuse or breaker somewhere in the Syrian grid, the meltdown continued, the humming growing louder as sparks flew out of the corrugated metal vents of the transformer building.

Several hundred employees of the various Free Zone businesses just stared in disbelief as the owners of cars near the transformer building frantically tried to move them out of harm's way. Othaina, braving smoke and mortal danger, ran back into the *Syria Today* offices, threw the main electricity switch, then ran back out. Thara, our office administrator, wept openly. "It's just chaos," she said to me in English, wiping tears away from her cheeks.

About twenty minutes later, someone somewhere turned off that entire sector of the Damascus grid to stop the meltdown, and the humming stopped. An olive-green Land Rover with blackened windows and stencils of Bashar's silhouette then arrived at the transformer building. The license plates indicated they were from one of the country's security branches. No one got out of the vehicle, which sat there for two or three minutes, then drove around to the junction boxes that were on fire, and sped down the street and out of the Free Zone.

Syria Today staff, their faces in shock, watched as firemen put out the flames. When it was over, I just told them to go home—we could operate without Internet service, but without power, there was simply nothing to do.

The July meltdown was just the latest sign that Syria's infrastructure was under considerable stress from increased demand and difficulty in performing maintenance due to US sanctions. In mid-June, ADSL Internet connections all over the city died, paralyzing businesses such as *Syria Today*, which had benefited from the "new economy" that Bashar's opening up to the outside world had made possible. In the past, a couple of phone calls and a few thousand pounds to our *wasta*, or influential friends, in the state-owned telecommunications establishment would have solved the problem. But this time was different: no matter how many times we called, no one was able to fix the problem.

The magazine's IT manager said that there was nothing she could do, as the problem was happening all over the country. Much slower dial-up connections still worked, however, so we set up an Internet-access terminal in the newsroom. Productivity ground to a halt, though, and most employees simply stayed home and used their personal dial-up accounts.

Flying on Syrian Arab Airlines, the state-owned national carrier that was later rebranded Syrian Air, had become an increasing problem as well. US sanctions on Syria banned all exports of goods with more than 10-percent American content. A waiver in the sanctions allowed exports of repair parts to Syria via export licenses, applications for which Syrian Air's suppliers had to file with the US Commerce Department in Washington. During the 1990s, when relations between Washington and Damascus were arguably at their all-time best (as Syria was involved in US-sponsored peace negotiations with Israel), the US government approved most of the export licenses for Syrian Air parts and also allowed the carrier to purchase a few used Airbus aircraft, which, because they had more than 10-percent US content, required an export license as well.

Despite the fact that Washington tightened sanctions in 2004, the waiver for aircraft parts was still in effect. However, as relations worsened, export-license applications were increasingly rejected. The Bush administration had adopted a hard line on the interpretation of the waiver, which allowed exports only for "safety of flight."

By the summer of 2007, Syrian Air had only six commercial jets remaining, which caused chaos for passengers traveling abroad. On a holiday trip to Milan, for example, I was unable to secure a confirmation for the flight, despite the fact that I had a ticket and a reservation to travel. Once onboard the aircraft, I saw that Bashar's "reforms" had not made it to Syrian Air. Most of the material on the seat cushions was threadbare, and the stuffing inside most seats was lumpy and uncomfortable. The trays used to serve food were crude and clearly not intended for use on an aircraft. Upon return, I was once again unable to secure a reservation, so I was forced to show up several hours early for the flight. Luckily I was able to make it, but scores of passengers—many of whom were Italian tourists—were left angry and stranded.

A few days after the meltdown, Syrian prime minister Muhammad Naji al-Otari—under intense criticism for the outages—blamed it on US sanctions. This contravened the Assad regime's public line that US sanctions had little or no impact on the country. According to Otari, as well as the deputy prime minister for economic affairs Abdullah Dardari, US sanctions had scared away the world's top five power-plant manufacturers, thus causing a lack of generating capacity when demand skyrocketed during the heat wave. Syria was also forced to cut electricity exports to Iraqi Kurdistan and Lebanon, robbing itself of revenue and influence there.

At *Syria Today*, the staff didn't buy Otari's explanation. While the prime minister's explanation possibly explained problems in genera-tion, the failures they had witnessed in the Free Zone a few days earlier were due to transmission and grid problems. Othaina, working with a foreign freelance journalist, came up with the best quote to summarize Syria's feeling on the meltdown: "The main problem for Syria is a total lack of planning for the future. Sanctions may be having an effect, but bad governance is the main factor, and we're seeing none of our offi-cials being held accountable for their mistakes."[20]

Damascus in August is like Washington, DC: it's hot, humid, and not much happens as people enjoy their summer vacation. While the electricity blackouts continued in some parts of the country, the much-hoped-for rapprochement between the United States and Syria not only failed to materialize, but this new "Cold War" began to affect relations between everyday Syrians and Americans.

The Syrian Ministry of Higher Education had failed to grant visas and residency permits to American teachers of the Damascus Com-munity School (DCS). Known as the "American School," DCS had been established in the 1950s with the help of former secretary of state John Foster Dulles. Unlike American schools elsewhere in the Middle East, the Syrian government didn't grant DCS a formal license but allowed it to operate nevertheless. Over four decades, DCS educated the children of the Syrian elite who were destined for universities in America and elsewhere.

Instead of dealing with Syria's perceived eagerness to engage diplomatically with the United States, America's chief diplomat in Damascus, chargé d'affaires Michael Corbin, ended up spending the month of August negotiating with the Syrian Ministry of Foreign Affairs to get the teachers' visas granted. With only a few days to go before the September start of the school year, Minister of Foreign Affairs Moallem intervened to allow the teachers entry.

I arrived early to the offices of *Syria Today* the morning of September 6, 2007, trying to avoid the daytime heat as much as I could. Reading through the state papers, I was researching recent parliamentary discussions on the Syrian fiscal budget, which amounted to a record $4 billion. Nicholas Blanford, a good friend and the correspondent for the *Christian Science Monitor* in Beirut, called.

"The Syrians are saying they chased Israeli aircraft out of eastern Syria last night," he said. "What could that be?"

The wheels started spinning in my mind. I had spent time in Washington the previous spring at various think-tank events concerning relations with Syria. At a particularly good seminar at the Washington Institute for Near East Policy, I was surprised that many analysts were predicting a possible war between Syria and Israel that summer. While they were not specific about the source of the tension, I assumed that Israel wanted to restore the psychological deterrence it had "lost" during the 2006 Israel-Hezbollah War.

Eastern Syria was not normally Israel's area of operations, however. In 2003 Israel had bombed the Palestinian camp at Ain Saheb outside Damascus, and in 2006 Israeli jets had buzzed Bashar's palace near the Syrian port city of Latakia. There was plenty of talk in the press and in op-ed pages about the likelihood of an Israeli raid on Iran's nuclear program, especially in light of European attempts that had repeatedly failed to convince Tehran to stop its enrichment of uranium. So after I made a few phone calls, I gave Nick what I thought was the safe answer: "There seems to be a consensus here that the Israelis were test-ing Syrian air defense systems."[21]

Downstairs in the newsroom, I found Othaina sitting at his com-puter terminal, reading the Syrian Arab News Agency (SANA) site and watching Al Jazeera on a TV set anchored to the wall above his desk. Othaina was from Deir Ezzor, a city in eastern Syria along the Euphrates River, so news of an Israeli incursion in northeastern Syria was a national and local concern for him. He motioned for me to step outside the office with him for a smoke.

"There are reports that people heard four or five jets around Tal al-Abyad on the Turkish border," he said. "I'm hearing the jets were Israeli, and there were American jets, too. Some people heard loud booms as well. What the hell is going on?"

Over the next few days, the story took an unexpected turn.[22] On September 7, SANA reported more details on the raid, saying that the jets had "infiltrated Syrian airspace through the northern border com-ing from the direction of the Mediterranean and headed toward the north-east territory, breaking the sound barrier. . . . The Syrian Arab Republic warns the government of the Israeli enemy and reserves the right to respond according to what it seems fit."

Information Minister Bilal told Al Jazeera that Syria was "giving serious consideration to its response . . . to this aggression. . . . This shows that Israel cannot give up aggression and treachery." Reuters quoted a Syrian official saying that the Israeli jets "dropped bombs on an empty area while our air defenses were firing heavily at them." The next day, Turkey asked Israel for clarification on two fuel tanks that it had found in the Turkish provinces of Hatay and Gaziantep along the Syrian frontier. Prime Minister Olmert continued to deny all knowl-edge of the incident, telling reporters, "I don't know what you are talk-ing about."[23]

After a few days' lull, a US official stated on September 11 that the incursion was a raid that had been targeting weapons destined for Hezbollah. On September 13, the *Washington Post* reported, quoting a former Israeli official, that the attack had targeted "a facility capable of making unconventional weapons." On September 15, there was another, much bigger bombshell. The same newspaper, quoting American sources, reported that Israel had recently provided the United States with evidence that North Korea was cooperating with Syria on a nuclear facility of some type. The evidence included "dramatic satellite imagery" but was restricted to senior officials.

The report also said—citing a "prominent US expert on the Middle East" who had interviewed Israeli participants in the raid—that the timing of the attack was related to the arrival of a ship from North Korea with cargo "labeled as cement" in the Syrian port of Tartous. The source added that the planes targeted an "agricultural research center . . . on the Euphrates River, close to the Turkish border." Israel had been monitoring the facility in the belief that Syria was "using it to extract uranium from phosphates."[24] This report seemed to dovetail with known cooperation between 1986 and 1992 as well as between 1992 and 1997 by Syria with the UN's International Atomic Energy Agency (IAEA), which provided Syria with a "micro-plant" facility to enable yellowcake to be extracted from phosphoric acid produced at a plant outside of Homs—that is, extract uranium from Syrian phosphates.[25]

There were more reports the next day, this time from the British press, that the raid—code-named Operation Orchard—had involved eight planes using five-hundred-pound bombs and that an Israeli commando team had gone into Syria before the attack to set targeting lasers for the jets. Although Israel continued to deny the reports, AFP (Agence France-Presse) reported that the head of Israeli military intelligence, Amos Yadlin, had told an Israeli Knesset committee that Israel had recovered its deterrent capability lost during its problematic showing in the 2006 Israel-Hezbollah War. The same day, John Bolton—the former US ambassador to the UN, who, in 2003, while undersecretary of state for arms control, voiced concerns to Congress over Syria's suspected WMD programs—said, "It will be very unusual for Israel to conduct such a military operation inside Syria other [than] for a very high-value target."[26]

Because Israel remained silent as well, this seemed to confirm something out of the ordinary, but in Damascus there was no way to get to the bottom of the accusations. The Syrian government completely denied the charges, mostly by ignoring them. Eastern Syria is completely controlled by Syrian military intelligence, which closely monitors all people—especially foreigners—coming and going from the Euphrates Valley, heading east to the Iraqi border. So a trip to the alleged site was impossible without permission from the Ministry of Information, which was not being forthcoming, according to Othaina.

Just as the story started to die, another report brought it back to life. Ron Ben-Yishai, an Israeli reporter with the Israeli newspaper *Yedioth Ahronoth*, wrote a story on September 26 about his trip to the area of the "Syria operation." It included a photo of him in front of a sign for the Deir Ezzor research station of the Arab Center for the Studies of Arid Zones and Dry Lands (ACSAD). Never before had an Israeli journalist filed a story from Syria, let alone from an area directly under the control of military intelligence. What made the story stick in my mind was that Yishai was allowed to interview local people, who told him, "There were a few Israeli planes here that made supersonic booms over the city and maybe even dropped something." What was even stranger was that Yishai interviewed a Syrian journalist, who told him that "all this talk about supposed tensions following an overflight of fighter planes is only meant to intimidate Israel" and who also said that Israel caused the booms in order to "bait Syria into shooting down the planes, and thus giving Israel reason to declare war."[27]

Given that Yishai didn't speak Arabic, he could not have arranged an interview without a "fixer" who reported to Syrian intelligence, and all Syrian journalists speaking with foreigners had to report their conversations to their intelligence minders. I suspected that the Syrian government was going out of its way to cover something up very subtly.

Strangely, however, the nuclear story didn't have much traction in the international press. One reason seemed to be the low credibility of the Bush administration. Most reporters I knew didn't want to get burned supporting a US administration that got Saddam Hussein's weapons programs so wrong. Despite lots of news of the incident from Washington and Israel, foreigners visiting Damascus and Beirut didn't even mention the story after a few weeks. The story that the Bush administration was looking for—that could be used to put international pressure on the Assad regime—was somehow, mysteriously, allowed to fade away.[28]

In the summer of 2007, as the US surge in Iraq and their "awakening campaign"—working with local tribes to undermine al-Qaeda in Iraq—in Anbar Province rolled out in earnest, Democratic members of Congress demanded that General David Petraeus return to Washington and report on the operation's progress. In full uniform, Petraeus testified before Congress on September 10, 2007, stating that the "military objectives of the surge are, in large measure, being met," with violence levels declining to their lowest levels since June 2006.

Petraeus's official comments on Syria consisted of only one line: "Foreign and home-grown terrorists, insurgents, militia extremists, and criminals all push the ethno-sectarian competition toward violence. Malign actions by Syria and, especially, by Iran fuel that violence."[29] But on the ground in Iraq, a new phase of the cold war with Syria was beginning. The following day, the sixth anniversary of the September 11 attacks, coalition forces overran a tent camp in the desert near Sinjar, an Iraqi village close to the Syrian border. There they uncovered a collection of databases belonging to an al-Qaeda in Iraq (AQI) cell responsible for smuggling fighters from Syria into Iraq. The databases provided details of more than seven hundred fighters crossing the border between August 2006 and August 2007 along a two-hundred-mile stretch of the Iraqi-Syrian frontier from the Euphrates River north to the border with Turkey.

The databases, which became known as the Sinjar documents, showed that 90 percent of all foreign fighters entered Iraq through Syria. And while Syrians only made up 8 percent of all fighters, they ranked third after Saudis and Libyans. The documents were quickly released to the Combating Terrorism Center (CTC) at West Point for analysis. What the CTC would eventually find, together with Israel's bombing raid at what would become known as Al Kibar, would challenge basic assumptions about the Syrian regime that would detrimentally affect its relations well into the next US administration.[30]

8

WEATHERING THE STORM

The loud boom stopped me in my tracks in the evening of February 12, 2008, as I entered the bedroom of my apartment in the Damascus neighborhood of Jisr al-Abyad. In Beirut, explosions were common, be they fireworks or car bombs, but in Assad's Syria, explosions were rare, as the regime kept a tight lid on security throughout the country. When I awoke the next morning, the news said that a car bomb in Damascus had killed Imad Mughniyeh, the senior Hezbollah operative.

Mughniyeh was perhaps the Middle East's most shadowy figure. The US government held him responsible as the mastermind behind the 1983 bombing of the US embassy in Beirut, which killed sixty-three people. Washington also blamed Mughniyeh for the bombing of the US marine barracks at Beirut's airport later that year. Mughniyeh was also indicted by a US court for the June 1985 hijacking of TWA Flight 847, in which Navy Airman Robert Stethem was murdered onboard and his body dropped from the plane onto the tarmac at Beirut's airport. Prior to the September 11 attacks, Mughniyeh was responsible for the deaths of more Americans than any other foreign national since World War II. As a good friend said to me on the day of his death, he was Osama bin Laden before Osama bin Laden.[1] It was the end of an era, and, while I didn't know it then, it signaled the beginning of the end of my time in Damascus.

The circumstances surrounding the blast were odd indeed. He had been killed in Kfar Suseh, a recently built upmarket housing development in Damascus where the country's first two shopping malls were being built. The area is adjacent the headquarters of a number of the country's seven security services. On the facade of the headquarters of the Palestine Branch of Military Intelligence—Syria's most feared intelligence agency and the one closest to the blast site—two neon signs above the building's main entrance read ASSAD FOREVER. If ever there was a geographic center of the dark side of the Assad regime, it was here.

As rumors and reports of the blast circulated throughout Damascus the following day, comparing notes just led to more questions. A foreign marketing executive with *Syria Today*, who had been walking back from the Cham City Center Mall in Kfar Suseh to a nearby hotel at the time, actually saw the blast—including a ball of flame extending three or four stories into the air. There were peculiarities about how the story broke as well. The first to report the blast was an Iranian TV station, which showed grainy cellphone video of the fire. This was highly unusual, as the state theoretically controlled all satellite uplinks in Syria. For whatever reason, Iranian news agencies used their own satellite uplink, giving viewers in Iran, as well as the outside world, live coverage of the event.[2]

Then there were larger questions. For example, how could this happen in a country renowned for security? It wasn't the first assassination by car bomb in Damascus, as an attempt had been made on the life of a Palestinian official a few years before, but it missed its target and was far too small to do the job. But if it was an outside power that organized this bomb, how could they have penetrated the security surrounding one of the world's most-wanted men, who had a twenty-five-million-dollar bounty on his head? And perhaps most importantly, what was Mughniyeh doing in Damascus?[3]

Iranian foreign minister Manouchehr Mottaki visited Damascus the next day for consultations with the Assad regime. The following morning, Iranian deputy foreign minister Ali Reza Sheikh Attar announced that Mottaki had agreed with the Syrians to establish a joint Iranian-Syrian-Hezbollah investigation to "look into the root causes and dimensions of the assassination to identify the perpetrators of this dirty crime."[4] Syria's state-run Syrian Arab News Agency branded Attar's announcement as "baseless," however, indicating a growing rift between Syria and its patron, Iran.[5]

Other signs over the next few months seemed to reinforce this idea. A high-profile project to replace Damascus's aging public-bus fleet with Iranian vehicles that ran on natural gas was mysteriously canceled and awarded to a Chinese company, even though the Chinese buses burned diesel fuel, of which Syria was running increasingly short.

The Syrian government continued to drag its feet on cutting import tariffs on two high-profile Iranian-Syrian joint ventures to assemble cars in Syria—the first in the country's history. This was particularly hard to understand, as the Syrian government owned a 35-percent stake in one of the projects. Syria's state investment office released statistics that put direct Iranian investment in Syria at $544 million, a mere 8 percent of total Arab investment in Syria. This contradicted earlier reports coming from Iran—citing Syrian government statistics—that put Iranian investment at 66 percent of all Arab investment in the country.[6]

In Washington, policy makers struggled to make sense of Syria's moves, especially as tensions continued to rise in Lebanon. The renewed term of the country's president, Émile Lahoud, had expired the previous November, leaving Lebanon in a constitutional vacuum. French president Nicolas Sarkozy launched a diplomatic initiative with Damascus to gain its support for the election of a successor. It bore early fruit: Lebanese parties and Damascus agreed on the commander of the Lebanese Army, General Michel Suleiman, to succeed Lahoud.

However, as the initiative unfolded, Hezbollah, with the support of Damascus, continued to insist on a "guaranteed third" of the deputies in the Lebanese cabinet. This would ensure Hezbollah's veto over all government decisions, most notably the tribunal into the death of Hariri. Since Hezbollah had suspended its participation in the cabinet in November 2006, Prime Minister Siniora's government had ruled without Shiite participation—which was something it legally could do, but which did not conform with the Lebanese state's tradition that all of the country's seventeen sects had to participate in government in order for it to be legitimate.

When Lahoud's term ended on November 23, he left the powers of the Lebanese presidency in the hands of the Suleiman-commanded Lebanese Army. After a number of attempts to reach a negotiated settlement, Sarkozy broke off talks with Damascus at the end of December.

Those advocating the "wedge theory"—engaging Syria and promoting peace with Israel to cut Syria off from Iran and Hezbollah—saw Mughniyeh's assassination and its aftermath as a sign that Syria was preparing to back away from Iran. Back in November, the United States had invited Syria to attend the Annapolis peace conference, and Syria's deputy foreign minister, Faisal Mekdad, attended the meeting. Since then, however, there seemed to have been few signs that Syria was preparing to bury the hatchet with its old foe, Israel.

Information on Syria quickly became a source of great contention. At an event hosted at Washington's Henry L. Stimson Center on April 23, 2008, I delivered a presentation opposite Daniel Levy, an advocate for peace negotiations between Israel and Syria, and Emile El-Hokayem, who put forward a tough line on Damascus. My presentation outlined recent events that showed Damascus was pushing back on Iranian influence in Syria. When it came to US policy, however, I said that US sanctions were having mixed effects. On the one hand, more US consumer goods, such as iPhones, software, and computers, were available from reexporters in Dubai and Lebanon, significantly watering down the effect of the US trade ban on Damascus. On the other, Washington's recent move to sanction President Assad's cousin, Rami Makhlouf, for "regime corruption" had made significant waves in Damascus, especially among the country's business elite.[7]

The next day, a version of my comments made it into the pages of the Kuwaiti Arabic daily *Al Rai*. While covering my comments on Syria's relationship with Iran was fine, the paper quoted me on the United States's sanctioning of Assad's cousin—it was "very smart, as the regime relies on him a lot"—which was going to get me in trouble. Making matters worse, I didn't even remember saying those words.

Later that same afternoon, I attended a hearing on Capitol Hill for the Syrian opposition in exile. As I walked up to the hearing room, an Arabic television channel was interviewing Ammar Abdulhamid, my former colleague from MAWRED who had moved to Washington and headed the MEPI-funded Tharwa project. He had recently met President Bush at the White House as part of a delegation from the Syrian opposition. His wife, Khawla Yusuf, ran up to me, pointed her finger in my face, and shouted, "You! You! Why did you say you bought an iPhone in Damascus?" When I answered that I had and it was simply the truth, she shouted, "It doesn't matter! Everyone is talking about it!" It seemed that no matter what I said about Syria, I was taking flak from both the regime and its opponents.

Other news on Syria that day would eclipse the conference, however. The CIA had briefed Congress on the site that Israel bombed in eastern Syria the previous September. A six-minute video showed that the site, located near the Syrian town of Al Kibar, was similar in structure to a North Korean–designed, gas-cooled, graphite-moderated nuclear reactor—the same model that International Atomic Energy Agency inspectors were trying to shut down outside Pyongyang. Only North Korea had constructed such nuclear reactors in the past thirty-five years.

The video included not only satellite photography—common to presentations on North Korea and Iraq's WMD programs—but detailed still photos of the reactor under construction. One picture even showed the director of Syria's nuclear program arm in arm with his North Korean counterpart; in the background of the photo was a car with Damascene license plates. The video reported that the reactor's water-pumping station along the Euphrates had been completed at the end of August 2007, meaning that the reactor was close to operation.[8]

The Syrian embassy in Washington immediately issued a statement denouncing the "campaign of false allegations," saying it was designed by the Bush administration to "misguide the US Congress and international public opinion in order to justify the Israeli raid in September of 2007, which the current US administration may have helped execute." The statement added that "this manoeuvre on the part of this administration comes within the framework of the North Korean nuclear negotiations."[9]

While analysts and journalists were reviewing the announcement, the Syrian embassy in Washington called a press conference the following afternoon at the residence of Syrian ambassador Imad Moustapha. He said that the CIA had "fabricated" the pictures, and he predicted that in the coming weeks the US story about the site would "implode from within."

When I returned to Damascus a few days later, I found that most people had chalked up the nuclear video to Washington's efforts to pressure North Korea to negotiate on its nuclear program. The release of the video had come at the end of a two-day meeting between US and North Korean officials in which Washington failed to reach an agreement with Pyongyang.

Syria tried to undermine the credibility of US intelligence as well. In an April 27 interview in the Qatar daily paper *Al-Watan*, President Assad said, "Does it make sense that we would build a nuclear facility in the desert and not protect it with anti-aircraft defences? . . . A nuclear site exposed to (spy) satellites, in the heart of Syria and in an open space?" Assad added that the building was an unused military building—which was the same explanation that the Syrian government had made following the attack.[10]

The spin didn't stop there. Syria's ambassador to the United Kingdom, Sami Khiyami, told *The Guardian* newspaper that US intelligence was unreliable, referring to secretary of state Colin Powell's presentation to the UN Security Council about Iraq's weapons of mass destruction program—allegations that ultimately proved untrue.

Samir al-Taqi, the director of the Orient Center for International Studies, a think tank rumored to be closely associated with Syria's foreign ministry and security services, told *Syria Today* that Syria would "make a full disclosure because they have the best defence: innocence. Syria will be able to demonstrate that it has adhered to all of its international obligations."[11] He questioned why the United States had waited so long to present the evidence: "If there had been any real evidence about a Syrian nuclear facility, the US and Israel would have gone straight to the UN because that would have been the most difficult thing for Syria to deal with. The fact that they bombed first and therefore destroyed any of their supposed evidence is proof they had no proof." He blamed the video's release on neoconservatives in the Bush administration. "They want to sink any possible peace accord and I think one is really possible. The Syrians are serious about it and it is the first time since Rabin that an Israeli leader has acknowledged the return of the Golan is the price Israel must pay for peace," he said.[12]

As the number of issues between the United States and Syria grew, the regime became increasingly sensitive to criticism. When I returned to my desk at the *Syria Today* offices following my Washington trip, I noticed that something was out of the ordinary. Staff members seemed a bit reticent to talk, and some seemed to be staying away from work. After a few days, a friend told me that someone from the Palestine Branch of Military Intelligence ("Palestine" referring to Israel) had stopped by the *Syria Today* offices to talk with people about my political beliefs.

I began asking around, and sources told me that someone from the Syrian embassy in Washington had reported me to Syrian intelligence regarding my presentation and a recent article I had written on the Syrian opposition. This was not a complete surprise—in the spring of 2007 I had a professional dispute with Joshua Landis, whose blog, Syria Comment, had become noticeably closer to the Syrian regime's line following the Hariri assassination and the 2006 war in Lebanon. It was a small but important matter; Landis had cited one of my articles in his autumn 2007 journal article on the Syrian opposition to prove his assertion that a Syrian opposition figure, Michel Kilo, had met the Muslim Brotherhood two days after Hariri's assassination. My article did not make that claim, as I could not prove the assertion and was sensitive to the fact that Kilo, who was standing trial at that time, could be affected. After a number of attempts to settle the matter, I asked the journal for a clarification, which they granted.[13] Landis is widely known to be close to Imad Moustapha, whom Landis quotes regularly on his blog. Only a few weeks before the Palestine Branch showed up at *Syria Today*, I interviewed Moustapha during work on a report on US-Syrian relations for the International Crisis Group. During the interview, the kind and welcoming Moustapha that I had known in the past seemed annoyed by my presence.[14]

The Palestine Branch was Syria's strongest intelligence agency. Just saying its name was enough to send shivers up the spine of any Syrian, as the agency dealt with espionage from Israel. Suddenly I was caught in a dilemma: if I left Damascus and spoke openly about what I knew, I would almost certainly be cut off from my professional livelihood. But if I stayed in Damascus, I would have to toe the regime's new hard lines on the nuclear file, on jihadists infiltrating Iraq from Syria, and on the deteriorating human rights situation in the country. As I didn't know where the new red lines would be set, the chances

were high that I would trip over them, putting not only my own position in Syria in jeopardy but my colleagues at *Syria Today* in jeopardy
as well.

It was time for me to go. I tendered my resignation to the magazine's owner, Abdul Ghani Attar, moved my base of operations to Beirut, and began writing this book.

After nearly five months without a president in Lebanon and sixteen
months with a capital divided between the tent cities of the Hezbollah-led opposition and the prime minister's palace, tensions in Beirut
finally came to a boil in early May. Walid Jumblatt, then a pillar of
Lebanon's pro-independence government and sharp critic of Syria and
Hezbollah, accused the latter of using cameras to monitor the runways
at Beirut's international airport. It was a sensitive area—it was located
in the Lebanese capital's Hezbollah-dominated southern suburbs and
was allegedly one of the group's ports for arms shipments from Iran.
Jumblatt also accused Hezbollah of operating its own fiber-optic telephone network, which could be used to monitor the calls of private
citizens. A few days later, the Lebanese cabinet ordered a judicial
investigation into the network. They also fired General Wafiq Shuqeir,
the head of security at Beirut airport and a close ally of the Lebanese
parliamentary speaker Nabih Berri, whose political movement, Amal,
was aligned with Hezbollah.

Hezbollah immediately branded the inquiry into the fiber-optic
system an "act of war," as the organization's military wing relied heavily on the network to communicate with its forces throughout the
country. Hezbollah fighters quickly set up checkpoints and road-
blocks throughout Beirut. They met only token resistance from private security guards hired by March 14 leader Saad Hariri. Hezbollah
also overran the Hariri-owned Future Television in west Beirut, setting its offices on fire. Hezbollah forces quickly surrounded Hariri's

mansion in the suburb of Koreitem as well as Jumblatt's nearby offices at Clemenceau.

In the space of a few hours, Hezbollah had completely taken over west Beirut, dealing Siniora's government a blow to its already embittered prestige.[15] Siniora issued a statement calling the takeover a "bloody coup" aiming "to return Syria to Lebanon and extend Iran's reach to the Mediterranean."[16] Fighting continued in and around Beirut for six days. The Lebanese Army stood by and watched, refusing to get involved. The reaction of both Damascus and Washington indicated that both wanted a negotiated settlement to the crisis. President Assad branded the eruption of violence an "internal matter," while Secretary of State Rice simply said that "the United States stands by the Lebanese government and peaceful citizens of Lebanon through this crisis and provides the support they need to weather this storm."[17]

Two weeks later in Qatar, Lebanon's factions met face to face, along with representatives from Syria, Saudi Arabia, and Iran. On May 21, 2008, an agreement was hammered out whereby General Michel Suleiman would immediately be elected president of Lebanon. Until the next parliamentary elections, which would be held in June 2009, the Lebanese cabinet would include eleven of the sixteen ministers from the Hezbollah-led opposition bloc, thus giving it a "blocking third plus one" of deputies and allowing them to veto any cabinet decision, most notably the Hariri tribunal.

As soon as word reached Beirut of the agreement, Hezbollah and its opposition supporters immediately began pulling down their tent cities in Beirut's central Martyrs' Square. The following morning, the army arrived, rolled up the barbed wire, and took down the opposition banners and posters. One of the last to be removed featured the head of Secretary of State Rice superimposed on the body of a school teacher; her eyes and mouth had been poked through. Sitting in front of her, wearing a dunce cap, was Fouad Siniora. The top of the poster read A LESSON IN THE NEW MIDDLE EAST.

As the Lebanese Army ripped down the barricades in Beirut, Israel announced that it would begin indirect peace talks with Syria under Turkish mediation. For months there had been rumors of Track II (civilian talks blessed by the authorities) and other secret talks between the two countries. A month before the showdown in Beirut, Assad had told the Qatari daily *Al-Watan* that Damascus and Jerusalem had been exchanging messages via Turkish prime minister Recep Tayyip Erdogan since April 2007. A statement from Prime Minister Olmert's office in Israel said that "both sides have declared their intention to hold these talks openly. . . . They decided to hold a serious and continuous dialogue, with the intention of arriving at an embracing peace treaty, in accordance with the framework [laid down by the 1991] Madrid peace conference."[18]

The first round of talks, held on June 15 and 16, reportedly ended with a "positive atmosphere." Both sides played down talk of direct negotiations, as they needed to work on a number of technical issues concerning the border. While details of the talks remained restricted, a Turkish source told the Israel daily *Haaretz* that "the talks are being held on the basis of an agreement in principle that Israel will withdraw from the Golan Heights in return for normalization of relations between Syria and Israel. The nature of that normalization, its extent and stages will be discussed at a later stage."

While the parameters of the potential agreement were nothing new—these more or less matched the last round of talks in Geneva in May 2000—the big news was that France was creating a diplomatic path for Assad to Washington. The Turkish source added that an invitation by President Sarkozy to the July 14 Bastille Day celebrations could be "a significant launchpad for furthering the process; however Assad is expecting American mediation and this can only happen following the presidential elections in the United States."[19]

When Assad arrived in Paris, Syrian TV broadcast video footage of him and Asma walking along a line of bronze-helmeted honor guards with swords drawn. A day before the Syrian first family's arrival in Paris, Assad and the Lebanese president Michel Suleiman had agreed to open embassies in each other's capitals for the first time, a decision that Sarkozy described as "historic progress." While Assad came up short on the details of demarcating the border between the two countries—a much larger hurdle, as it underlined the issue of Shebaa Farms and the justification for Hezbollah's arms—Sarkozy saw Assad's decision as an opportunity to dangle the Syrian president's possible Western-oriented future in front of him.[20]

While most coverage focused on Assad meeting Sarkozy in front of the cameras, other shots included his wife at the Pompidou Center and the Louvre, looking glamorous and very much relieved to be back in the limelight.[21] Sarkozy was launching his new "Union for the Mediterranean," which nominally included the countries of the European Union and both Israel and Syria. Following the military parade on the Champs-Élysées, the paparazzi focused on Assad and Olmert as they weaved through the crowd on the VIP grandstand, each trying to avoid publicly shaking the hand of the other. At times, they were a mere five feet apart. At one point, after a brief conversation with the Emir of Qatar, while Olmert spoke with Egyptian president Hosni Mubarak, Assad was left awkwardly standing alone in the grandstand.[22]

While Assad's isolation was effectively over, not everyone was happy about his presence in Paris. A group of French veterans accused Syria of supporting the 1983 bombing of the French paratrooper barracks in Beirut—which occurred simultaneously with the attack on the US marine barracks near Beirut's airport—and said that Assad should not have been invited to France's national festival celebrating human rights. An opposition Socialist Party leader, François Hollande, said that Assad "tainted" the ceremony, citing Syria as one of the most repressive regimes in the Arab world.[23]

In Damascus, the mood ironically turned suddenly more authoritarian. No journalism visas were issued for foreigners during the last two weeks of June, which delayed my first post–*Syria Today* visit to Damascus. From June 22 to 25, Syria allowed IAEA inspectors to visit the site bombed by Israel in September 2007 at Al Kibar.[24] While no details were known about the site, satellite photographs showed that the regime had cleared the rubble and constructed a square-shaped building in its place. The inspectors visited the site to take samples, then visited the country's research reactor outside Damascus, a facility that had been declared to the IAEA in keeping with the country's safeguards agreement.

The regime intensified its crackdown on the Damascus Declaration as well. Syria's state security services arrested more than forty activists following a meeting held by the Damascus Declaration on December 1, 2007. The meeting, which attracted more than one hundred sixty Syrians, resulted in the creation of the Damascus Declaration's "National Council"—the body of opposition and pro-democracy groups that activists had attempted to set up in the spring of 2006, shortly before the outbreak of the Lebanon War. Those elected to the National Council were detained and charged in January 2008 with breaking provisions of Syria's Civil Code, including "weakening national sentiments," "spreading false information," and actions "encouraging conflict among sects." Included in the group was Dr. Fida al-Hourani, a gynecologist and the woman elected as the National Council's first president. All were transferred to Syrian prisons, where their lawyers claimed they were tortured. In October 2008, the National Council was collectively sentenced to two and a half years in prison.[25]

With Assad in Paris and Syria talking to Israel in Ankara, the way now seemed open for Syrian contact with the United States. In the last two weeks of July, the US-based organization Search for Common Ground hosted a group of Syrian pundits and academics in Washington. Tom Dine, a former head of the American Israel Public Affairs Committee

(AIPAC), had formed what he called the US-Syria Working Group to "find ways to overcome the very bad state of US-Syrian relations." Search for Common Ground had visited Damascus in July 2007 on the advice of Robert Malley, head of the Middle East section of the International Crisis Group. It was the only think tank to have an official office in Damascus, which was staffed by Peter Harling, a Frenchman with extensive experience in Iraq.

The chief of the Syrian delegation was Samir al-Taqi. In the year leading up to the meeting, the center's previously humble offices along the Mezze highway in Damascus had more than doubled in size. Also on the delegation was Samir Seifan, a former economic adviser to President Assad and one of the country's "new guard" reformers who were sidelined in the years after Bashar's rise to power. Rounding out the delegation was Sami Moubayed, a historian at Syria's Kalamoun University and the founder of the English-language magazine *Forward*.

Visitors from US think tanks and newspapers packed the hall at the Brookings Institution's Saban Center for Middle East Policy to hear what they had to say. While a number of Syrians or people closely associated with Syria had visited Washington during the Bush administration's isolation of the regime, the Syrian participants' close ties to their government meant that their visit signified not just Track II negotiations, but something closer to "Track 1.5." In his opening remarks, Dine said that the visit was designed "to find ways to build trust, to find ways to overcome the very bad state of US-Syrian relations."[26]

Al-Taqi laid out Syria's position at the start: the Bush administration's attempt to isolate the Syrian regime had failed, and its huge effort to destroy the regional state system had given rise to nonstate actors such as Hezbollah and Hamas. Al-Taqi added that the situation was getting "very, very, very risky" and that the region needed a "safety network" involving the United States "to hug it, to prevent it from collapsing." He added that if the Bush administration's "confrontational attitude is withdrawn vis-à-vis Syria," which he added had been "very much fabricated," then Syria was ready to be a "solution provider."

During the question-and-answer session, various participants asked questions about what Syria believed that solution might look like. On the question of what Syria would do concerning the IAEA's recent investigation into its alleged nuclear program, al-Taqi predicted that Syria would fully cooperate, as something about Israel's bombing of the facility seemed "funny." Using a metaphor, al-Taqi said that Israel had "killed a man, buried him, and then accused him," and he compared the allegations to Colin Powell's testimony before the Security Council on Iraq's WMD program prior to the 2003 invasion of Iraq. On Syria's relationship with Hezbollah, al-Taqi refused to say if Syria would cut off arms to Hezbollah, but instead he said that Syria would be "cooperative" if Lebanon found that "it's time to gradually integrate Hezbollah within the army." Concerning Iraq, al-Taqi said that the Syrian government no longer saw its biggest danger from Lebanon but from a "federal confessional state in Baghdad, a weak confessional state." In dealing with all these major issues, however, al-Taqi said, "Unless there is a real perspective towards peace, all the other elements of the conflict will continue to be there. There is no prepayment. . . . Syria will not close all, any of its opportunities just in case, you never know."

After al-Taqi finished his talk, Sami Moubayed took the microphone. He described the problem between the United States and Syria as a "difference in perception. If the Bush administration has been saying we are agents of destabilization . . . if that is correct . . . that means, by default, we are agents of stability as well." To prove his point, Moubayed said that Syria had "played a role" in setting free BBC reporter Alan Johnston, who had been kidnapped by Hamas, as well as the fifteen British sailors who had been captured by Iran in 2007. Echoing al-Taqi's talk, Moubayed said that Syria's number one priority had shifted to Iraq, where Syria now had an interest "to play a stabilizing role." He concluded by saying, however, that there were limits to what Syria could do to patrol Syria's 605-kilometer frontier with Iraq. "So, to the best of our abilities, we have been trying to keep a secure border."[27]

When the group returned to Damascus, they brought with them a notable sense of triumphalism. The US-Syria Working Group had traveled to Houston, Texas, where they were hosted by Edward P. Djerejian, head of the James L. Baker III Institute for Public Policy at Rice University and the former ambassador to Syria who had helped build the last period of "constructive engagement" during the 1990s. Djerejian told his visitors an anecdote about his discussion with the late Israeli prime minister Yitzhak Rabin about the highlight of his career: his appointment as US ambassador to Syria. Rabin wished Djerejian luck and warned him to be careful of "loopholes" in what the United States was offering Syria, as "Hafez al-Assad will drive a truck through it."

Picking up on Djerejian's theme, Moubayed penned an op-ed entitled "Driving Trucks Through US Loopholes," which outlined how Bashar had "driven a truck" through US policy in the Middle East. On Iraq, Moubayed said that the United States had failed to bring security to Iraq and that Syria could offer to help the United States with exiled Iraqi Baathists in Syria "through dialogue, or aggressively, by threatening . . . to return many busloads of Iraqis to [prime minister Nouri] al-Maliki's Iraq."

Concerning Iran, Moubayed said that US isolation had driven Damascus into the arms of Tehran but that the United States could now capitalize on that by using Syria as a broker with Tehran to convince it to stop enriching uranium. On peace with Israel, Moubayed said that isolation hadn't worked and that a peace accord between Syria and Israel would be a "complete strategic package that would redefine the balance of power" in the region.

Echoing al-Taqi's comments in Washington, Moubayed said Syria would not break its ties with Hamas and Hezbollah but would instead play the role of "back-channel to people like Hamas' exiled leader Khaled Meshaal and Hezbollah leader Hassan Nasrallah." Moubayed also warned Israel not to drag its feet, as "non-state players may work hard at changing the mood in either Israel or Syria to drown the peace treaty. . . . The Syrians aren't suffering if peace is not signed; it is Israel that suffers."

On Lebanon, Moubayed declared complete victory, calling the Doha Accord ending the standoff "tailor-made for the Syrians," as they had got all they were asking for and "pro-Syrian figures were brought back to government and Michel Suleiman, a pro-Syrian general, was made president."

Concluding his story, Moubayed used a quote from the comment section of Syria Comment. A Syrian who lived abroad had recently returned to Damascus and wrote about what he saw: "I found people going about their daily lives as they did before, but this time with a strong sense of Syrian pride of standing together and surviving the storm that was hatched in the dark alleys of the White House. The feeling was that the whole world conspired against them and the Syrians finally won."[28]

EPILOGUE

THE EXPECTATIONS GAP AND THE ADVENT OF THE ARAB SPRING

A s the sun prepared to set on October 26, 2008, over the farms of Al-Sukkariya, a Syrian enclave five miles west of the Iraqi frontier city of Qaim, three US helicopters hovered over a group of buildings. According to reports by Syria's state news agency, a number of US troops descended "from helicopters and attacked a civilian building under construction and opened fire on workers inside—including the wife of the building guard—leading to [the deaths] of eight civilians. . . .The helicopters then left Syrian territory towards Iraqi territory."[1] One witness in the area, who was somehow able to log onto the BBC website despite the regime's close monitoring of Internet traffic in the country, said that those killed were from the al-Mashada tribe, which has members near the Iraqi city of Tikrit—the hometown of late Iraqi dictator Saddam Hussein and the heart of the Sunni insurgency in the country. The mystery source said that the people there were "very relaxed, laid-back people, not very religious—there's no Mujahideen from this tribe. The guard and the woman who died were very simple people."[2]

The following morning, however, US sources quietly confirmed the death of someone far more complex and lethal: Badran Turki Hishan al-Mazidih, an Iraqi national sanctioned by the US Treasury Department back in February for "facilitating and controlling the flow of money, weapons, terrorists, and other resources through Syria to al-Qaeda in Iraq (AQI)." A US military official said the raid demonstrated that US forces were "taking matters into [their] own hands" to shut down the networks of al-Qaeda–linked foreign fighters moving between Syria and Iraq and using the former as a safe haven.[3] In the coming days, reports emerged that the attack was one of a dozen of previously undisclosed US special-forces raids on al-Qaeda militants in Syria and Pakistan.[4] The details of the raid differed from the line that Syrian members of the US-Syria Working Group had sold in Washington the previous summer. If Syria's primary interest now focused on Iraq—over fears of sectarian strife in that country spilling into Syria—what were al-Qaeda fighters still doing camped out on its territory?

Damascus responded by closing the Damascus Community School—the American academy attended by Damascus's elite that had remained formally unlicensed since its establishment in 1957 as part of a general effort to keep Syria out of the Soviet camp in the Cold War.[5] The state also closed the American Cultural Center, which was housed in a building adjacent to the US embassy in Damascus and which organized community outreach and hosted the weekly and very popular "American movie night." The center was preparing for a US election party, scheduled for the early hours of November 5 as the polls closed in the United States. The regime also closed the American Language Center (ALC), which is associated with the US embassy.

The center's closure was also the preemptive end of my relationship with Syria. I had planned to travel from Beirut to Damascus to attend the event and write about people's reactions—a natural scene to conclude this story and set the stage for what I thought would be a reconciliation between Damascus and Washington. Following the attack, however, the regime clamped down on visas for Americans, and I stayed in Beirut. I never had a chance to say good-bye to my friends in Damascus or my colleagues at *Syria Today*.

A little over a week later, on November 4, the American people elected Barack Hussein Obama as the forty-fourth president of the United States. His early campaign promises to engage unconditionally with Iran and Syria led many close to the Syrian regime to believe that the new president would quickly come knocking on the doors of Damascus. Two days later, Syria's state-run newspaper *Al-Thawra* ran an article saying that Syria "extends its hand" to president-elect Barack Obama. Sami Moubayed—the editor in chief of *Forward*, the English-language monthly magazine, and a member of the US-Syria Working Group—also penned the piece "Abu Hussein's Invitation to Damascus." He wrote that Damascus would "use its weight in the region to moderate the behavior of non-state players like Hezbollah in Lebanon and Hamas in Palestine, and find solutions for the US standoff with Iran over its nuclear program." In return, Moubayed listed ten things that Obama had to do to be "greeted with open arms in Damascus, like Jimmy Carter and Bill Clinton." While Moubayed later insisted that his article reflected only his own views, journalists and analysts widely regarded them as reflecting those of the Syrian regime.[6] The requirements included the following:

- The appointment of a US ambassador to Syria. This would be accompanied by greater room to maneuver for Syria's ambassador to the United States, Imad Moustapha, who was spurned by the Bush administration because of his criticism of how Bush treated Syria.
- An end to the anti-Syrian rhetoric coming from the White House and the State Department since 2003. That would automatically reduce the anti-Syrian sentiment in the US media.
- Recognition of Syria's cooperation with Iraq on border security.
- Cooperation with Syria to deal with the 1.5 million Iraqi refugees in Syria.

- The lifting—in due course—of the sanctions that were imposed on Damascus.
- The abolition of the SAA.
- Willingness to sponsor Syria's indirect peace talks with Israel, currently on hold in Turkey. That was something Bush curtly refused to do since the talks started in April 2008; he claimed that Syria was more interested in a peace process than a peace treaty. Syria is sincere, and the new White House must acknowledge that to deliver peaceful results in the Middle East. The United States's willingness to serve as an honest broker could make the talks successful, the Syrians believe. Its participation could transform the talks from indirect to direct negotiations. Syria is determined to regain the occupied Golan Heights (taken by Israel during the Arab-Israeli war of 1967), and Obama must help Syria achieve that if he is sincere about change in the region.
- Recognition that no problems can be solved in the Middle East without Syria with regard to the Palestinians, Iraqis, and Lebanese. Bush launched his famous "roadmap" for peace between Israel and Palestine, but he bypassed the Syrians. If another roadmap were to be launched, Syria would have to be included.
- Help Syria combat Islamic fundamentalism, which has been flowing into its territory from north Lebanon and Iraq.
- An apology, compensation, and explanation for the air raid on Syria that left eight Syrian civilians dead in October 2008.
- Help normalize relations between Syria and America on a people-to-people level, which have been strained since 2001 when Bush came to power. That would include giving visas to Syrians wanting to study or work in the United States.

From Damascus and the region, Syria's "triumphalism" must have seemed justified.[7] The Assad regime had outlasted not only the Bush administration's isolation and confrontation policy but also the administration itself. However, to accomplish this, the Assad regime had concocted an eclectic and potentially volatile mixture of policies. To fight the United States and its allies in Iraq, Damascus allowed al-Qaeda–affiliated foreign-fighter networks to cross its territory into Iraq, where they were responsible for some of the conflict's most spectacular attacks. This policy undermined the notion I and others had entertained following the September 11 attacks that a minority-led Alawite regime would never allow its territory to be used by Sunni extremists like al-Qaeda. That action plus the regime's domestic outreach to Islam increased Assad's domestic legitimacy at the expense of weakening the secular regime his father, Hafez, had built. He also continued the repressive aspects of his father's rule by arresting regime opponents and perpetuating horrific human rights abuses. In Lebanon, Damascus had deepened its ties with Hezbollah to historic levels to contain the March 14 coalition, including frequent public meetings between President Assad and Hezbollah leader Hassan Nasrallah, a man that Bashar's father had always held at arm's length. To cement this relationship, Assad brought his country into a closer orbit with Iran, forming the "resistance axis" of countries allied against US and Israeli interests in the region. Last but not least, Assad appeared to have started a nuclear program, either as a deterrent against Israel or as part of a second Iranian nuclear program or, perhaps, both.

While the Assad regime might have survived the worst that the Bush administration would throw at it, the things the regime had to do to survive made reconciliation with the United States even more difficult, and the high-level engagement Damascus had hoped for didn't materialize. An expectations gap rapidly grew between both countries.

Less than a week after Moubayed's article, the IAEA put Syria on the agenda of its November 19 board of governors' meeting. Among the environmental samples taken during its June 2008 inspection of the Al Kibar site, the IAEA had found traces of uranium that were not part of Syria's declared inventory of nuclear material. Damascus later blamed the presence of uranium on Israeli depleted-uranium munitions that might have been used to destroy the facility, but nuclear experts doubted that the kind of uranium found at the site—anthropogenic, or man-manipulated, uranium—was in any way similar to depleted uranium. In subsequent reports, the IAEA said that it found the same type of particles at Syria's declared research reactor outside Damascus as well. While the Syrian regime stopped answering questions on Al Kibar in September 2008, it continued to allow inspectors access to Syria's research reactor and provided two sets of explanations for the presence of the particles. The IAEA rejected both explanations, and in June 2011 the IAEA board announced publicly what was known privately: Syria appeared to have constructed a nuclear reactor. As of the time of writing, the investigation was still ongoing.[8]

With tensions between the two countries mounting and Damascus anticipating high-level engagement with the incoming Obama administration, the regime began a comprehensive crackdown on journalists in Syria, forcing them to toe the regime's line. Given what I knew about Syria's recent behavior, investigations by the Syrian authorities into my political beliefs, and my inability to obtain a visa, I accepted a new fellowship with the Washington Institute for Near East Policy—a think tank that had been critical of Syrian policies during the Bush administration. My fellowship dealt with how to engage Syria and maintain US national-security interests. In the United States, I visited Leila, who had left Syria in May 2007 to study journalism. While Leila didn't like the Washington Institute's position on Syria and was critical of my work, she understood that I was leaving Syria behind.

Those advocating a quick rapprochement with Damascus pointed to rumors that the indirect peace talks between Israel and Syria under Turkish auspices in Ankara were getting tantalizingly close to a deal. The specifics of the talks were not officially announced, but by spring 2009, some details had emerged.

Syria was rumored to have asked Israel for clarification regarding six points along the "line of June 4, 1967"—the line of separation between Israeli and Syrian forces before the former captured the Golan

Heights two days later. Syria was also rumored to have agreed to cede its riparian rights to the Sea of Galilee, though not of the Jordan River, and to the immediate exchange of ambassadors and the "normalization of relations" with Israel while Israeli forces disengaged from the Golan Heights in stages over three to eight years. The Golan would be demilitarized and turned into a "peace park," which would allow Israelis access without visas. This was an idea first developed by Frederic Hof—a longtime Levant observer and a close associate of Senator George Mitchell—whose report on the Palestinian-Israeli conflict in 2001 had recommended rebuilding the Palestinian Authority following the al-Aqsa intifada, ending all Israeli settlement activity and Palestinian violence. Last but not least, Syria had apparently agreed to allow Lebanon to pursue its own negotiations with Israel.

These hopes for progress were dashed on December 22, 2008, however, when Hamas refused to renew the ceasefire with Israel and began shooting hundreds of rockets per day into Israel. Israel responded with a massive incursion into Gaza, code-named Cast Lead. Syria then broke off the indirect talks in Ankara. When the conflict ended in early January, Israelis had become increasingly cynical about the benefits of returning territory for peace. In elections on February 10, 2009, the Kadima Party, led by Tzipi Livni, earned one more Knesset seat than Benjamin Netanyahu's Likud Party. However, other right-of-center parties gathered around Likud did better, causing Israel's president, Shimon Peres, to ask Netanyahu to form a government. The coalition that Netanyahu formed was skeptical of progress on the Syrian track and refused to return to indirect talks. Instead, it advocated talks with no preconditions (that is, no commitment to the June 4, 1967, line) under American auspices.

So with peace talks on hold, secretary of state Hillary Clinton dispatched assistant secretary of state for Near East affairs Jeffrey Feltman on February 26, 2009, for talks with the Syrian ambassador to Washington, Imad Moustapha. The president was rumored to have given Clinton two instructions. The first was that his administration was elected on the idea of engagement with America's adversaries and that Washington would work with Damascus as part of that effort. The second was that a victory by Hezbollah and its allies in the elections scheduled for June 7 should be avoided at all costs—therefore, engagement with Syria should not come at the expense of US allies in Lebanon.

Feltman was not the engager that Syria had in mind, given his previous tenure as ambassador to Lebanon during Syria's forced withdrawal from the country following Hariri's assassination in February 2005. Syrian foreign minister Walid al-Moallem had once quipped to UN secretary-general Ban Ki-moon that "Feltman should leave [Lebanon]; I'm prepared to pay for his vacation to Hawaii."[9] In the first meeting with Moustapha, Feltman raised the issues of Syria's "support to terrorist groups and networks, acquisition of nuclear and nonconventional weaponry, interference in Lebanon, and worsening human rights situation."

Syrian-regime analysts immediately attacked Feltman in the press for using the "language of the neocons." Following the meeting, however, both sides labeled the talks "constructive," leading to another round of discussions in Damascus on March 7 between Feltman and National Security Council Middle East director Daniel Shapiro and Moallem. Following the talks, Feltman announced that both sides had found "a lot of common ground" and that instead of setting "benchmarks" for Damascus, each side was watching the future "choices" of the other.

Two days later, Assad stepped into the fray. In the ensuing twenty-three days, he gave six interviews to international media—this was unprecedented for a Syrian president over such a short period of time. Rather than dealing with the issues discussed during Feltman and Shapiro's visit, however, Assad targeted Israel, offering it only a cold peace. He blamed outgoing Israeli prime minister Ehud Olmert for the failure of recent indirect Syrian-Israeli negotiations and refused to talk about cutting ties with Hezbollah, Hamas, and Tehran. In another interview, Assad implied that he had been asked to mediate between

Washington and Tehran. Then, in his first-ever e-mail interview with an American journalist, Assad told *The New Yorker*'s Seymour Hersh that he not only sought US mediation with Israel, but he also wanted direct contact with President Obama.

In the June 7, 2009, Lebanese elections, the pro-West March 14 coalition achieved an unexpected victory over the Hezbollah-led opposition. A little over a week later, US Middle East peace envoy George Mitchell—together with his new special coordinator for regional affairs and point man on Syria-Israel peace talks, Frederic Hof—headed to Damascus for a first round of talks with President Assad. The discussions focused not only on getting Syria involved in possible Middle East peace talks but also on repairing bilateral relations between the two countries, most notably over the issue of foreign fighters traveling through Syria to Iraq.

Unexpectedly, Syria reiterated its earlier demand that the United States lift its sanctions—measures that until then the Syrian government had claimed had had little effect on the country. Days after the visit, the State Department announced that the United States would return its ambassador to Syria. In Mitchell's second meeting with Assad that July, the US envoy was said to have spent hours with Assad personally going over the US sanctions regime—an unusual topic for a Syrian president to be discussing with Washington's chief Middle East peace negotiator.

Signs that US sanctions were having an increased impact had been steadily growing. The Syrian economy had performed relatively well in recent years, posting an average annual economic growth rate of around 5 percent, which was fueled by high oil prices and increased investment from the Gulf. However, there were big problems. Oil production—proceeds from which account for a little less than a third of state revenues—had declined by 30 percent since 2005. And Syrian industry—accounting for 28 percent of the gross domestic product (GDP)—had contracted 15 percent as a result of its free-trade agreement with Turkey. A record three-year drought had also devastated the Syrian agricultural sector, which accounts for a quarter of Syrian economic output.

Following the global economic downturn, Syria's economic situation worsened. The collapse in oil prices forced the state to revise its budget oil price downward to $51 for light crude and $42 for heavy, which resulted in an estimated record budget deficit of $4.8 billion, or roughly 10 percent of its GDP. Although the state usually makes up for budget shortfalls by slashing investment spending—a line item that accounted for 40 percent of its 2009 budget—this tactic was becoming increasingly difficult. Syrians born in the 1980s and early 1990s, when the country was among the top-twenty fastest-growing populations in the world, were flooding the job market. According to an interview in January 2009 with the Syrian deputy prime minister for economic affairs, Abdullah Dardari, Syria needed $14 billion of investment over the next two years to meet the 6 to 7 percent economic-growth targets required to create enough jobs for the expanding workforce.

The bad economic news explained Damascus's demand that Washington drop its sanctions. In an interview with Reuters in February 2009, Dardari said that "to have normal relations between Syria and the United States, sanctions should be lifted. . . . This is going to be a very important part of any dialogue." His statements echoed those of Sami Moubayed's "Invitation to Abu Hussein" article.

These statements represented a reversal of the regime's standard rhetoric on sanctions. When the Syria Accountability and Lebanese Sovereignty Restoration Act (SAA) was implemented in May 2004, analysts that I interviewed in Damascus bragged that the sanctions would have little effect due to historically small amounts of bilateral trade. At the time it made sense. Many Syria observers—including me—questioned the effectiveness of US sanctions, as spiraling food, commodity, and oil prices drove the dollar value (but not volume) of US-Syrian trade to all-time highs.

Slowly but surely, US sanctions on Damascus had an increasing impact. The SAA, which bans all US exports to Syria (except food and medicine), hit Syrian aviation particularly hard. State-owned Syrian Air could not obtain parts for its fleet of American-made Boeing jets nor purchase new aircraft from Europe's Airbus, which also has substantial US content in its planes. The SAA also complicated Syrian oil and gas production by denying companies that operated in Syria the necessary US technology to reverse the diminishing output of Syrian crude. Indeed, in the summer of 2007, Damascus blamed electricity blackouts on the "knock-on effect" of US sanctions; companies specializing in major high-tech projects shunned operations in Syria for fear of running foul of US law. The only legal exceptions to the sanctions were export licenses for US goods for certain humanitarian purposes, such as to promote the exchange of information and to help maintain aviation safety.

At the same time, US actions targeting the state-owned Commercial Bank of Syria (CBS) exacerbated Damascus's financial woes by making it more difficult to repatriate critical oil revenues. In March 2006, the US Treasury Department's designation of CBS—the depository for the lion's share of Syria's estimated eighteen to twenty billion dollars in foreign-currency reserves—as a "primary money-laundering concern" under the USA Patriot Act led all US banks, as well as a number of European ones, to close their correspondent accounts. In anticipation of the move, Damascus switched state foreign-currency transactions from dollars to euros. Since oil, the regime's lifeline, is denominated in dollars, the switch complicated the regime's ability to fund itself. In addition, the designation scared businessmen away from CBS and toward the country's new private-sector banks, which operate under less regime control, effectively reducing the amount of cash the regime could access.

Executive orders freezing the US assets of Syrian officials likewise made global banks and investors wary of doing business with Syrian officials and regime businessmen. In May 2008, two American executives of Gulfsands Petroleum—a company contracted to boost crude output in eastern Syria—resigned, and the company moved its headquarters from the United States to the United Kingdom after one of the company's partners, business tycoon and President Assad's cousin, Rami Makhlouf, was targeted by an executive order focusing on public corruption in Syria.

Later, Washington successfully pressured the Turkish mobile-phone provider Turkcell to abandon its bid to buy Syriatel, another Makhlouf-owned business. The US move was hailed by Syria's business community, which views Makhlouf, according to a 2009 International Crisis Group report, as "a symbol of crony capitalism, resented by many colleagues for having bullied them into forced partnerships or out of lucrative deals."

By late summer 2009, rumors swirled around Washington and the Middle East that the White House was preparing to turn a new page with Damascus. The first test of this new relationship would be over the issue that caused the breakdown in US-Syrian relations more than six years before: the flow of jihadi militants from Syria to Iraq. A CENTCOM-led delegation visited Damascus and concluded a tentative agreement with Syria on a "technical assessment of Iraqi-Syrian border posts."

Iraqi prime minister Nouri al-Maliki, miffed at being initially left out of these promising talks, visited Damascus on August 18 to seal the tripartite deal. The string of bomb blasts that greeted him upon his return to Baghdad the next day—the bloodiest in more than eighteen months and later claimed by an al-Qaeda affiliate—led Iraq to demand that Syria expel Iraqi Baathists and jihadi militants from its soil and recall its ambassador. Damascus responded in kind, effectively blowing up Washington's initiative on the launch pad.[10] The jihadi issue proved so explosive that even when Damascus had wanted to show its ability to turn a new page with the United States, it was unable to deliver. A month later, deputy foreign minister Faisal Mekdad arrived in Washington for talks that dealt almost exclusively with US sanctions and how they could be lifted.

Mekdad's visit signaled the end of the cold war between Washington and Damascus. It was replaced with a cold détente to solve the pile of bilateral issues between the two countries and achieve the Obama administration's goal of fostering "comprehensive Middle East peace." Damascus might have expected that negotiations with Israel would solve other outstanding issues between the United States and Syria, but with Israel and Syria unable to even come to terms on returning to talks, it was unclear when this would happen. Perhaps the best summary of the Obama administration's position on Syria came in an interview on December 1, 2009, by the left-of-center think tank, the Center for American Progress (CAP) with Middle East peace envoy George Mitchell. After answering numerous questions on the administration's failed efforts to get Israeli-Palestinian talks off the ground, Mitchell turned his attention to Syria in the final question:

Question: What is the prospect of resuming talks on the Syrian track? How do these efforts tie in with the administration's policy toward Syria and with the broader regional strategy for the Middle East?

Mitchell: President Obama is committed to comprehensive Middle East peace. . . . President Obama has directed that we engage Syria diplomatically. His objective is to assess Syria's readiness to improve the US-Syria bilateral relationship so that Syrian policies and actions that have been problematic for successive US administrations will change in ways that permit the relaxation and eventual elimination of US economic and political sanctions. If the US and Syria were to share a substantially common regional, strategic outlook the implications for Middle Eastern political stability and economic progress would be quite positive.

The key problem affecting the US-Syria relationship is Syrian support of terrorist organizations, including Hezbollah and Hamas. If Syria truly wants a better relationship with the United States and a stable, prosperous future for its people, it must end its support for terrorist groups and move toward resolution of its conflict with Israel through peaceful negotiations.

We are encouraging Syria and Israel to re-engage in negotiations as soon as possible. We have offered to facilitate their discussions in any way they see fit. We recognize there will be a major US role in helping them implement a peace treaty. We intend to continue encouraging the Parties to engage by helping them come to agreement on certain understandings that would enable each to have a positive and compelling idea of what peace between them would look like once it is achieved.

Finally, on February 17, 2010, the administration dispatched undersecretary of state William Burns to Damascus to meet President Assad. Burns became the highest-level US official to visit the capital since former deputy secretary of state Richard Armitage did so in January 2005. Washington simultaneously announced that Robert Ford, a former ambassador to Algeria then serving as deputy chief of mission in Iraq, would be President Obama's choice as ambassador to Syria. For the better part of a year, the name of the administration's candidate for ambassador had been a closely held secret, leading to wild rumors in the press. Finally, it seemed, engagement was getting off the ground in earnest. On February 24, Secretary of State Clinton told a Senate committee that the United States was "asking Syria to move away from Iran."[11]

The following day, Assad invited Iranian president Mahmoud Ahmadinejad and Hezbollah leader Hassan Nasrallah to Damascus for meetings and a public dinner, which was branded in the press by pundits as the "Axis of Evil Banquet." While Ahmadinejad and Nasrallah's comments slamming Israel and hailing the "resistance" were predictable, what was unexpected was an especially defiant tone from President Assad. Openly mocking Clinton's request, Assad said, "We must have understood Clinton wrong because of bad translation or our limited understanding, so we signed the agreement to cancel the visas. . . . I find it strange that [Americans] talk about Middle East stability and peace and the other beautiful principles and call for two countries to move away from each other." Ahmadinejad added that "Clinton said we should maintain a distance. I say there is no distance between Iran and Syria. . . . We have the same goals, same interests and same enemies. Our circle of cooperation is expanding day after day."[12] Shortly thereafter, reports began to surface of Syria transferring advanced weaponry—including Scud missiles—to Hezbollah in Syria and Lebanon.[13]

During his nomination hearing before the Senate Foreign Relations Committee on March 16, 2010, Ford outlined the five things that the Obama administration sought with the Assad regime. First, the United States sought Syria's help in stabilizing Iraq, which he specifically clarified as stopping the networks that fed foreign fighters into Iraq. Second, the administration wanted help in maintaining stability in Lebanon. The third goal was to gain Damascus's support for peace talks with Israel, and the fourth was to obtain Syria's cooperation with the IAEA. Finally, the United States wanted improvement of the deteriorating human rights situation in the country. Ford added that US sanctions on Syria would not be lifted unless Syria changed its position on those key issues.

With Syria's behavior worsening and engagement not going according to plan, Washington policy makers launched an informal review of US-Syria policy in the summer of 2010 as the Obama administration tightened sanctions on Iran and stories began to appear in the international press that Israel was contemplating striking Tehran's nuclear program. The debate quickly fell into the old pattern. Advocates of a US approach based on engagement to foster Syria-Israel peace talks pointed to the strategic advantages of "realigning" Assad away from Iran and Hezbollah via a peace treaty, championing deeper diplomacy with no pressure or negative inducements as the best way to get Assad back to the negotiating table. This policy echoed the constructive engagement policy of the 1970s and 1990s, when Washington believed it had more ability to reward good behavior than punish Damascus's problematic policies. Critics of this approach, most notably those in the Republican Party, said that the best way to deal with the Iranian problem and proxies like Hezbollah is to stop engagement and pressure Assad until his regime changed its behavior.

But a look back at the cold war between Washington and the Assad regime showed that the neither peace talks nor pressure alone were likely to work. Basing a policy of engaging Damascus with only the goal of reaching a peace treaty and thus fundamentally changing the Assad regime's behavior has historically had limited success. Unlike the case of Muammar el-Qaddafi's Libya, which Washington engaged successfully to end its nuclear program, the primary carrot Damascus seeks—the Golan Heights—is controlled by a third party, Israel. Because Israel and Syria are such bitter foes, and handing back the Golan would actually require an Israeli referendum, the best the United States has achieved to date is a "peace process" that allows Syria to carry on with policies that have grown worse over time. While brokering a Syrian-Israeli peace treaty should remain an important objective, the slow pace of the peace process combined with the growing list of problems with Assad's regime make the possibility of "flipping" Syria into a Western orbit difficult at best.

On a domestic level, the Assad regime continues to use Syria's state of war with Israel to justify an authoritarian form of government that reforms with only half measures, generating one of the highest corruption rates in the world. Without a firm legal foundation, Syrians are forced to bribe the minority-dominated networks that dominate the regime. This corruption has become the mortar holding Syria's regime together. Even in the event of a Syrian-Israeli peace treaty, unless Damascus institutes fundamental domestic reforms on the issues of human rights and rule of law, it is unclear how the United States can underwrite a treaty the same way it did in Egypt and Jordan.

Basing a policy solely on pressure and isolation hasn't worked well either, with US unilateral and multilateral pressure failing to change the Assad regime's behavior. Following Rafik Hariri's 2005 murder, US allies fell into line to compel the Assad regime to pull its forces out of Lebanon—a primary goal of the Syria Accountability and Lebanese Sovereignty Restoration Act (SAA). It also relaxed its domestic repression and allowed signatories of the Damascus Declaration to organize openly. Economically, the withdrawal from Lebanon caused the Assad regime to follow through on promises to liberalize its finance sector and lift its ban on imported goods, bringing prosperity to Syrians—at least to those who could afford it. In all cases, Assad only changed course when faced with a dilemma of the lesser of two evils.

Damascus was able to roll back some of these changes, however. Sensing its survival was at stake, the Assad regime was simply more ruthless and flexible than the United States and its Western allies in obtaining its objectives. To fight the United States in Iraq, the Assad regime made a tacit Faustian bargain with Sunni al-Qaeda networks who otherwise despise Syria's minority Alawite-based regime. It was a deal many foreign-policy analysts said in the past was impossible. Syria deepened its relationship with Iran to unprecedented levels and provided Hezbollah with sophisticated arms from its own stockpile, including the Kornet-E antitank weapon, which Hezbollah used to decimate Israeli tank columns and command posts in Lebanon.

On the domestic scene, the regime reached out to Syria's majority Sunni Muslim community in unprecedented ways that changed the nature of Hafez al-Assad's secular Syria. It also launched the biggest crackdown on the Syrian opposition since the regime's brutal repression of the Muslim Brotherhood in the 1980s. The Assad regime used all these factors to divide the United States and its allies on what to do when things did not go according to plan—most notably during the 2006 Lebanon War. Assad's plan of "flexibility and steadfastness"— which was announced at the Baath Party conference of 2005 but implemented in the aftermath of the October 2005 report on the murder of Rafik Hariri—allowed Syria to pragmatically adopt and adjust policies to resist and reverse Washington's pressure campaign.

Washington's ability to deal with Damascus's responses improved substantially after the United States launched the "Surge" and "Awakening" campaigns in Iraq. Washington also showed great skill by cooperating with Israel in its firm but nuanced response to Syria's nuclear reactor at Al Kibar. But in Syria and Lebanon, the United States was simply not creative or flexible enough to counter Assad's moves. An unfortunate ancillary side effect of American isolation was Washington's inability to respond to the Assad regime's skillful use of the chaos of sectarian bloodshed in US-occupied Iraq and war in Lebanon to rally the Syrian people around the flag and arrest domestic pressure on the regime. Washington's lack of a response to Hezbollah's "takeover" of west Beirut in May 2008 and the subsequent veto power given to the Party of God over the Lebanese state showed that when push came to shove in Lebanon, the Bush administration was unwilling—and perhaps ultimately unable—to push back. It also was unable to develop a diplomatic strategy to arrest Hezbollah's rise in Lebanon.

When US engagement finally resumed in 2009 in the name of creating tension between Iran and Syria, the Assad regime's deepening of relations with the Iranian-backed Hezbollah in Lebanon clashed directly with the Obama administration's objective of using a Syrian-Israel peace treaty to reorient Syria away from Iran. Insisting that he sought peace with Israel but was unwilling to give up Syria's close relations with Iran and Hezbollah, Assad attempted to have his political cake and eat it too.

But then the winds of change blew through Syria. In January 2011, anti-regime protests in Tunisia and Egypt brought down the Ben Ali and Mubarak regimes. Suddenly the strongly held notion in Washington and throughout the world that autocratic Arab regimes were stable was called into question. Dramatic scenes spread around the world of knife-wielding regime thugs riding horses and camels and assaulting pro-democracy protestors, who were using Facebook and Twitter accounts via smartphones to demand civic and human rights, in Cairo's Tahrir Square. Clearly, there was a gap between these regimes' anachronistic and brutal idea of governance and the protestors living their lives in the twenty-first century.

True to form, Assad reacted with hubris. In an interview with the *Wall Street Journal* on January 31, 2011, Assad claimed that his regime was impervious to the kind of protests that brought down the governments of Ben Ali and Mubarak, because his policies were so "closely linked to the beliefs of the people."[14] He quickly lifted the regime's Internet firewall—which blocked Facebook and Twitter—as a sign of his domestic legitimacy, seemingly daring antiregime activists to test him.

And they did. On March 15, a small antiregime protest broke out in front of Damascus University, followed by unrest in the southern Syrian city of Der'a, the capital of the southern Houran region of Syria from which my business partner, Leila Hourani, and her family hail. The protests were instigated when security officials arrested a group of children aged ten to fourteen for scrawling on a wall, "The people want the fall of the regime"—a slogan seen widely in Cairo's Tahrir Square. After failing to convince the regime to release the children, their families flooded the streets of Der'a to demand their release. The regime responded with force on March 18, killing six and injuring scores of others.

On March 21, the regime sent a delegation of high-level officials native to Der'a, including deputy foreign minister Faisal Mekdad, to engage with local tribal leaders and quell the violence. The children were released and the governor of Der'a was sacked, but the regime continued to use force to disperse demonstrators on March 22, killing another six. While the protests were non-Islamic in nature, on March 23 the protestors also chanted "No to Iran, no to Hizballah!" and "We want a leader who fears God!" The latter of these slogans constitutes a reference to the Assad family's roots in the Alawite faith, the heterodox offshoot of Shiite Islam that dominates the Syrian regime.

Perhaps more notable than the scale of the protests was the protestors' demographic base. The tribal Sunni population of the Houran region has played a key role in stabilizing the Assad regime. For hundreds of years, tensions had flared between Syria's Alawite community and its Sunni majority. The flash point for this simmering conflict had last occurred in February 1982, when the Sunni-based Muslim Brotherhood threw Hafez al-Assad's security forces out of the northern Syrian city of Hama. The regime responded by shelling the city, killing an estimated thirty thousand people, and arresting thousands of suspected Muslim Brotherhood supporters all across Syria, many of whose whereabouts remain unknown to this day. To stabilize the regime, Hafez gave it a veneer of Sunni legitimacy by co-opting tribal Sunnis from the Houran region and the Jazeera region of eastern Syria—as well as the Sunni Damascene and Aleppine merchant trading families—to join the regime's core of Alawites, Druze, Ismailis, and Christians. The protests in Der'a began to crack and break away that Sunni veneer.

In response to the 2011 uprisings, Assad delivered a speech before the Syrian parliament on March 30, 2011. Despite multiple reports that Assad would announce sweeping reforms, the president instead gave a defiant speech with no specific details. Nearly two dozen times, Assad blamed the protests on a vague conspiracy of some type coming from the United States and Israel, and he dismissed the notion that an "old guard" or other hard-line faction was holding him back from launching domestic reforms. The protests quickly spread to other Sunni areas and cities, including Homs, Latakia, and Banias on the Syrian coast. The regime reacted with lethal fire as well as the deploying of *Shabbiha* (Ghosts), bands of Alawite thugs and militia that threatened and terrorized Sunni communities. Sectarian tensions increased, and Sunni refugees from the village of Tal Khalak, which is surrounded by a constellation of Alawite villages located along the Lebanese frontier southwest of Homs, fled into Lebanon. By late April, around one thousand Syrians had perished, and the regime had arrested another ten thousand in what had quickly become its biggest crackdown under Bashar al-Assad, dwarfing its arrests following the 2000 to 2001 Damascus Spring and the 2005 Damascus Declaration.

The unrest created a problem for the Obama administration in terms of how to punish the Assad regime for the crackdown. The Bush administration, for all its emphasis on democracy promotion, had not included provisions for human rights. On April 29, the Obama administration issued Executive Order 13572, which declared the Syrian regime's "continuing escalation of violence against the people of Syria, including through attacks on protestors, arrests and harassment of protestors and political activists, and repression of democratic change" a national emergency. The administration targeted Assad's brother Maher, the commander of Syria's Fourth Armored Division who played a key role in suppressing protests in Der'a; Atif Najib, Assad's cousin and head of the Political Security Directorate; Ali Mamlouk, chief of the General Intelligence Directorate (GID); and the organization itself. Unexpectedly, the administration also sanctioned Iran's Islamic Revolutionary Guard Corps–Quds Force (IRGC-QF) for "providing material support to the Syrian government related to the crackdown." While the nature of that support was unclear, it was widely rumored in policy and activist circles that Iran had provided software to track Facebook and Twitter users, thus helping to explain the apparent reason for Assad's magnanimous gesture of lifting his regime's Internet block on both platforms.

Then, in a speech on May 19 that outlined US policy on what had become known as the Arab Spring, Obama chided Assad by saying the Syrian president had to lead a transition to democracy or "get out of the way." The same day, Obama issued another order sanctioning Assad himself, vice president Farouk al-Shara, prime minister Adel Safar, interior minister Mohammad Ibrahim al-Shaar, defense minister Ali Habib Mahmoud, military intelligence chief Abdul Fatah Qudsiya, and Political Security Directorate head Mohammed Dib Zaitoun for responsibility for the crackdown.

Assad responded with more force and defiance, and the protests spread to Syria's Idlib governorate in the country's northwest region. In the village of Jisr al-Shughour, protestors under the threat of government forces picked up guns and, along with support from unknown gunmen, forced the regime's forces from the town. As the Syrian army approached Jisr al-Shughour, nearly eleven thousand refugees fled over the border into Turkey. When the regime forces arrived, they claimed those defending the village were *takfiri* extremists—Sunni Islamists who deem non-Sunnis apostates.

Turkish prime minister Recep Tayyip Erdogan, who had a long history of positive rapport with Assad, unleashed rare public criticism of the president, describing the crackdown as "barbaric" and saying that his telephone conversations with Assad indicated he was "taking the issue lightly." Rumors soon spread that Erdogan said Assad had to ask his brother Maher to leave the country and implement reform or risk Turkey's wrath.

In response, Rami Makhlouf—who, only a few weeks before, had threatened in a *New York Times* interview that the regime would essentially fight to the death and warned that "if there is no stability here, there's no way there will be stability in Israel"—announced that he would divest his shares in the country's lucrative mobile-phone carrier, Syriatel, as well as real estate investments, and he would donate the proceeds to charity.[15] Then, on May 20, Assad delivered a speech at Damascus University in an attempt to quell three months of antiregime protests sweeping Syria. While recognizing some of the protestors had legitimate concerns, Assad continued to blame the demonstrations on a "conspiracy" of "outlaws," "vandals," and "*takfiri* extremists." Perhaps most offensively, Assad refused to recognize the regime's brutal crackdown on the protesters. He also dismissed "rumors related to the president and his family"—a reference to reports that Maher was leading efforts to snuff out the demonstrations.

But the fact that Assad dedicated his speech to themes of reform demonstrates that the Assad family was beginning to see the need for change under the pressure of growing antiregime protests and international pressure from Turkey, France, and the United States. Assad promised to address corruption (which, Transparency International's figures show, has skyrocketed under his reign), a new law for elections, increased media freedoms, and local administrative reform. Assad also dangled the prospect of constitutional reforms in response to a "new political reality in Syria."

Instead of immediately implementing the measures by presidential decree—which he could easily do under Syria's presidential system—he chose to push responsibility for the decision into various committees ahead of a "National Dialogue" that he vaguely said would roll out sometime in the next two months.

All the measures Assad outlined had been under consideration by the regime for years, so it was unclear how much discussion would be required for passage, other than that of Assad's willingness to sign the measures into law. In addressing the issue of why reform in Syria has been so slow, Assad said there was "no reason"—a reference to his speech on March 30 in which he dismissed the notion that a group of hard-line or old-guard figures were holding him back. Finally, Assad indicated that Syria's parliamentary elections, which were originally set for August, might be rescheduled before the end of 2011.[16]

As Washington officials struggled to come up with a further policy response to the Syrian uprising, it was clear that any strategy they chose going forward had to cut through the ambiguity and duplicity that was the hallmark of Bashar al-Assad's reign. In speeches on March 30 and June 20, he blamed the unrest sweeping his country on foreign "conspiracies" and refused to announce any specific reforms, indicating that he was not about to change his ways—at least not without a push from the outside.[17]

Assad had spent the last eleven years promising political "reform," but he had never delivered on the promise. This pattern is a well-established one. He talks about peace with Israel and at the same time sends Scud missiles to Hezbollah. He promises to keep his hands off Lebanon but worked with Hezbollah to bring down the government in Beirut. He says that as a signatory to the Nuclear Non-Proliferation Treaty he wants a nuclear-free Middle East, but he stonewalls International Atomic Energy Agency inspectors investigating the rubble of his North Korean–designed nuclear program.

Until the uprising, the Obama administration had engaged Assad with the primary goal of restarting peace talks between Syria and Israel while trying to mitigate the regional damage from Syria's worsening policies. Washington has attempted to test Assad's intention and ability to reorient his country away from Iran and toward the West in Syria-Israel peace talks by putting him on the horns of a dilemma: Either you get back the Golan Heights, or you keep supporting Hezbollah—but not both. Those well-intentioned efforts failed to break the gridlock. Israel watched Assad's transfer of weapons to Hezbollah, doubted his peaceful intentions, and refused to make the risky political decision to rejoin talks. With Washington unable to deliver Israel to the negotiating table, Assad was not compelled to show his hand.

The Obama administration was right to use dilemmas as a negotiating strategy; a dilemma can force a clear choice and reveal the other side's character and intentions. But the dilemma has to fit the context. Assad, who repeatedly attributed the unrest to Israeli and American meddling, has lost significant public support by using live fire on protesters, and he is not likely to risk further alienating his supporters by signing on the dotted line with Israel—at least anytime soon.

Dilemmas also only work if they are set up properly. The Obama administration tried to conduct its test by talking behind closed doors with Assad about peace with Israel and his destructive policies while keeping US sanctions in place. But it had not introduced new negative incentives in response to Assad's regional meddling and hardhanded tactics that diametrically oppose US interests or values. And Assad had little fear that Washington would, especially when US officials made his case for him by repeatedly emphasizing their lack of leverage in Damascus. Pressure alone, much like engagement alone, would not be enough to change Assad's policies. Both stood a far better chance of being effective if used in concert. That required focus and creativity— two things Washington's Syria policy has historically lacked.

The unrest sweeping Syria and the rest of the Middle East provided Washington with an opportunity to launch a Syria policy that would allow the administering of more tests in better ways. First, Washington should continue to shine a light on the Assad regime's human rights violations by bringing it before the UN Security Council. On the multilateral front, the administration should be working closely with European allies and Turkey to establish an effective sanctions regime—including diplomatic isolation—against Assad to push him to stop his bloody crackdown on protesters and follow through on his reform promises. Second, the Obama administration should continue to issue sanctions and executive orders targeting individuals responsible for human rights abuses in Syria. Third, it should use this remit to designate more Syrian officials and figures under Executive Order 13460, which targets rampant regime corruption—the mortar that holds Assad's regime together and a key issue that has brought protesters out into the streets. Elite defections could play a key role in pressuring the regime either to cut a deal with the country's Sunni majority or leave power. Along those lines, Washington should impose costs on other Syrian businesspeople who continue to back the regime. One way to do so is to lengthen the list of US Treasury Department designations aimed at businesspeople close to the regime, many of whom are the exclusive importers of a wide variety of goods on the Syrian market. This would not only create fissures in the regime's traditional alliance with the Sunni business elite, it would also diminish government revenue, since many major trading families pay an increasingly larger share of state revenues via a flat 20-percent corporate tax.

Fourth, the Obama administration should target Syrian energy. Syrian oil production has been in steady decline since the mid-1990s and is now around 390,000 barrels per day. Of that, Syria exports around 148,000 barrels per day, with revenues accruing directly to the state. According to International Monetary Fund (IMF) and US government estimates, oil sales account for between a quarter and a third of state revenue, with the remainder increasingly made up through corporate and public-sector employee taxes. As the protests decrease tax receipts, Damascus is likely to become increasingly reliant on oil revenue, forcing the regime to tap reserves and/or resort to deficit spending. This in turn would constrain the regime's ability to maintain market subsidies (for example, for diesel fuel) and payoffs to patronage networks.

Accordingly, the Obama administration should prod the chief buyers of Syrian oil—Germany, Italy, France, and the Netherlands—to stop purchasing the regime's heavy crude. It should also pressure multinational energy companies operating in Syria—Royal Dutch Shell; Total; Croatia's INA Nafta; India's Oil and Natural Gas Corporation (ONGC); Canada's Petro-Canada; and the China National Petroleum Corporation (CNPC) and Sinochem—to exit the country. In addition, it should ask Britain to halt the operations of Gulfsands Petroleum, the one-time Houston-based company specializing in extracting heavy oil from depleted fields. The firm relocated to Britain in 2008 to avoid US sanctions on Rami Makhlouf, Assad's cousin and the regime's primary businessman.

With these additional measures in place, Washington can rally allies around a common cause, send a strong message to Assad that his crackdown will cost him, and lead Assad toward a soft landing with his people and a transition toward a more accountable government in Damascus. In the meantime, Washington can also use these instruments on Assad's worsening domestic position to extract concessions on his relationship with Iran, be it his relationship with Hezbollah or— eventually, if he holds on in some capacity and the time is right—peace talks with Israel. It will also teach Assad that Washington will judge him on his actions, not just his words to US officials behind closed doors.

In terms of regional dilemmas, perhaps the most intriguing—and the one with deep implications for the Syrian-Iranian alliance in the short term—remained the Special Tribunal for Lebanon (STL) investigation into the 2005 murder of Rafik Hariri. On June 30, 2011, the tribunal indicted a number of members of Hezbollah for the murder operation itself based on forensic and communications evidence. While the Assad regime must have breathed a collective sigh of relief for being spared, the indictments of Hezbollah members placed the Assad regime in an awkward position—especially following a diplomatic effort by Saudi Arabia in 2010 to reconcile Assad and the former Lebanese prime minister Saad Hariri and a simultaneous attempt by Hezbollah chief Hassan Nasrallah to shift blame for Hariri's assassination to Israel. Would Syria back Hezbollah as indictments were issued? Would Syria support a Hezbollah attempt to cut off Lebanon's 51-percent share of funding for the tribunal?

The second dilemma involved the IAEA investigation into Syria's nuclear program. As Syria continued to deny all access to the Al Kibar site, the IAEA and the Obama administration considered issuing a "special inspection" of suspected Syrian nuclear sites.[18] The urgency had less to do with the Syrian program—by all accounts whatever was going on at Al Kibar was destroyed by Israeli aircraft—than with what kind of example Syria's case held out to other would-be nuclear proliferators looking to buck the international nonproliferation regime. If the special inspection were ordered, Syria faced referral to the Security Council and possible UN sanctions. Would the Assad regime come clean on its activities in the face of a showdown with the IAEA that threatened the international community's courting of the Assad regime? Or would it attempt to deflect pressure from the international community by reducing its demands for entering into peace talks with Israel?

The third dilemma involved the Assad regime's economics. With oil revenue declining as a percentage of government revenue and waves of young Syrians hitting the job market every year, the Assad regime faced increasingly stark choices. While it could continue its alliance with Hezbollah and Iran against Israel, it would have a hard time maintaining its war footing and the corruption it generates while attracting the kind of foreign investment necessary for job creation. The deep economic problems these policies produce for the Assad regime's finances presented the Obama administration with what would seem ample leverage through easing or tightening US sanctions.

But in the end, the hardest part for Washington will be reading Assad's response. For if there is one thing I learned from my engagement with Bashar al-Assad's Syria, it's that there are at least three answers for every question—yes, no, and no response. In the words of a good friend, "The Assad regime cannot exist in a world of black or white—only shades of gray."

NOTES

1. THE ARAB WORLD'S TWILIGHT ZONE

1. "The American–Syrian Crisis and the End of Constructive Engagement," *Middle East Intelligence Bulletin*, vol. 5, no. 4, April 2003.
2. Member of US embassy staff in Damascus, Syria, interview with the author, July 2008.
3. "Background Note: Syria," US State Department Bureau of Near Eastern Affairs, March 18, 2011, http://www.state.gov/r/pa/ei/bgn/3580.htm.
4. Former ambassador to Syria Edward Djerejian, interview with the author, April 2008.
5. The embargo included all countries designated as US state sponsors of international terrorism under the "Embargoed Countries," US Department of State, Directorate of Defence Trade Controls, 56 FR 55630, http://www.pmddtc.state.gov/docs /frnotices/56FR55630.PDF.
6. Following its addition to the state sponsor of terrorism list in 1993, Sudan remains the only other designated country with which the United States maintains diplomatic relations.
7. The request was still pending as of March 2010.
8. Michael Evans, "Syrian Pipeline Helps Iraq Evade UN Sanctions," *The Times*, December 16, 2002.
9. A book published in 2001 in Syria by the defense minister Mustafa Tlass was rumored to have said that Rifaat received a large chunk of Syria's foreign-exchange reserves in return for his peaceful departure.
10. Robert McMahon, "Syria's U.S. Ambassador: Syria Can Play 'Constructive Role' in Resolving Lebanese War," Council on Foreign Relations, August 7, 2006.
11. Alfred Prados, "Syria: U.S. Relations and Bilateral Issues," Congressional Research Service, January 23, 2003. Syria reportedly provided intelligence stemming from its interrogations of a German-Syrian national, Mohammed Haydar Zammar, suspected of playing a role in the September 11 attacks. Damascus also provided information on Mohamed Atta, one of those directly involved in the World Trade

Center attack, who worked in Aleppo in the 1990s. Valuable information was also given about Ma'mun Darkazanli, a Syrian businessman who allegedly served as a financial conduit to al-Qaeda members. See International Crisis Group Report, no. 23, *Syria Under Bashar (I): Foreign Policy Challenges*, February 11, 2004. See also Seymour M. Hersh, "The Syrian Bet," *The New Yorker*, July 28, 2003. However, Syrian intelligence did not give American investigators access to Zammar, leading analysts to question the degree of cooperation. See Ryan Mauro, "Has Damascus Stopped Supporting Terrorists?," *Middle East Quarterly*, Summer 2009, pages 61–67, citing Washington Institute senior fellow Matthew Levitt.

12. Syria, which was the uncontested candidate of the UN's Asia Regional Group for a rotating seat on the Security Council, received support from 160 of 178 nations voting in the UN General Assembly. As is the case in all elections to the Security Council, the United States did not disclose its vote. "Syria Gains Seat on U.N. Security Council," *United Press International*, October 8, 2001.

13. My hard feelings about Egypt did not last long, and I continue to enjoy visits there and value my Egyptian friends. See Andrew J. Tabler, "Making Peace with Egypt," Institute of Current World Affairs (newsletter), May 2006.

2. THE GREAT UNRAVELING

1. "U.S. Secretary of State Colin Powell Addresses the U.N. Security Council," White House press release, February 5, 2003, http://www.whitehouse.gov/news /releases/2003/02/20030205-1.html#20.

2. UN Resolution 68 1441 became the basis for the US-led "coalition of the willing," which invaded Iraq on March 20, 2003.

3. Cuba and Yemen voted against Security Council Resolution 678, which gave legal justification for the Gulf War of 1990–1991. It passed by a vote of 12 to 2 (China abstaining) on November 29, 1990.

4. "Security Council Wraps Up Two Days of Debate on Iraq," UN News Centre, October 17, 2002, http://www.un.org/apps/news/story.asp?Cr=iraq&Cr1 =&NewsID=5078.

5. Nicholas Blanford, "London Journalist Arrested in Syria," *The Times*, January 1, 2003, http://www.timesonline.co.uk/tol/news/world/article807352.ece.

6. Asma al-Assad, interview with the author, February 2003; CV of Asma al-Assad.

7. Syria Accountability and Lebanese Sovereignty Restoration Act, December 12, 2003, Section 2, Point 9.

8. *As-Safir* (Lebanon), March 27, 2003.

9. Neil MacFarquhar, "For Arabs, New Jihad Is in Iraq," *New York Times*, April 15, 2003; Gary C. Gambill, "The American-Syrian Crisis and the End of Constructive Engagement," *Middle East Intelligence Bulletin*, April 2003.

10. Neil MacFarquhar, "Syria Wants U.S. to Lose War, Its Foreign Minister Declares," *New York Times*, March 31, 2003.

11. As cited in Gambill, "The American-Syrian Crisis."
12. Ibid.
13. MacFarquhar, "For Arabs, New Jihad."
14. As cited in Gambill, "The American-Syrian Crisis."
15. Bill Gertz, "Iraqi Oil Pipeline to Syria Closed," *Washington Times*, April 16, 2003, http://www.washtimes.com/national/20030416-1723360.htm.
16. As cited in Gambill, "The American-Syrian Crisis."
17. Neil MacFarquhar, "Syria Fears the Unknown: What's Behind U.S. Threats," *New York Times*, April 15, 2003.
18. As cited in Gambill, "The American-Syrian Crisis."
19. Paul Kerr, "Senior US Officials Voice Concern over Syria's WMD Capability," Arms Control Today, May 2003, http://www.armscontrol.org/act/2003_05/syria_may03.
20. Ziad Abdelnour, "The US-Syrian Crisis: Why Diplomacy Failed," *Middle East Intelligence Bulletin*, October 2003.
21. Judy Miller, "Senior U.S. Official to Level Weapons Charges Against Syria," *New York Times*, September 13, 2003.

3. PARADISE LOST

1. "Trying to Fit In," *Syria Today*, zero edition, March 2004.
2. "Bush Signs Syria Sanctions Bill," CNN.com, December 13, 2003, http://www.cnn.com/2003/US/12/12/bush.syria/.
3. "US Sanctions Are Work of Israel's Friends in Congress: Syria," AFP, December 11, 2003.
4. Andrew J. Tabler, "US Sanctions Unjust, Unjustified," *Daily Star*, May 13, 2004.
5. Executive Order 13338—Blocking Property of Certain Persons and Prohibiting the Export of Certain Goods to Syria, Federal Register, May 13, 2004.
6. Ibid.

4. PRESSURE YIELDS RESULTS

Portions of this chapter originally appeared in the Institute of Current World Affairs member newsletter.

1. "Lebanon's Government Quits in Face of Mass Protest," Reuters, February 28, 2005.
2. Andrew J. Tabler, "The Gathering Storm," Institute of Current World Affairs (newsletter), March 2005.
3. "Security Council Declares Support for Free, Fair Presidential Election," Security Council press release 8181, September 2, 2004, http://www.un.org/News/Press/docs/2004/sc8181.doc.htm.
4. Nicholas Blanford, *Killing Mr. Lebanon* (New York: I.B. Tauris, 2006).
5. "Rice on Death of Former Lebanon PM Rafik Hariri," US Department of State press release, February 14, 2005.

6. White House press conference transcript, February 17, 2005.
7. Joel Brinkley, "Rice Says Syria Is at Least Indirectly Responsible for the Blast," *New York Times*, February 17, 2005.
8. "Syria Must Withdraw from Lebanon: Bush," *Daily Times*, February 24, 2005.
9. "Rice Turns Up the Heat on Syria," BBC News, March 2, 2005.
10. Hassan Fattah, "Saudis Join Call for Syrian Force to Quit Lebanon," *New York Times*, March 3, 2005.
11. Robin Wright, "U.S. Rejects Syria's Withdrawal Plan for Lebanon," *Washington Post*, March 6, 2005.
12. "Adviser to the Syrian President: Establish a Foreign Investment and We Expect Revenues of $7 Billion over the Next Five Years," *Al-Sharq al-Awsat*, February 26, 2005.
13. The initial signatories of the Damascus Declaration were the NDR, the Kurdistan Democratic Alliance, the Kurdish Democratic Front, the Committee for the Revival of Civil Society and the Future Party. Prominent opposition figures included Riad Seif, Jawdat Sa'id, Dr. Abd al-Razzaq Id, Samir Nashar, Dr. Fida al-Hourani, Dr. Adil Zakkar, Abd al-Karim al-Dahhak, Haitham al-Maleh, and Nayif Qaysiyah. Damascus Declaration, October 16, 2005.
14. Sami Moubayed, interview with the author, Damascus, Syria, October 20, 2005.
15. "Landis: Damascus Rife with Rumors on Whether UN's Lebanese Investigation Implicates Syrian Leadership," Bernard Gwertzman, consulting editor, Council on Foreign Relations, October 21, 2005.
16. United Nations Security Council, 5,297th meeting, October 31, 2005.
17. "Security Council Demands Syria's Unambiguous, Immediate Response to Commission Investigating Assassination of Former Lebanese Prime Minister Hariri," Security Council 5,329th Meeting (PM), December 15, 2005.
18. Abdel Khalim Khaddam, interview on Al Arabiya, December 30, 2005, transcript, http://www.alarabiya.net/articles/2005/12/31/19936.html#8.

5. THE ENEMY OF MY ENEMY IS MY FRIEND
Portions of this chapter originally appeared in the Institute of Current World Affairs member newsletter.

1. Katherine Zoepf, "Syrian Leader Says His Nation Is Being Made a Scapegoat," *New York Times*, November 10, 2005.
2. Bashar al-Assad, "Comprehensive Political Speech Delivered by H.E. President Bashar al-Assad at the Damascus Auditorium," official copy of speech issued by *Tishreen* newspaper, November 10, 2005.
3. Sami Moubayed, "Allied to, Created by or Friends of the Ba'ath," *Gulf News*, March 7, 2006. Moubayed predicted that a multiparty law would be issued within a month. As of mid-2011, the law had yet to be enacted.
4. Michel Kilo, interview with the author, Damascus, Syria, March 24, 2006.
5. "Michel Kilo Detained," *Syria Monitor*, May 15, 2006, http://syriamonitor.typepad.com/news/2006/05/michel_kilo_det.html.

6. NO VOICE LOUDER THAN THE CRY OF BATTLE

Portions of this chapter originally appeared in the Institute of Current World Affairs member newsletter.

1. "Mic Picks Up Bush: 'Get Hezbollah to Stop This S***,'" *Times Online*, July 17, 2006.
2. Helene Cooper and David E. Sanger, "U.S. Plan Seeks to Wedge Syria Away from Iran," *New York Times*, July 23, 2006, http://www.nytimes.com/2006/07/23 /washington/23diplo.html.
3. Seymour Hersh, "Watching Lebanon: Washington's Interests in Israel's War," *The New Yorker*, August 21, 2006.

7. PLAYING WITH FIRE IN EASTERN SYRIA

1. George W. Bush, "President's Address to the Nation," White House, Washington, DC, January 10, 2009, http://georgewbushwhitehouse.archives.gov/news/releases /2007/01/20070110-7.html.
2. "Iran, Forerunner in Syria Investment Among Non-Arab States," Islamic Republic News Agency, January 24, 2007, http://www.irna.ir/en/news/view/menu-237/07 01242933180528.htm.
3. For a partial account of this meeting, see Andrew Lee Butters, "Guess Who Is Coming to Dinner," *Time*, February 8, 2007.
4. Andrew Tabler, "The Shiitization of Syria?," *Executive*, June 2009.
5. Grand mufti of the Syrian Arab Republic Ahmed al-Hassoun, interview with the author, March 2007.
6. Andrew Tabler, "Catalytic Converters," *New York Times Magazine*, April 29, 2007.
7. Barack Obama, interview on MSNBC, January 11, 2007. Viewed via YouTube, July 10, 2009.
8. Joseph R. Biden Jr., "A Plan to Hold Iraq Together," *Washington Post*, August 24, 2006.
9. Elizabeth Williamson, "Pelosi Plans Trip to Syria Next Week," *Washington Post*, March 31, 2007.
10. "Bush: Pelosi Meeting With Syria's Assad Sends Wrong Signal," Fox News, April 3, 2007.
11. Hassan Fattah, "Pelosi's Delegation Presses Syrian Leader on Militants," *New York Times*, April 4, 2007.
12. "Pratfall in Damascus," *Washington Post*, April 5, 2007.
13. US diplomat, interview with the author, March 2008.
14. CNN newscast, May 3, 2007.
15. Dominic Moran, "Rice–Syrian FM Meet Eclipses Iraq Plan," International Relations and Security Network (ISN), May 4, 2007.
16. "Syria: Writer Michel Kilo Sentenced," PEN, May 16, 2007.
17. For another account of the polls, see Hassan Fattah, "Syrian President's Fortunes Revive for Election," *New York Times*, May 27, 2007.
18. "Dialogue with Syria: Opportunity or Ambush?," Saban Center for Middle East Policy, transcript, page 79; Adam Zagorin, "Syria in Bush's Cross Hairs," *Time* December 19, 2006.
19. Andrew Tabler, "To Help Israel, Help Syria," *New York Times*, August 5, 2006.

20. Hugh Naylor, "Tired of Energy Ills, Syrians Doubt the West Is to Blame," *New York Times*, August 15, 2007.
21. Nicholas Blanford, "Why Did Israeli Planes Enter Syria?," *Time*, September 10, 2007.
22. For an excellent account of statements following the raid, see "06 September 2007 Strike" on GlobalSecurity.org, last modified October 27, 2007.
23. Yoav Stern and Mazal Mualem, "Israel Mum on Any IAF Entry into Syria Airspace," September 6, 2007, http://www.haaretz.com/.
24. Glen Kessler, "Syria–N. Korea Reports Won't Stop Talks," *Washington Post*, September 15, 2007.
25. "Extracting Uranium from Phosphates," Arms Control Wonk (blog), September 20, 2007, http://armscontrolwonk.com/.
26. "06 September 2007 Airstrike," GlobalSecurity.org, October 29, 2007, http://www.globalsecurity.org/military/world/war/070906-airstrike.htm.
27. Ron Ben-Yishai, "Ynet Reporter Visits Site of 'Syria Operation,'" *Yedioth Ahronoth*, September 26, 2007, http://www.ynetnews.com/articles/0,7340,L-3453679,00.html. For another account of the visit, see Hugh Naylor, "Syria Tells Journalist Israeli Raid Did Not Occur," *New York Times*, October 9, 2007.
28. American and Israeli sources later said that they didn't push the nuclear issue immediately so that Assad would not overreact and launch a retaliatory strike on Israel.
29. General David H. Petraeus, "Report to Congress on the Situation in Iraq," September 10–11, 2007.
30. Richard A. Oppel, "Foreign Fighters in Iraq Are Tied to Allies of U.S.," *New York Times*, November 22, 2007.

8. WEATHERING THE STORM

1. Nicholas Blanford, "Hizballah Mourns Its Shadowy Hero," *Time*, Feburary 13, 2008.
2. Ibrahim Hamidi, "No More Secrets," *Syria Today*, March 2008.
3. Andrew Tabler, "Speculation Rages over Imad Moughniyah Assassination," Eighth Gate (blog), February 13, 2008, http://www.andrewtabler.com/2008/02/speculation-rages-overimad-moughniyah.html.
4. "Iran Joins Syria in Hunt for Killers of Militant," Associated Press, February 15, 2008.
5. "An Official Information Source Denies Reports on the Formation of a Joint Committee to Investigate Moghnia Assassination," Syrian Arab News Agency, February 16, 2008.
6. Andrew Tabler, "The U.S. Can Help Tackle Syrian Corruption," *Daily Star*, July 29, 2008.
7. "Syria: From Isolation to Acceptance," roundtable presentation at the Henry L. Stimson Center, April 24, 2008.
8. "Syria's Covert Nuclear Reactor at Al Kibar," Central Intelligence Agency, April 24, 2008.
9. Embassy of the Syrian Arab Republic, press release, April 24, 2008.
10. Fay Ferguson, "Radioactive Allegations," *Syria Today*, May 2008.
11. Ibid.
12. Ibid.
13. For a summary of the dispute, see "Perhaps It Was the Genie in the Lamp?," http://www.andrewtabler.com/search?q=Landis.

14. Imad Moustapha, interview by the author and Robert Malley, February 2008.

15. Nicholas Blanford, "Spectre of War Returns to Haunt Lebanon," *The Times*, May 8, 2008.

16. "Hezbollah Takes Over West Beirut," BBC News, May 9, 2008.

17. Ibid.

18. "Israel Announces Indirect Peace Talks with Syria," DPA, May 21, 2008.

19. "Official: Latest Israel–Syria Talks End in 'Positive Atmosphere,'" June 16, 2008, http://www.haaretz.com/.

20. Steven Erlanger and Katrin Bennhold, "Sarkozy Helps to Bring Syria Out of Isolation," *New York Times*, July 14, 2008.

21. For another account of Syrian coverage of the event, see Andrew Lee Butters, "The Syrians Take Paris," *Time*, July 14, 2008.

22. "No Comment," Euronews Television, July 14, 2008, recovered from YouTube as "Cat-and-Mouse between Syrian President Bashar al-Assad and Israeli Prime Minister Ehud Olmert in Paris" on August 20, 2009, http://www.youtube.com/watch?v=tY5Z4OKq28o.

23. "Syria's Assad Stirs Controversy at France's Bastille Day," AFP, July 14, 2008.

24. "IAEA Team to Inspect Syria's Alleged Nuclear Site," DPA, June 22, 2008.

25. This paragraph is a summary of Radwan Ziadeh's chapter on Syria in *Freedom of Association in the Euro-Mediterranean Region: 60 Years after the Universal Declaration of Human Rights* (Copenhagen: Euro-Mediterranean Human Rights Network, December 2008), pages 44–47.

26. Brookings Institution, "Engaging Syria: New Negotiations, Old Challenges," July 23, 2008, http://www.brookings.edu/–/media/Files/events/2008/0723_syria/0723_syria.pdf.

27. Ibid.

28. Sami Moubayed, "Driving a Truck Through Syrian Loopholes," *Asia Times*, August 6, 2008.

EPILOGUE: THE EXPECTATIONS GAP AND THE ADVENT OF THE ARAB SPRING

Portions of this chapter originally appeared in *PolicyWatch* (http://www.washingtoninstitute.org/templateI05.php?&newActiveSubNav=PolicyWatch/PeaceWatch&activeSubNavLink=templateI05.php%3F&newActiveNav=analysis), an online publication of the Washington Institute for Near East Policy.

1. "'US Helicopter Raid' Inside Syria," BBC News, October 27, 2008.

2. "Syrian Witness Reacts to US Raid," BBC News, October 27, 2008.

3. Albert Aji, "U.S. Special Forces Launch Rare Attack Inside Syria," Associated Press, October 26, 2008.

4. Eric Schmidt and Mark Mazzetti, "Secret Order Lets U.S. Raid Al Qaeda in Many Countries," *New York Times*, November 9, 2008.

5. Sami Moubayed, "American Dream Expelled from Syria," *Asia Times*, November 4, 2008.

6. Despite the fact that Moubayed published a denial on the blog Syria Comment stating the views were only his own (http://www.joshualandis.com/blog/?p=1486),

many journalists—especially in Israel—believed Moubayed's views reflected those of the Assad regime at that time. For a thoughtful discussion of the issue by one Israeli journalist who quoted Moubayed, see "Yoav Stern Discusses His Coverage of Syrian Affairs," Syria Comment (blog), November 9, 2008, http://www.joshualandis .com/blog/?p=1500. For further background of Syria's spring 2009 public relations offensive to woo Obama, see Andrew J. Tabler, "Will Mitchell's Trip Bypass Damascus?," April 13, 2009, http://www.washingtoninstitute.org/templateC05 .php?CID=3043.

7. For a discussion of "Syrian triumphalism" and its ultimate impact on engagement with the Obama administration, see Steven Heydemann, "Why Syria Needs to Get a Grip," *Foreign Policy*, April 20, 2010, http://mideast.foreignpolicy.com/posts/2010 /04/20/why_syria_needs_to_get_a_grip.

8. For more information, see "Implementation of the NPT Safeguards Agreement in the Syrian Arab Republic," Director General's Report, International Atomic Energy Agency, February 18, 2010.

9. Cecile Hennion, "Dialogue de sourds entre Bachar Al-Assad et Ban Ki-moon," *Le Monde*, June 28, 2007.

10. Excerpt from Andrew Tabler, "Assad Clenches His Fist," *Foreign Policy*, August 28, 2009.

11. "Clinton Presses Syria to Abandon Iran, Halt Hizbullah Arms," AFP, February 25, 2010.

12. Khaled Yacoub Oweis, "Syria and Iran Defy Clinton in Show of Unity," Reuters, February 25, 2010.

13. Charles Levinson and Jay Solomon, "Syria Gave Scuds to Hezbollah, U.S. Says," *Wall Street Journal*, April 14, 2010.

14. Jay Solomon, "Interview with Syrian President Bashar al-Assad," *Wall Street Journal*, January 31, 2011.

15. Anthony Shadid, "Reviled Tycoon, Assad's Cousin, Resigns in Syria," *New York Times*, June 16, 2011, http://www.nytimes.com/2011/06/17/world /middleeast/17syria.html.

16. Excerpted from Andrew Tabler, "Another Deeply Disappointing Speech by Bashar al-Assad," CNN Global Public Square (blog), June 20, 2011, http:// globalpublicsquare.blogs.cnn.com/2011/06/20/another-deeply-disappointing -speech-by-bashar-al-assad/.

17. The following argument is based on an edited excerpt from Andrew Tabler, "Twisting Assad's Arm," *Foreign Policy*, April 14, 2011, http://www.foreignpolicy. com /articles/2011/04/14/twisting_assads_arm.

18. Jay Solomon, "U.S. Considers Push for U.N. Action in Syria," *Wall Street Journal*, August 6, 2010, http://online.wsj.com/article/SB10001424052748704657504575411 762167580080.html.

INDEX

and corruption, 71, 92, 230–31, 236, 239, 242

and economic downturn, xix, 242

and Hariri assassination investigation, 113–15, 117–20, 140–41, 176

and Hezbollah, xx, 13, 156, 158, 219, 232, 237–38, 241

and human rights, 177–78, 239

and Islam, 131, 133–34

and Israel, 48, 148, 150, 159–60, 176, 206–8, 222–23, 229–30, 237, 241–42

and Lebanon, xix, 13, 81, 83–85, 154, 206

marriage of, 36

and protest crackdowns, xviii, 151, 233–36, 239

reelection of, 179–82, 186

and reform, 4, 8, 26, 30, 66, 69, 88, 93, 107, 117, 160, 183–84, 236–37, 239

speech at Baath Conference, 95–100

and Syria's nuclear program, 202, 219–20, 241

trip to China by, 70–74

and the US, xvii–xx, 13, 41–42, 48, 66, 83–88, 118, 159, 174–77, 187–189, 212, 218–19, 223, 228–33, 237–40, 242

Assad, Bushra al-, 110

Assad, Hafez al-, 4, 6, 14–16, 19, 39–40, 51, 57, 72–73, 100, 106–7, 110, 161, 179, 212, 219, 231, 234

Assad, Maher al-, 111–12, 117, 235–36

Assad, Rifaat al-, 19

Associated Press, 99

associations law, 36, 37, 50–51, 57

Assyrian Democratic Organization, 108–9, 141

Attar, Abdul Ghani, 182, 205

Attar, Abdul Rahman, 182

Attar, Ali Reza Sheikh, 199

Azm, Amr al-, 53, 56

Azm, Sadiq Jalal al-, 53

Baath Day, 133

Baath Party, 5–6, 8, 43, 57, 81, 86–91, 93, 119, 124–26, 133–34, 145, 226

conference of, 94–108, 117–18, 231

Baker, James, 15, 161

Barak, Ehud, 15

Battat, Joseph, 61, 73

Bayanouni, Ali Sadreddin al-, 90–91, 144

Bayda, Rola, 20, 25–26, 32, 34, 38–39, 44–46, 48–49, 55–56, 59–61, 64–67, 71–74

BBC World Service, 100

Beirut-Damascus/Damascus-Beirut Declaration, 146

Ben Ali, Zine el-Abidine, 232–33

Ben-Yishai, Ron, 193

Berri, Nabih, 87, 205

Bashir, Sheikh Nawaf al-, 108

Biden, Joe, 173

Bilal, Mohsen, 148, 168–69, 191

bin Laden, Osama, 21–22, 197

Blair, Tony, xvii, 148

Blanford, Nicholas, 111, 190

blue line (1949 cease fire line on Lebanon's southern border), 149

Bolton, John, 43–45, 193

Bunni, Anwar al-, 146, 177

Burns, William, 228

Bush, George W., administration, xvii, xix, xxi, 25, 30, 41, 43–44, 49–50, 54, 62–63, 66, 83–84, 87, 128, 132, 141, 145–46, 148, 151–52, 158, 160–61, 163–67, 169, 173, 175–78, 181, 184, 194, 201–3, 210–11, 217–18, 220, 232, 235

Butters, Andrew, 168–69

Andrew Tabler is a fellow with the Washington Institute for Near East Policy and one of the most sought-after voices on contemporary Syria. His articles have appeared in the *New York Times*, the *New York Times Magazine*, *Newsweek*, the *International Herald Tribune*, *Foreign Policy*, and *Foreign Affairs*. His opinion is regularly sought by CNN, NBC, and PBS. After seven years of living and working under Assad's regime, Tabler left Damascus for Beirut. He currently resides in Washington, DC.

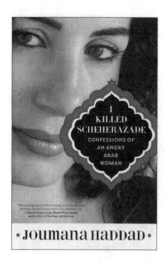

I Killed Scheherazade
Confessions of an Angry Arab Woman
Joumana Haddad

Foreword by Etel Adnan

978-1-56976-840-2

$14.95 (CAN $16.95)

"A very courageous and illuminating book about women in the Arab world. It opens our eyes, destroys our prejudices and is very entertaining."
—Mario Vargas Llosa, author and Nobel Laureate

"*I Killed Scheherazade* . . . is many things: a coming-of-age memoir, a sexual polemic and a spirited call to Arab women to stand up for themselves. There is something in it for Western women, too. . . .The fate of the honor-killed, acid-scarred, burqa-bound Arab female has implications for the status of women worldwide."
—*New York Times Magazine*

"Joumana Haddad is a revolutionary, this book is the manifesto. Read it or be left behind." —Rabih Alameddine, author of *The Hakawati* and *Koolaids: The Art of War*

"Courageous. . . . Haddad breaks down the taboo of the Silent Absent Arab Woman."
—Elfriede Jelinek, novelist, playwright, and Nobel Laureate

"Surprisingly entertaining." —*Publishers Weekly*

Available at your favorite bookstore,
(800) 888-4741, or
www.lawrencehillbooks.com

Lawrence Hill Books

Our Way to Fight
Israeli and Palestinian Activists for Peace

Michael Riordon

978-1-56976-778-8

$16.95

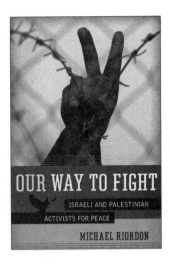

"[*Our Way to Fight*] is an exercise in humility. The author, Michael Riordon, limits his commentary to a minimum, and lets the activists speak for themselves. They describe the injustice with their own words, and in the book their humanity and individual stories become inseparable from the stories of repression and resistance in Palestine."
—*Dissident Voice*

"Lyrical. . . . Even while maintaining a sober assessment of the difficult road activists face, simply by demonstrating that Israelis and Palestinians can and do work in common cause, Riordon offers an important corrective to the standard tale of an intractable conflict."
—*Publishers Weekly*

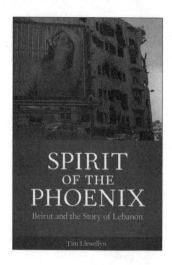

Spirit of the Phoenix
Beirut and the Story of Lebanon
Tim Llewellyn
978-1-56976-603-3
$16.95 (CAN $18.95)

"Part travelogue, part political vignettes, part personal reminiscences, [*Spirit of the Phoenix*] captures the essence of this unique and troubled country." —David Hirst, author of *The Gun and the Olive Branch*

"Llewellyn, a bright and brave BBC correspondent during many of Lebanon's earlier seemingly endless little and big wars, has returned decades later to scrutinize Beirut and its still largely unresolved problems. Read his compelling *Spirit of the Phoenix* and understand how and why that fabled bird of resilient rebirth has survived in Lebanon, but just barely, alas, and missing many of its feathers."
—Jonathan Randal, former *Washington Post* Middle East correspondent and author of *Osama: The Making of a Terrorist*

"With a sense of the richness inherent in real voices [Llewellyn] celebrate[s] the spirit of the country's indomitable people. . . . The loving eye that traces the changes in fast-food joints and pubs during a sunset walk down Hamra has a particular appeal." —Ellen Hardy, *TimeOut Beirut*

**Available at your favorite bookstore,
(800) 888-4741, or
www.lawrencehillbooks.com**

Lawrence Hill Books